TRIALS OF EUROPEANIZATION

TRIALS OF EUROPEANIZATION
TURKISH POLITICAL CULTURE AND THE EUROPEAN UNION

Ioannis N. Grigoriadis

First published in 2009 by PALGRAVE MACMILLAN® in the
United States—a division of St. Martin's Press LLC, 175 Fifth
Avenue, New York, NY 10010.

Where this book is distributed in the UK, Europe and the rest of
the world, this is by Palgrave Macmillan, a division of Macmillan
Publishers Limited, registered in England, company number 785998,
of Houndmills, Basingstoke, Hampshire RG21 6XS.

Palgrave Macmillan is the global academic imprint of the above
companies and has companies and representatives throughout the
world.

Palgrave® and Macmillan® are registered trademarks in the United
States, the United Kingdom, Europe and other countries.

ISBN-13: 978-0-230-61215-0

Library of Congress Cataloging-in-Publication Data is available from
the Library of Congress.

A catalogue record of the book is available from the British Library.

Design by Scribe Inc.

First edition: January 2009

10 9 8 7 6 5 4 3 2 1

Printed in the United States of America.

Transferred to Digital Printing in 2009

To my parents, Niko and Efi

Contents

List of Figures   ix

Foreword   xi

Acknowledgments   xiii

Abbreviations   xv

1   Introduction: Methodological Considerations   1

2   The Historical Background to the Debate on   21
Turkish Political Culture

3   Civil Society   41

4   The State   65

5   The Secularism Debate   95

6   Turkish National Identity   123

7   Conclusions: Prospects of Turkish Political Culture   155

Postscript   181

Notes   185

Index   227

FIGURES

2.1   EU Eastern Enlargement and Turkey's   36
      Accession Prospects

3.1   "Don't stay silent about torture!"   60

4.1   Anitkabir, Ataturk's Mausoleum in Ankara,   71
      a symbol of Kemalism

5.1   The Mevlana Shrine in Konya, an icon of   98
      Turkish Islam

5.2   A group of headscarved women on a busy   115
      Istanbul street

7.1   Turkey's Prime Minister, Recep Tayyip Erdogan, 174
      a former football player, in probably the most
      difficult shot of his career

7.2   The uncertain future of EU-Turkey relations   177
      succinctly illustrated

FOREWORD

Istanbul, May 4, 2008

Turkey's European vocation has attracted the interest of scholars, journalists, and the general public alike. Furthermore, as Turkish accession progresses, albeit slowly, paradoxes and controversies both in Europe and in Turkey emerge and flourish. This naturally has resulted in the production of a considerable amount of academic literature and policy-oriented discussion on EU-Turkey relations. Yet, little scholarly work has been done in the field of political culture and the setting it provides for the accession process. Turkish political culture, especially as related to European accession, has remained an understudied topic, although it is probably the most critical factor to be studied in terms of Turkey's democratic consolidation.

Dr. Grigoriadis' book successfully fills this gap and provides an eloquent and comprehensive study of the impact of the European Union on Turkey's democratization process. The insight he provides as a Greek scholar of Turkish politics is a very valuable asset of the volume you are about to read. This is also a reflection of what will probably be billed by historians as the most spectacular reform that Turkey has experienced since the years of Kemal Ataturk. It is a very informative and balanced work, a valuable companion for scholars and students of democratization and European and Turkish politics, as well as a great source of knowledge for the nonspecialist reader interested in contemporary Turkey.

Prof. Ustun Erguder
Sabanci University

ACKNOWLEDGMENTS

I would like to thank all my interviewees who greatly assisted my field-work in Turkey in the academic year 2004–5.

I would also like to express my gratitude to my PhD supervisor, Prof. William M. Hale, whose tireless support throughout my PhD studies cannot be overstated.

ABBREVIATIONS

ABGS	*Avrupa Birliği Genel Sekterliği*—General Secretariat of European Union
AKP	*Adalet ve Kalkinma Partisi*—Justice and Development Party
AKUT	*Arama Kurtarma Dernegi*—Search Rescue Association
ANAP	*Anavatan Partisi*—Motherland Party
AP	*Adalet Partisi*—Justice Party
CHP	*Cumhuriyet Halk Partisi*—Republican People's Party
DEHAP	*Demokratik Halk Partisi*—Democratic People's Party
DSP	*Demokratik Sol Partisi*—Democratic Left Party
DGM	*Devlet Guvenlik Mahkemesi*—State Security Court
DP	*Demokrat Parti*—Democrat Party
DYP	*Dogru Yol Partisi*—True Path Party
FP	*Fazilet Partisi*—Virtue Party
HADEP	*Halkin Demokrasi Partisi*—People's Democracy Party
IHD	*Insan Haklari Dernegi*—Human Rights Association
MGK	*Milli Guvenlik Kurulu*—National Security Council
MHP	*Milliyetci Hareket Partisi*—Nationalist Action Party
MNP	*Milli Nizam Partisi*—National Order Party
MSP	*Milli Selamet Partisi*—National Salvation Party
MUSIAD	*Mustakil Sanayici ve Isadamlari Dernegi*—Independent Industrialists' and Businesspersons' Association
OYAK	*Ordu Yardimlasma Kurumu*—Armed Forces Mutual Assistance Fund

PKK	*Partiya Karkaren Kurdistan*—Kurdistan Workers' Party
RP	*Refah Partisi*—Welfare Party
RTUK	*Radyo Televizyon Ust Kurulu*—Higher Radio-Television Board
SP	*Saadet Partisi*—Felicity Party
TESEV	*Turkiye Ekonomik ve Sosyal Etudler Vakfi*—Economic and Social Studies Foundation of Turkey
TIHV	*Turkiye Insan Haklari Vakfi*—Human Rights Foundation of Turkey
TMSF	*Tasarruf Mevduat Sigortasi Fonu*—Savings Deposit Insurance Fund
TUSEV	*Turkiye Ucuncu Sektor Vakfi*—Third Sector Foundation of Turkey
TUSIAD	*Turk Sanayiciler ve Isadamlari Dernegi*—Turkish Industrialists' and Businesspersons' Association
VGM	*Vakiflar Genel Mudurlugu*—General Directorate of Foundations
YOK	*Yuksek Ogretim Kurulu*—Higher Education Council

Chapter 1

Introduction

Methodological Considerations

The Scope of this Study

Turkey and Europe in Historical Perspective

The relations between Turkey and the European Union and the future of Turkey's EU vocation have attracted considerable public interest in both the EU countries and Turkey. The European identity of Turkey, the economic, social, and political consequences, as well as the practicality of Turkey's potential membership in the European Union, have been discussed at length. Based on Turkey's history and religion, some argued that Turkey is not a member of the "European family" for geographical and cultural reasons and, therefore, not eligible for EU membership.[1] Driven by Turkey's relative large size and economic underdevelopment, it was also argued that Turkey's membership would disrupt EU economic and population balances. Others stressed that the European Union is based on values and a culture of which Turkey is not a part. According to this opinion, EU-Turkey relations could at best reach the level of institutionalized close political and economic cooperation, a "privileged partnership." Hence, Turkey could never become a full member of the European Union. On the other hand, it was also argued that tolerance and multiculturalism are the key properties of the emerging European identity and that Turkey's EU candidacy comprised an excellent opportunity for the European Union to show its inclusive character.

Turkey's quest to join Europe is by no means novel or without historical precedents. A campaign aiming at the recognition of a European Ottoman identity had marked Ottoman foreign policy agenda since the initiation of the Ottoman modernization program (*Tanzimat*) in 1839. A first success was marked in March 1856 when the Ottoman Empire was invited to participate in the "Concert of Europe" under the provisions of the Treaty of Paris, which marked the end of the Crimean War (1855–56).[2] Yet the failure of the *Tanzimat* leaders to bring about political, economic, and social change in the Ottoman Empire and the relapse into authoritarianism under the rule of Sultan Abdulhamid II (1876–1909) reinforced existing European stereotypes about the Oriental essence of the Ottoman Empire. The Ottoman Empire might have been *in* Europe, as it had successfully invaded and occupied vast parts of Southeastern and Central Europe in the past and still ruled over a large part of Southeastern Europe in the late nineteenth century. Nonetheless, it was not viewed as being an integral part *of* Europe, a part of the European continent in historical, cultural, and political terms.[3] On the contrary, the Ottoman "Turk" was the geographically proximal manifestation of the Oriental "Other," against which Europeanness was measured.[4] Despotism, underdevelopment, brutality, and all the other stereotypical properties of the Orient were epitomized in the Ottoman Empire. The 1908 Young Turk revolution, which ended the despotic rule of Sultan Abdulhamid II, raised hopes for political and social change that would bring the Ottoman Empire closer to Europe. However, these hopes were soon refuted, as the failure of the Young Turk leadership was much more serious than that of the *Tanzimat* leaders. The situation deteriorated even further when the Ottoman Empire was caught in the maelstrom of the Balkan Wars and the First World War, which made it a belligerent against Great Britain and France, the two states whose civilizations had arguably contributed the most to what was then understood as Europeanness. The Ottoman defeat did not signal the end of hostilities, as Mustafa Kemal [Ataturk][5] resumed the armed struggle in Anatolia. Nonetheless, despite continued hostilities, Ataturk reckoned that Turkey's political and economic development could only come from the West, from Europe.[6] The concept of "Westernization despite the West [*Bati'ya ragmen Batililasma*]" gained crucial importance in Ataturk's campaign to integrate Turkey into the European political, cultural, and social paradigm. Despite the recurrence of atavistic nationalistic suspicions, Europe would always remain the model for Turkey's political, economic, and social transformation.

Yet, the focus of this study will not be on the intricacies of Turkey's Westernization project or what its potential membership in the European Union would mean for both it and the European Union. This study aims to explore Turkish political culture under the prism of improving Turkey-EU relations since the 1990s. Given that political culture is an accurate indicator of political and social transformation, a change of Turkish political culture under the impact of its ever-closer relations with the European Union and its membership perspective would constitute a significant step toward its effective Europeanization.

AIM

The aim of this study is to evaluate the impact that Turkey's decision to pursue full membership in the European Union has had on its political culture. Through the Copenhagen Criteria, the European Union required the introduction of political liberalism in all states interested in EU membership. Turkey, which had adopted republican ideas since its foundation, had now to imbue its political culture with political liberalism, the element of Western political thought that was disregarded in the process of Turkey's political and ideological Westernization. The impact of political liberalism on Turkish political culture has been significant. Kemalist nationalist ideology, which has been dominant since the foundation of the Republic, has come under considerable pressure. Turkish national identity has been reconsidered, as Turkish nationalists of all kinds, as well as Turkey's minorities, have enjoyed increased protection of their rights and have also been exposed to the debate that the introduction of the European supra- or postnational model has opened. Turkey's state tradition has also been influenced by liberal ideas espoused by the European Union. State intervention in the public sphere has been reduced, while the concept of national security has been openly discussed for the first time. Turkey's human rights legislation has undergone extensive reform aiming at increased protection of citizens' human rights. The convergence process with the EU human rights standards has led to a compromise of state interests for better protection of individual rights and freedoms. Islam, whose role in the public sphere was historically severely restricted by the secular state, could aspire to improved protection of religious freedom. Civil society has also benefited from the political liberalization process. State-independent socialization and expression and advocacy of group interests against the state have never been more profound and vibrant. Political and cultural pluralism has been aided through increased protection of individual and social rights. The Turkish state, economy, and society have already undergone substantial transformation; their full convergence with the European Union standards, though, is yet to be accomplished.

Turkey's membership in the European Union would be the culmination of a perennial quest for participation in European political and cultural space. Turkey's accession to the European Union would also require the successful completion of its transformation process, leading to complete liberalization of Turkish political culture. On the other hand, Turkey's EU membership would also leave a heavy imprint on the European Union itself. Current debates on European identity would then have to be then reconsidered, and a more inclusive interpretation of Europeanness would need to be adopted.

THE IMPORTANCE AND CONTRIBUTION OF THIS STUDY

The importance of studying Turkish political culture lies in the fact that the liberalization of Turkey's political culture in view of its integration into the European Union would have a profound impact on Turkey itself and the European Union, and it would directly affect regional politics. Notwithstanding the impact of Turkey's economic situation, the Cyprus question, and Greek-Turkish disputes, Turkey's illiberal political system has so far been the biggest domestic obstacle to its membership in the European Union.[7] Its political liberalization would lift the most serious obstacle for its EU membership. Nonetheless, Turkey's prospective EU membership is of critical importance for the European Union as well: The membership of a liberal, democratic Turkey would comprise an acid test for the political values the European Union stands for. As Turkey's population is almost entirely Muslim, the integration of a liberal, democratic Turkey would affirm the inclusive, multicultural, tolerant, and universalistic character of the European Union. Besides, Turkey's EU membership—despite its obvious functional difficulties, due mainly to its size and relative poverty—would multiply the strategic capabilities of the European Union in regions as sensitive as the Middle East, the Balkans, the Caucasus, and Central Asia.

Studying the debate on Turkish political culture that Turkey's approach toward the European Union and subsequent political liberalization steps have initiated, would also contribute to a better understanding of the challenges faced by liberalizing developing countries with a strongly authoritarian past and provide valuable insights for the global questions of democratization and liberalization. Although the number of democratic states has risen considerably in the recent years, this has not meant that democracy has dominated the sphere of world politics, especially in the Middle East. The difference between procedural and substantive democracy has become clearer than ever. Democratic institutions and elections cannot guarantee the existence of a fully functioning democratic political system if a democratic political culture is not present. There is a clear need to assist the development of a civic, participant political culture that will then enable the successful functioning of democratic institutions. Transition to political liberalism and the introduction of participant political culture elements are universal demands, and the political liberalization of Turkey, a Muslim-populated state with strong historic and political links with Europe and a secular political tradition, would be highly indicative of the prospects of the same experiment at a regional level. Turkey's success would weaken the argument that Islam and Western liberal and democratic tradition are incompatible.

THEORETICAL CONSIDERATIONS

Studies focusing on Europeanization, historical institutionalism, path-dependence theory and the two-level games model comprise the theoretical framework of this book.

UNDERSTANDING EUROPEANIZATION

This study has greatly benefited from the theoretical framework on Europeanization proposed in the volume *Transforming Europe: Europeanization and Domestic Change*, which focuses on the impact of Europeanization on the domestic structures of the EU member states. Europeanization is thus defined as "the emergence and development at the European level of distinct structures of governance."[8] EU member states change under the exertion of *adaptational pressures*, whose strength is inversely proportional to the compatibility of preexisting domestic conditions (*goodness of fit*). If domestic structures are largely compatible, convergence occurs at relatively low cost. Nevertheless, when domestic structures turn out to be both incompatible and enduring, the process of Europeanization becomes synonymous with radical domestic reform, which often meets serious reaction and whose success is uncertain.[9]

The process of adaptation is further affected by the presence or absence and activity of mediating factors. Multiple veto points in the domestic structure, facilitating formal institutions, the organizational and policymaking cultures of a country, the differential empowerment of domestic actors, and learning are cited as examples of mediating factors.[10] Structural adaptation can be seriously hampered by the existence of multiple veto points within a given policy-making structure,[11] while mediating formal institutions provide social actors with material and ideational resources to induce structural change. Organizational and policymaking cultures have their own impact on the ability of domestic actors to bring about structural change through the use of adaptational pressures, while differential empowerment of actors in the process of Europeanization provides them with incentives to pursue reform with zeal. The extent to which learning mechanisms become operational and domestic actors thereby modify their goals, identities, and preferences is also instrumental for the successful implementation of structural change. Learning constitutes "an agency-centered mechanism to induce such transformations."[12] The relative strength of elite learning and grassroots societal pressure on elites in the process of structural change is also a function of domestic structures. Societal pressure is prevalent in liberal and less so in corporatist structures, while elite learning prevails in elitist and less so in statist ones.[13]

Differentiating between the Europeanization and globalization processes and their effects is also of critical importance. As Europeanization and globalization trends are often interlinked, identifying the effects of Europeanization on the domestic political structures of EU member states can often become difficult. In some cases, Europeanization itself might constitute a response to the globalization processes by reinforcing their trends or by protecting EU member states against their undesired effects. Careful process-tracing and attention to the time sequences between EU policies and domestic changes allow us to distinguish between Europeanization and globalization effects. The same method can be useful for identifying whether specific structural changes can be attributed to domestic factors, with minor or no independent effects of Europeanization.[14]

Turkey is not directly in the focus of this analysis, as the concept of Europeanization *stricto sensu* relates to states that have already joined the Union. Nevertheless, states in the process of fulfilling the criteria for EU membership face similar challenges and undergo significant structural changes in their effort to meet the Copenhagen Criteria and become eligible for EU membership. In that respect, the concept of Europeanization could also be understood in the wider sense, so that it becomes applicable in the cases of states in the process of joining the European Union. Improving EU-Turkey relations and Turkey's desire to join the European Union have resulted in increasing adaptational pressures on Turkey's domestic political structures, depending on their *goodness of fit*. Meanwhile, mediating factors similar to those described in the study have emerged and been of critical importance in influencing the convergence process of Turkey's political structures to EU norms. Distinguishing between the effects of Europeanization, globalization, and domestic factors on political structures is an equally challenging task, and the aforementioned methodological tools can be successfully applied in the case of Turkey as well. The model of Europeanization can, therefore, be useful in understanding the impact of improving EU-Turkey relations on Turkish political culture.

THEORIES OF EUROPEAN INTEGRATION

Among the theories that have attempted to explain the political role of institutions in the context of European integration, four have attracted considerable interest: functionalism, liberal intergovernmentalism, constructivism, and historical institutionalism. Functionalism stresses the autonomous power and energy of society, especially when coupled to entrepreneurial institutions and agents.[15] What matters in politics is the economy, the society, and the efforts of individuals trying to solve practical problems cooperatively.[16] In this approach, institutions have little bearing on policies and political structures. What really matters is the self-sustainability of European integration, which becomes possible as a result of a spillover process. Initial cooperation efforts are amplified due to endogenous economic and political dynamics and result to further integration. This spillover can be functional or political: It is functional when problems resulting from incomplete integration enforce deeper policy coordination, mainly in the economic field. It is also political when existing EU institutions mobilize a self-reinforcing process of institution-building. Functionalism lost ground when the development of the European Economic Community turned out to be neither cumulative nor smooth. This showed that institutions had much more bearing on political developments than functionalists had predicted. Neofunctionalist views attempted to bridge the gap between functionalism and political developments at the European level by addressing the deficiencies of functionalist arguments in regard to the definability of European cooperation outcomes[17] and the persistence of national interest considerations within supranational institutions.[18] Nonetheless, they failed to produce a theory offering a satisfactory account of European integration.[19]

According to liberal intergovernmentalism, states are the primary decision makers, while governments are able to structure agendas and control other organizational agents. Moravcsik identified three essential elements at the core of liberal intergovernmentalism: the assumption of rational state behavior, a liberal theory of national preference formation, and an intergovernmentalist analysis of interstate negotiation.[20] The "liberal" aspect of liberal intergovernmentalism refers to the way social and economic interests use domestic political systems to influence central decision makers.[21] Interdependence in different fields of politics influences state decision-making processes. Thus, economic interdependence becomes the main determinant of state policies in the field of economics, while political-military interdependence has a crucial bearing on foreign policy decisions. Rationalist bargaining and institutional choice theories are additionally applied in order to explain how states reach compromises on disputed issues.[22] In their study of the EU Amsterdam Treaty, Moravcsik and Nicolaidis came up with "four categories of evidence confirming the overriding importance of a rational ranking of concerns about issue-specific interdependence in the formation of national preferences and positions." First, the positions of major state governments on important issues did not disprove the most common theories of issue-specific incentives for cooperation. Second, rational, issue-specific preferences were what was assumed and reported by officials. National policies were also relatively stable before and during the negotiations. Finally, "exceptional cases of salient policy reversal were positively correlated with salient, predictable and structural changes in domestic politics."[23] When it came to the question of how agreements were reached, interstate bargaining to achieve a substantive outcome was based on asymmetrical interdependence formation. International actors might have been very active, yet their activity was not in direct proportion with their real influence. States decided to cede sovereignty rights to international actors only where necessary to increase the credibility of their commitments. In view of their findings, Moravcsik and Nicolaidis stressed that the governments of the EU member states and not the EU institutions are the primary actors shaping EU politics.[24] Moravcsik elaborated his position by adding the role of institutions in the process of preference formation and bargaining.[25] This does not mean an approach toward institutionalism. Institutions are not recognized as primary actors in shaping preferences or affecting identities. Yet, they help enforce agreements, make bargains credible, and provide a rule-based structure as a bulwark against defection.[26]

Constructivist views of Europeanization argued that critical decisions for the future of the European Union were made on the base not of rational but of normative arguments. The Eastern enlargement is a characteristic case of a norm-based decision within the European Union. The decision to incorporate ten new member states, whose level of economic development was in most cases far behind the EU average levels, could hardly be explained on the basis of the national interests of existing member states. The enlargement decision could only be made under the influence of "rhetorical action," the strategic use of norm-based arguments. Given that liberal democracy has acted as the core and legitimating basis of the European integration project, it provided the bulk of norm-based arguments, which were used for the further deepening and widening of the European Union. Since the new candidate states adopted a rhetoric heavily influenced by political liberalism and democratic ideals, it was virtually impossible for EU institutions and member states to give priority to their economic grievances over the need to prove their loyalty to the constitutive values and norms of the European Union.[27] Identity politics also significantly influence political decision-making within the European Union. Collective nation-state identities define the realm of interests considered legitimate and appropriate in a given political discourse. The responses of Germany, France, and the United Kingdom to the introduction of a single European currency in the late 1990s differed because of the unequal identification of their respective national identities with a common European identity. An increasingly Europeanizing national identity in the case of Germany coincided with strong support for the Euro. In the case of the United Kingdom, anti-European sentiment and emphasis on British national identity was followed by strong opposition to the Euro, while in France fluctuations in the European vs. national identity debate were mirrored on the French stance regarding the introduction of the Euro.[28]

While functionalism, liberal intergovernmentalism, and constructivism adopt an essentially bottom-up approach, in which social actors rather than institutions are important, institutionalism adopts a top-down approach. Institutions are political vehicles that can crucially affect political structures and policies, sometimes against the wish of domestic actors. Hall and Taylor have identified four key features of historical institutionalism: "First, historical institutionalists tend to conceptualize the relationship between institutions and individual behavior in relatively broad terms. Second, they emphasize the asymmetries of power associated with the operation and development of institutions. Third, they tend to have a view of institutional development that emphasizes path dependence and unintended consequences. Fourth, they are especially concerned to integrate institutional analysis with the contribution that other kinds of factors, such as ideas, can make to political outcomes."[29]

Historical institutionalism becomes distinctive by emphasizing the effects of institutions on politics.[30] In contrast with functionalist views that institutions have been deliberately designed by contemporary actors for the efficient performance of specific functions, historical institutionalists argue that institutional choices made in the past can persist and thereby shape and contain actors over time.[31] Temporary setbacks may occur due to contemporary actor activities, yet institutional choices in the end prevail. Putnam has outlined three basic principles that explain differences in democratic performance.[32] According to the first, "social context and history profoundly condition the effectiveness of institutions." Institutions do not operate in a historical or social vacuum, and the lack or existence of civic cooperation, democratic government, and public trust traditions have a profound influence on institutional performance. As Putnam puts it, "effective and responsive institutions depend, in the language of civic humanism, on republican virtues and rights."[33] According to the second principle, "changing formal institutions can change political practice." Institutions do matter in shaping public policy and can become the means for the implementation of policies and change of identities, values, power, and strategies. This means that states and communities are not prisoners of their own history and tradition. Political reform programs can be successful in their efforts to bring about change in political practice and institutional performance, yet there is little room for overambitious expectations. As the third principle states, "most institutional history moves slowly." In the short run, it is virtually impossible to overcome adverse political and social legacies and build thriving networks of civic cooperation, democratic government, and public trust. Political and social reform can only be successful through planned efforts for social capital[34] building. Historical knowledge is crucial in order to understand diversity in institutional development and why some possible outcomes prevailed upon others.

PATH DEPENDENCE THEORY

The concept of *path dependence* is instrumental in this respect. According to Pierson, early decisions provide incentives for actors to perpetuate institutional and policy choices inherited from the past, even when the resulting outcomes are manifestly inefficient.[35] Levi attempts to give a more detailed approach:

> Path dependence has to mean, if it is to mean anything, that once a country or region has started down a path, the costs of reversal are very high. There will be other choice points, but the entrenchments of certain institutional arrangements obstruct easy reversal of the initial choice. Perhaps the better metaphor is a tree rather than a path. From the same trunk, there are many different branches and smaller braches. Although it is possible to turn around or to clamber from one to the other—and essential if the chosen branch dies—the branch on which a climber begins is the one she tends to follow.[36]

Risse adds that a path dependent process is "one in which positive feedback loops lead to increasing returns."[37] In the context of the European Union, the Maastricht Treaty could be seen as an example where path dependence crucially affected European politics. Once the steps leading to the Economic and Monetary Union (EMU) were finalized, the costs of reversing the agreed policies eventually became unaffordable for both the public and the private sector. The socialization process, "the gradual adaptation and internalization of new norms and rules," was a necessary step for the success of the EMU. This process was reinforced by the implementation of the EMU and "modified the standard operating procedures of existing public and private institutions."[38] Shaped as either a tree or a path, the concept of path dependence sheds light on the role of history in the course of institutional reform. As North has stressed: "Path dependence means that history matters. We cannot understand today's choices (and define them in the modeling of economic performance) without tracing the incremental evolution of institutions. . . . We need to know much more about culturally derived forms of behavior and how they interact with formal rules to get better answers to such issues."[39]

THE TWO-LEVEL GAME MODEL

The model of *two-level games* introduced by Putnam can also be applied to explain the process of the Europeanization of Turkish political culture. With the introduction of this term, Putnam examined the interactions of domestic and international politics during diplomatic negotiations, using the example of the 1978 Bonn Accord between the United States, Japan, and West Germany.[40] A negotiation at the international level (Level I) takes place simultaneously with a negotiation at the domestic level (Level II) between the negotiators and their respective political constituencies. Negotiators have to constantly think how a possible compromise agreement would resonate domestically and, more importantly, whether the agreement would be so unpopular that it would fail to be ratified. A compromise agreement is then reached, and parties are forced to accommodate the positions and interests of their counterparts. However, it appears that the observed policy shifts were initially supported by domestic political factions, which were outnumbered in the process of domestic decision policy-making.[41] In their view, the achieved compromise was favoring rather than curtailing national interest. Nonetheless, this policy shift would not have occurred had there not been a negotiation at the international level. International negotiations, on the other hand, are limited in their scope by the necessity to have their outcomes ratified by domestic institutions. To outline the limits of the agreement spectrum, Putnam has defined "win-sets" as the set of all possible international agreements that would "win" ratification at the domestic level.[42] The outer limits of a win-set are defined by the domestic constraints that would render the ratification of the agreement impossible. The size of the win-set depends on the distribution of power, preferences, and possible coalitions among domestic constituents and institutions, as well as on the strategies of international negotiators.[43] The two-level approach recognizes the inevitability of domestic conflict on the definition of national interest and accepts that domestic and international imperatives are simultaneously compromised.[44]

A HISTORICAL INSTITUTIONALIST APPROACH

This study has been informed by a broader historical institutionalist approach. Liberal intergovernmentalism provides a clear insight into the process of Europeanization but cannot account for all its complexities. EU member states maintain a great leverage inside the European Union; EU institutions, however, still retain a considerable degree of autonomy in their actions, which has often shaped EU political developments contrary to the perceived interests of EU member states. The existence of this slack means that the character of EU institutions is primarily political. Their function is not limited to facilitating EU member state negotiations by means of reducing transaction costs, managing interdependence, and locking in agreements. Institutions are crucial in helping to implement policies and diffusing norms and expectations, often against the wishes of key domestic institutions, which might not approve of their formation.[45] In the context of the European Union, the establishment of autonomous enforcement mechanisms reinforces the role of EU institutions. Moreover, the European Union constitutes a *sui generis* type of politics that is neither domestic nor interstate, as it creates additional options for domestic political actors. The European Union can sometimes become involved in domestic politics and have considerable impact on policies and institutions.[46] The historical institutionalist approach does not underestimate existing differences between historical institutionalism, sociological institutionalism, and rational choice theory.[47] Rational choice theory can offer useful insights in historical institutionalism debates, yet its incorporation as a subcategory of historical institutionalism is problematic, as this would challenge the social ontology of historical institutionalism. Institutions are perceived as structures, whose functionality is open to empirical and historical research rather than functional means of reducing uncertainty. The ineffective and inefficient nature of social institutions, institutions as the subject and focus of political struggle, and the contingent nature of such struggles whose outcomes cannot be derived from the existing international context have all attracted the interest of historical institutionalists.[48] In the words of Thelen and Steinmo, "The institutions that are in the center of historical institutionalist analysis . . . can shape and constrain political strategies in important ways, but they are themselves also the outcome (conscious or unintended) of deliberate political strategies of political conflict and of choice."[49]

Nonetheless, the historical institutionalist account of European integration should not be understood as merely establishing a principal-agent relationship between EU member states and institutions.[50] While Pierson correctly argues that gaps in member state control over institutions can arise from "altered circumstances or new information" and changes in government,[51] this account needs to be expanded so it includes "the partial autonomy of EU institutions, politicians' restricted time horizons, the ubiquity of unintended consequences and shifts in domestic preferences." Institutions are thus perceived as having a distinct political effect by bringing to the fore tensions and inconsistencies between European and domestic institutions, which spark in turn adaptational pressures at the domestic level. These pressures corroborate the active role of Europeanization in inducing domestic change.[52]

DEFINING POLITICAL CULTURE

Aims

The following section aims to explore the concept of political culture. Various approaches to the term "political culture" will be outlined, and the intellectual debate on the function and impact of political culture will be explored. The views of advocates and critics of the usefulness of political culture as an analytical tool of comparative politics will be juxtaposed, and a working definition will be selected. The last part of this chapter will refer to the empirical basis and structure of this study.

Definitions of Political Culture

The sociocultural tradition of political analysis was by no means a product of the twentieth century. Plato first argued in his *Republic* that governments vary in according to the dispositions of their citizenry. This idea was furthered by Alexis de Tocqueville in his treatise *Democracy in America*.[53] Tocqueville stressed the link between the mores of a society and its political practices. In the case of the United States, the number and variety of civic associations reinforce the "habits of the heart" that are essential to stable and effective democratic institutions.[54]

The political culture approach gained impetus in the mid-twentieth century, when the failure of purely institutional descriptions of political systems to offer adequate explanations of post-Second World War political developments led scholars to delve into the reasons why similar political institutions performed so divergently in different countries. Gabriel Almond and Sydney Verba attempted with the introduction of the term "political culture" to offer a new tool for the study of political systems.[55] This soon attracted the interest of academics, and the debate gained intensity in the ideologically polarized environment of the Cold War. Before embarking on the debate on Turkish political culture, it would be, therefore, useful to discuss definitions of and the intellectual debate on political culture, the term that will be the crux of this study. According to Pye, political culture is "the sum of the fundamental values, sentiments and knowledge that give form and substance to political processes."[56] Hague and Harrop have identified the "knowledge, beliefs, opinions and emotions of individual citizens toward their form of government" as the "building blocks" of political culture.[57] Kavanagh argues that the study of political culture is concerned with "*orientations* towards *political objects.* Orientations are predispositions to political action and are determined by such factors as traditions, historical memories, motives, norms, emotions and symbols. We can break these down into their component parts as follows: cognitions (knowledge and awareness of the political system); affect (emotional disposition to the system); and evaluation (judgment about the system)."[58]

Inglehart maintains that, according to the political culture approach, "People's responses to their situations are shaped by subjective orientations, which vary cross-culturally and within subcultures. . . . These variations in subjective orientations reflect differences in socialization experience, with early learning conditioning later learning."[59]

Inglehart adds that cultural theory implies that culture cannot be changed overnight, though the young are easier to influence; observed cross-cultural differences reflect the experience of generations, even centuries, rather than relatively short-run factors.[60]

In what follows, political culture will be understood as a set of citizens' orientations toward political objects based on their knowledge, beliefs, opinions, and emotions. The classification of political cultures into parochial, subject, and participant, as suggested by Almond and Verba in their groundbreaking study of political culture, will also be followed. In *parochial* political culture there are no specialized political roles in societies, and for members of these societies political orientations to these roles are not separated from their religious and social orientations. In *subject* political culture there is a high frequency toward a differentiated political system and toward the output aspects of the system, but there are almost no orientations toward specifically input objects and toward the self as an active participant; it is essentially a passive system as far as government influence is concerned. In *participant* political culture, citizens tend to be explicitly oriented to the system as a whole. Close attention is paid to politics, while popular participation is regarded as both desirable and effective.[61]

The Debate on Political Culture

Since its introduction in the early 1960s, the term "political culture" has attracted considerable interest and sparked intellectual debate. Almond and Verba were the first to launch a comparative study of the political culture of the United States, the United Kingdom, Italy, West Germany, and Mexico. In their book they argued that "civic culture" is a blend of parochial, subject, and participant political culture, which differs in each state and reconciles the participation of citizens in the political process with the vital necessity for government to govern. Democratic stability was underpinned by a political culture character- ized by a blend of parochial, subject, and participant political cultures on the side of the citizens and a balance between obligation and per- formance on the side of the government.[62] The pioneering work of Almond and Verba was followed by a considerable number of scholars who applied behaviorist social science techniques to study the political culture of both capitalist and communist states. Meanwhile, the first critical views of the new political culture "school" appeared and were formed into four main groups.

The first group of—predominantly leftist—critics argued that Almond and Verba's work was undermined by hidden assumptions. It seemed to have assumed that all political systems should develop along relatively homogeneous paths toward some form of largely capi- talist economic system and largely nonideological liberal economic polity. It was also pointed that Almond and Verba showed no interest in subcultures, either class-, or ethnic-based, implicitly seeing them as "un-modern," while they ignored that other forms of stable democ- racy seemed possible, notably "consociational" ones based on "elite accommodation" in "pillared" societies like Belgium or the Nether- lands. In other words, Almond and Verba's work was accused of merely celebrating the "actually existing" Anglo-American democracy.[63]

The second argument was based on more specific methodologi- cal issues. The problems of using opinion polls, especially for prob- ing complex attitudes, were addressed. Matters became even more difficult when transnational comparisons were made. Besides, there was still vagueness in the content of the Almond and Verba's term "civic culture." Their research failed to anticipate crucial problems that the U.S. and UK civic cultures faced in the 1960s and 1970s, when decline in system support and the rise of ethnic nationalism in the United Kingdom were observed.[64]

According to the third group of critics, the political culture approach faced problems with the causality and primacy implied. Many schol- ars argued that it was vital to discover how attitudes were formed in the first place or to stress how powerless individuals were—even in democratic states. It was also argued that the political culture school by focusing on the power of socialization and tradition seemed more suited to explain continuity, while it was incapable of explaining the causal process by which political change took place. From a Marxist viewpoint, political and social attitudes reflected class or ethnic status differences and were formed by capitalist-controlled institutions such as schools, universities, and media. This "false consciousness" did not need to be researched; it needed to be replaced, instead, by a socialist political culture, which would guarantee political and social development.[65] Moreover, it was argued that the causality between civic culture and stable democratic government did not run from the former to the latter, as Almond and Verba had argued, but vice versa.[66]

Criticism of the political culture approach was also articulated by economists. The introduction of market and bargaining models into political studies resulted in the development of rational and public choice theories. The common assertion of all economics-based political theories was that all political actors were rational, short-term interest maximizers. Since political behavior could be accurately predicted through the use of economics-based models, the study of political culture was unnecessary. Public choice theories gained great popularity in the late 1970s and 1980s, and alternative approaches of studying political behavior lost part of their popularity.[67]

A second point of debate among disciples of the political culture approach was whether or not political culture is a fixed, unchangeable feature of states and citizens. Pye and Pye argued in their study of Asian political culture that political culture is "remarkably durable and persistent" because of its roots both in national histories and in the personalities of individuals.[68] On the other hand, Diamond opposed cultural determinism, arguing that historical, theoretical, and normative reasons affirm the changeability of political culture. Research has shown that cognitive, attitudinal, and evaluational dimensions of political culture can change in response to regime performance and—in many cases—have undergone considerable change. Political culture is also influenced by state economic and social structure, international factors, and the functioning of the political system. The examples of states like Germany, Japan, Spain, and Italy, which managed to liberalize and democratize their political culture, prove that efforts to influence political culture can bear fruit.[69]

The debate certainly pointed out weak points in the formation of the political culture approach; on the other hand, critics could not successfully deny the usefulness of political culture as an analytical tool in the field of comparative politics. The question of how to sustain and promote democracy, the main theme of Almond and Verba's work, has remained among the focal points of comparative politics research. The political culture school greatly benefited from various responses of academics, as well as alternative theories (e.g. neoinstitutionalism and rational choice theory). The political culture approach was thus elaborated and advanced. While rational choice models confirmed their usefulness in analyzing short-term fluctuations within a given system, taking cultural and institutional factors as constant, political culture proved indispensable in the study of long-term change.[70] It was also widely accepted that political culture is not something static but undergoes constant change, influenced by a series of social and political factors. In their later study of political culture, Almond and Verba highlighted a number of shifts in the civic culture of the five states they had first researched.[71] Robert Putnam was the scholar who later had the biggest influence on the political culture debate; his work focused on two states whose political culture was first studied by Almond and Verba. With his book on Italian civic tradition, Putnam revisited Italian political culture, shedding light on civic diversity among Italian provinces.[72] Diverging efficiency levels of Italian regional governments were directly correlated with the regional political culture. In the regions where communal trust and participation were higher, institutional performance was also high. Putnam related divergence of political cultures with the historical background of each Italian region.[73] His book on American political culture in the end of the twentieth century also illustrated the decline of political activity and community engagement in the United States. Putnam attributed the decreasing popularity of U.S. civic values in the last third of the twentieth century to a series of factors ranging from pressure of money and time to suburbanization and electronic entertainment.[74] In his view, only recuperation of social capital through individual and social initiative could reverse the declining process of the U.S. civic culture.

It should, however, be explained that applying the political culture model is not tantamount to endorsement of culturalist theories.[75] Political culture should not be understood as an immutable property that precludes the possibility of political change and favors the perpetuation of the status quo. Processes of political socialization are highly important for the formation of political culture. School, family, and other social groupings have their contribution to the formation of perceptions, affects, and evaluations that constitute political culture. Although historical memories and political socialization have considerable impact on the formation of political culture, political culture can be—to a large extent—considered as an independent variable in political science research. While the relationship between political culture and political structures is interactive, the survival of "traditional" attitudes even in the states where the most intensive political socialization programs were enforced has indicated that there are certain limits to the plasticity of political culture.[76] In other words, political culture should not always be considered as an independent variable in the study of political behavior and institutions. Whether political culture is influenced by or influences political behavior or institutions, is to be examined *ad hoc*, on the basis of the idiosyncrasies of the political phenomenon under examination. As Putnam succinctly puts it, "Social scientists have long debated what causes what—culture or structure. In the context of our argument this debate concerns the complicated causal nexus among the cultural norms and attitudes and the social structures and behavioral patterns that make up the civic community. . . . Most dispassionate commentators recognize that attitudes and practices constitute a mutually reinforcing equilibrium. Social trust, norms of reciprocity, networks of civic engagement, and successful cooperation are mutually reinforcing."[77]

Kavanagh's categorization of political culture as an amalgam of cognitions, affect, and evaluation will be applied in this study. The knowledge, emotions, and opinions of Turkish citizens and state officials on the issues that form the content of Turkish political culture will be examined, so that continuity and change in Turkish political culture since EU-Turkey relations started improving can be assessed. The predominantly subject nature of the traditional Turkish political culture outlines the properties of the Turkish political system and provides with explanations of popular behavior and choice.

Applying the political culture approach in the case of Turkey is highly illuminating. Both Ottoman and republican Turkish social context and history legacies were such that any modernizing institutional reform efforts would be seriously hampered. Nonetheless, as intensive and radical modernization programs have dominated both late Ottoman and republican Turkish elite politics, Turkey can be seen as a case where the success of radical top-down institutional reform programs can be gauged. The success of Turkey's conversion from an "Oriental" to a Western European state could provide us with evidence that elite-based institutional reform programs have some chance of success, no matter how adverse the political and social environment. Turkey, indeed, made several important steps in the direction of joining the European political and social paradigm but also failed to keep track of equally significant developments focusing on bringing political liberalism to the heart of European politics. According to the political culture approach, Turkey's social context and history did not facilitate modernizing institutional reform efforts; nonetheless, while the possibility that Turkey can endorse the European liberal paradigm is not precluded, the reasons why there has been a delay in its adoption are explored. Institutional change is not a process that can be successfully dictated or enforced in a short period of time, and understanding the reasons for its partial failure is the first step in the effort for its full implementation. Although Turkish political culture is treated in this study as one of the reasons why political liberalism failed to influence Turkish politics until EU-Turkey relations started improving, it is not viewed as an insurmountable obstacle in Turkey's effort to join the European Union. On the contrary, political culture is treated as a changeable attribute that can be affected by major political or social developments and become the object of political reform programs, even though change may be slow. A liberal shift in Turkish political culture in view of improving EU-Turkey relations would be a first significant signal that Turkey's political liberalization is not a chimera and that Turkey's full membership in the European Union is a realistic long-term task.

TIME FRAME-OUTLINE

The time frame of this study is defined by two crucial decisions of the European Council on the future of EU-Turkey relations. The first is the Helsinki European Council decision of December 1999, which awarded Turkey the status of candidate for EU membership. The second is the decision of the Brussels European Council in December 2004, which set October 3, 2005, to be the start date of EU-Turkey accession negotiations. Following an introduction to the historical background to the debate on Turkish political culture, the impact of improving EU-Turkey relations on Turkish political culture will be assessed, with an examination of four key areas: civil society, state-society relations, secularism, and national identity. The stance of social actors who played a key role in supporting or obstructing the reform process will be scrutinized, as well as the incidence of social learning, a crucial indicator for the change of political culture. In the concluding chapter, the liberalizing effect of the European Union will be assessed in whole.

CHAPTER 2

THE HISTORICAL BACKGROUND
TO THE DEBATE ON TURKISH
POLITICAL CULTURE

THE EMERGENCE OF THE REPUBLIC

Warfare, massacres, and population exchanges in the first quarter of the twentieth century had altered the multireligious character of Anatolia, establishing a formidable Muslim preponderance. Turkish national identity was not embedded in all the Muslim populations of Anatolia, which were often of diverse ethnic origin. Kurds, Arabs, Lazes, Bosnians, Albanians, Circassians, Chechens, and other Caucasian peoples were only a few of the existing Muslim ethnicities in Anatolia, while a substantial Muslim Alevi[1] religious minority challenged the Sunni majority. Under the leadership of Ataturk, the Turkish nation-state, which emerged in the aftermath of the First World War, made quick steps toward what was thought to be the "Western" political and civilizational model. A Republic was proclaimed and the Caliphate abolished. The new Turkish state was based on secularism; the Latin alphabet was substituted for Arabic, while Ottoman and Islamic culture was systematically purged, and Western European culture was—even forcibly—introduced.[2] While the young republic denounced the legacy of the Ottoman Empire and severed its legal, political, and cultural links with its predecessor state, Kemalist modernization belonged to the intellectual tradition of late Ottoman Westernization. Influenced by the anti-Islamic and nationalist features of Young Turk ideology, which were reinforced through the dismemberment process of the Ottoman Empire, Ataturk aimed to establish a Turkish nation-state in Anatolia. This project did not allow for ethnic or religious diversity. The authoritarian structure of early republican Turkey facilitated a campaign for the forging of a strong Turkish national identity. Individual rights were ignored when they contradicted the interests of the state, as defined by Ataturk and his staff.

Things started to change in 1946, when Turkey made a crucial transition to multiparty democracy. Nonetheless, human rights violations remained common, and minorities were particularly affected. Moreover, Turkey's democracy was repeatedly hit by military coups, which allegedly aimed to forestall anti-Kemalist revisionism. While constitutional reforms established a tutelary role for the military, they also allowed for the diversification of Turkish politics with the rise of Islamist, leftist, and minority movements. The rise of Kurdish nationalism seriously challenged republican Turkey's nation-building project and culminated in terrorist attacks and guerrilla warfare in the eastern and southeastern provinces of Turkey in the 1980s and 1990s. Turkish security forces managed to contain the direct secession threat but, on the other hand, could not prevent the consolidation of a distinct Kurdish national identity in a significant part of Turkey's population. Kemalism managed to create a Turkish nation-state, yet Turkey's full convergence with the Western political and civilizational paradigm remained unfinished. The nature of Turkish political culture was one of the issues that manifested the incomplete character of the Kemalist Westernization project.

THE REPUBLICAN IMPACT ON
TURKISH POLITICAL CULTURE

The founding of a modern Turkish nation-state did not cause a fundamental change in the dominant Ottoman political culture. A perennial center-periphery cleavage persisted,[3] as the Republican People's Party (*Cumhuriyet Halk Partisi*—CHP) took over in republican Turkey the functions of the Ottoman state bureaucracy.[4] Besides, Ottoman state autonomy implied that status-oriented values, rather than market-oriented values, were dominant. As Ozbudun argues, "The relationship between economic and political power was the reverse of its equivalent in Western Europe. Instead of economic power (ownership of the means of production) leading to political power, political power (high position in the state bureaucracy) gave access to material wealth."[5]

Subject political culture, which prevailed over the parochial model in the late years of the Ottoman Empire as a result of extensive centralization efforts in the nineteenth century, was not enriched by elements of participant political culture, a characteristic of Western European liberal democracies. On the contrary, reverence toward the state persisted and even increased. Despite the lip service usually paid to Turkish rural society as the "standard-bearer of Turkishness," the unity and continuity of the nation-state were perceived to be under constant threat by local notables, traditional groups, and rural populations. Therefore, the central bureaucracy had to employ absolute political control and social-engineering policies to secure state interests against those centers of "counterofficial culture."[6] According to Ataturk, sovereignty was to "belong to the people without any qualifications and conditions." Yet, in practice, this meant that the state elite, which allegedly understood the interest of the people better than the people itself, would exercise sovereignty in the name of the people. As Heper put it, "transcendentalism stressed the priority of the community and the state over the citizens, whose interest is identified with the common rather than their individual interest."[7] The Ottoman tradition of the benevolent father state (*devlet baba*) with an emphasis on equity enshrined a political culture accepting the legitimacy of an interventionist state.[8] As Mardin points out, "It is conceded in the abstract that the state and its leaders have a right and obligation to set a course for society and to use public resources to pursue that course. . . . The emphasis is on the ends of state intervention, and checks and balances are not seen as preventing abuse of power but rather as impeding the state's course toward its goal. Therefore, to some extent, there has been an acceptance of a high concentration of power—economic, administrative and military."[9]

On the other hand, the imposition of Kemalist imperatives and views as regards the formation of Turkish identity could not remain unchallenged. The Kemalist nation-building and civilizational project was so ambitious in its objectives that established groups and ideologies that could not be reconciled with the new image of Turkish political culture faced marginalization or even persecution. In the field of national identity, both the religious base of the Ottoman Turkish national identity and the multiethnic origins of the Ottoman population were removed from the fabric of the newly constructed Turkish national identity. Islamists, minorities, and liberals were the main opponents of this policy. Islamists claimed that Islam was the crucial factor in defining Turkish national identity. This view was in harmony with traditional Ottoman opposition to any forms of ethnic nationalism; the only meaningful division it saw was between believers and nonbelievers in Islam, a division institutionalized in the *millet* system.[10] Minorities also opposed the Kemalist nation-building project. Since the Greek and Armenian minorities had shrunk in republican Turkey, the Kurdish minority took the lead in opposition of Kemalist plans. The Sheikh Said rebellion of 1925 and other less important Kurdish uprisings, which also had religious underpinnings, showed that even Muslim ethnic groups of republican Turkey did not abandon their distinct identity.[11] The 1930 "Menemen Incident [*Menemen Olayi*]" provided additional evidence that the secularization program faced serious grassroots challenge also from the Turkish majority of the population.[12] And Turkish liberals, despite their overall support for the Kemalist modernization project,[13] opposed the forced imposition of official Turkish national identity on the population, as it meant severe human rights violations and was one more of the characteristics of an increasingly authoritarian state. Their political position and influence in the early republican years were, however, too feeble to affect the course of political events.

EARLY REPUBLICAN ENCOUNTERS WITH POLITICAL LIBERALISM

The Profile of Liberalism in Early Republican Turkey

Ideas like liberalism and democracy—already not very popular in the political context of the interwar years—did not attract the interest of the Kemalist leadership. The liberal faction within the Young Turk Committee of Union and Progress (*Ittihat ve Terakki Cemiyeti*) had been defeated, and subsequent political developments had eliminated its political stature.[14] Public opinion had linked Ottoman liberals with military defeat in the Balkan wars and collaboration with foreign occupation forces between 1918 and 1922.[15] Ottoman liberals comprised the backbone of the Ottoman Istanbul governments, which sided with Western powers and signed the Treaty of Sevres, thereby accepting the partition of Anatolia. The position of Ottoman liberals was further strengthened by the political support provided by the Ottoman Sultan Mehmed VI Vahdettin. Only the military victory of the Ankara-based Kemalist forces decided the power struggle between the Istanbul and Ankara governments. As the Istanbul government disintegrated, tarnished by its cooperation with Western forces, and Kemalist nationalists were taking over control of the whole country, the public appeal of political liberalism reached a nadir: liberalism became inextricably linked with capitulation, concession, and sacrifice of national interests, and particularly with the lethal—for the Ottoman Empire—Treaty of Sevres. Given that political environment, it is no wonder that the influence of Ottoman liberals in the newly established Republic of Turkey was minimal. In the early republican years, liberal ideas could only be advocated by politicians whose Kemalist credentials were indisputable. Yet loyalty toward Kemalist orthodoxy could hardly be compromised with a liberal view of politics.[16] This contradiction became apparent in the works of Ahmet Agaoglu, one of the most prominent representatives of liberal thinking in republican Turkey.[17] Nonetheless, even this version of qualified political liberalism could hardly be tolerated. Although Ataturk was at times doubtful of the validity of political authoritarianism and seemed to realize the benefits of political pluralism, in the end he decided to eliminate liberal political opposition expressed in the form of the Progressive Republican and the Free Republican Parties.[18]

The First Liberal Attempt: The Progressive Republican Party

The first attempt to introduce liberal policies in republican Turkey took place in November 1924 with the establishment of the Progressive Republican Party (*Terrakiperver Cumhuriyet Firkasi*).[19] Increasing tension between the radical and the moderate wing of Ataturk's People's Party led Rauf [Orbay] and thirty-two deputies of the Turkish National Assembly to the decision to found an opposition party. The party manifesto and program showed that the new party remained nationalistic and secular, yet it also opposed the authoritarian tendencies displayed by the radical wing of the People's Party (*Halk Partisi*). Decentralization, the separation of powers, evolutionary rather than revolutionary change, as well as a more liberal economic policy, were some of its political objectives.[20] The appeal of the views expressed by the Progressive Republican Party was considerable, and Ataturk had to remove Prime Minister Ismet [Inonu], who had sided with the radical authoritarians of the People's Party. The appointment of the moderate Fethi [Okyar] to the Prime Minister office aimed to prevent massive deputy defections to the newly established opposition party. Yet the radicals retained key positions in the new government, and following events gave them the upper hand. The 1925 Sheikh Said rebellion shook the state. Martial law was proclaimed in the eastern provinces, and increasing pressure was exercised on the opposition party leaders to disband voluntarily. Okyar eventually resigned. Inonu returned to his former post and pushed through the parliament the

Law of the Maintenance of Order (*Takrir-i Sukun Kanunu*). Two special "Independence Tribunals [*Istiklal Mahkemeleri*]"[21]—one for the east and one for the rest of the country—were reinstated. Mounting state suppression affected not only the Kurdish minority but also all Turkish dissident voices. Eight opposition newspapers were closed down, while prominent journalists were arrested. Under those adverse circumstances, the fate of the Progressive Republican Party was sealed. On the advice of the Independence Tribunal, the party was closed down by the government on June 3, 1925, on the grounds that some of its members had allegedly supported the Sheikh Said rebellion and tried to exploit religion for political purposes.[22] The "Izmir Conspiracy"[23] of June 1926 gave radical Kemalists the pretext to ban the leaders of Progressive Republican Party from Turkish politics and secure the insulation of republican Turkey against any liberal influences.[24]

The Second Liberal Attempt: The Free Republican Party

Despite his strong opposition to the Progressive Republican Party, it was Ataturk himself who encouraged the establishment of the second opposition party in the history of republican Turkey. The growing authoritarianism of the governing CHP[25] and the severe economic crisis that hit the country as a result of the Great Depression caused serious social discontent. Ataturk attempted to defuse this through the establishment of a legal opposition party that could challenge official policies. It seems that he was also concerned about the increasingly authoritarian character of the Turkish Republic and his despotic image. In 1930 Ataturk approached the former Prime Minister and known moderate Fethi [Okyar] and asked him to found a new party, arguing that "our present appearance more or less conforms to that of a dictatorship. . . . but I don't want to leave as a legacy to the nation an institution of despotism and go down in history like this."[26]

Following Ataturk's instructions, Okyar founded the Free Republican Party (*Serbest Cumhuriyet Firkasi*) and was joined by fifteen deputies, all prominent CHP members. Ataturk showed his goodwill by persuading his oldest friend Nuri [Conker] and his sister Makbule to join the new party. Ahmet Agaoglu was also among its founding members. The political orientations of the new party had a liberal essence similar to those of the Progressive Republican Party. Liberal economic policies, freedom of speech, and direct elections were among the party's main political positions. However, the reaction of the established CHP radical wing was vehement and effective. Skirmishes with party supporters and the police in Izmir in September 1930 and increasing political tension in the aftermath of the October 1930 local elections induced Ataturk to abandon his formerly neutral position, side with the CHP and support its policies. Okyar, who had no intention to oppose Ataturk himself, had no option but to close down the party on November 16, 1930.[27] The Kemalist elite showed its unwillingness to tolerate even "loyal" opposition and its inability to mobilize popular support for its reform program. Ataturk even came to the point of declaring that "liberalism is a system applied in colonies! Yet we are not and will not become a colony. Considering liberalism is denying the revolution."[28]

While the Turkish people seemed willing to endorse any dissenting political movement that could loosen the grip of the Kemalist elite over the state and society,[29] democracy and political liberalism seemed to be a very low priority at that time. The need to forge the unity of a Turkish nation-state and build a modern, secular national identity necessarily involved illiberal policies violating fundamental human rights. Subject political culture remained dominant in the mix of Turkish civic culture. The concurrent rise of authoritarianism and totalitarianism all over Europe and the outbreak of the Second World War could not but strengthen the illiberal character of the Turkish Republic in the following years.

POST-SECOND WORLD WAR DEVELOPMENTS

The Rise of the Opposition

Official Kemalist policies affecting political culture faced opposition.[30] This opposition, however, was not as clear-cut as in the case of national identity, because both the preceding Ottoman and the newly championed Kemalist political cultures could be classified as predominantly subject and had much in common. The focus switch from the Caliph and the Empire-cradle of the Islamic *ummah* to the modern Turkish state certainly caused a lot of friction among Islamists and minorities; nonetheless, it did not require a radically different form of political socialization. It was only the liberals who advocated the introduction of participant elements into Turkish political culture and—with their sparse forces—objected to the establishment of a subject republican political culture.

The introduction of multiparty politics in 1946 constituted a big leap forward as regards Turkey's democratization and paved the way for a gradual reconsideration of Turkish political culture. The free elections of 1950 and the peaceful transfer of power from the CHP to the DP, the loosening of restrictions on religious activities and increasing cooperation with Kurdish chieftains confirmed the change that the introduction of multiparty politics had brought about. The latter also allowed for the emergence of instrumentalist views of political culture. Authoritarian government policies and a series of military coups, however, reversed the "instrumentalization" process of Turkish political culture.[31] Participant elements of political culture faded under the dominant influence of a strong, centralized Turkish state. Turkey was transformed into an illiberal democracy, a feature of many states outside the Western core, in which democratic procedures—above all free elections—were observed, yet respect of civil liberties was missing.[32] Despite this, advocates of Turkey's political liberalization still championed the introduction of participant elements into Turkish political culture. The process of Turkey's political liberalization would be neither smooth nor cumulative.

The Introduction of Multiparty Politics and the Democrat Party

In the aftermath of the Second World War, the introduction of multiparty politics was the first step in the process of Turkey's political liberalization. Both domestic distress and external pressure influenced the decision of Ataturk's successor Ismet Inonu to allow for the establishment of opposition parties. The CHP was increasingly unpopular with the majority of the population, and resentment increased due to acute economic and social problems. Meanwhile, territorial demands made by the victorious Soviet Union against Turkey forced it to hastily join the Western bloc and strengthen its political bonds with the new emerging world power, the United States.[33] Instrumental in that effort would be Turkey's—even partial—convergence to the U.S. political and economic paradigm. The democratic and liberal principles could no more be bluntly ignored by the incumbent Kemalist elite. In a speech on November 1, 1945, Inonu declared the lack of an opposition party to be the main shortcoming of Turkish democracy.[34] On January 7, 1946, a new opposition party, the Democrat Party (*Demokrat Parti*—DP), was registered. Its leaders were Celal Bayar and Adnan Menderes, former CHP members and Members of Parliament. Freedom in the press and universities improved, while direct elections were also adopted.[35] The 1946 elections, however, outlined the limits of the liberal shift in Turkish politics: a CHP victory against the DP was only secured through grassroots organizational superiority and incidents of electoral fraud.[36] The DP continued exercising pressure for more liberal reforms and eventually took over power in the 1950 elections. The peaceful transfer of power from the CHP to the DP—despite dissident views within the incumbent CHP—was the first big success in the establishment of Turkish democracy. The DP broadened the scope of popular participation in Turkish politics and showed interest in the marginalized segments of Turkish society, especially the peasantry. Nonetheless, it soon relapsed into authoritarian policies highly reminiscent of those of CHP. The military coup of April 27, 1960, dealt the first blow against the young Turkish democracy and its liberalizing policies.

The 1960 Coup and the 1961 Constitution

The 1960 coup was followed by arrests and purges of officers and academics with suspected liberal and leftist leanings. The Kemalist bureaucracy reasserted its dominant position in the Turkish state and society, which had come under considerable threat when peripheral forces increased their influence during the DP era. Nonetheless, the Constitution proclaimed by referendum on July 9, 1961, included more liberal clauses than its predecessor of 1924 had. A greater scope for political activities became tolerated; the activities of new parties, trade unions, and religious groups enjoyed wider freedoms; and individual human rights were better protected. This apparent paradox can be explained by referring to the proceedings of the constitutional committees set up by the military regime. Given the experience of the DP governments in the 1950s, the military bureaucracy decided to curb the political powers of the executive through the establishment of a checks-and-balances system. Proportional representation in national elections, the introduction of a bicameral legislature, and a Constitutional Court were seen as effective political safeguards against abuse of power by the executive.[37] The views of this political school of thought eventually prevailed and exerted the main influence upon the 1961 Constitution. Sanctioning considerable freedom in the activities of political parties affirmed that Turkish democratic institutions were trusted and that tolerance for political activity was thought to constitute the most appropriate means of preventing a potential future relapse to authoritarian majoritarian politics, which had characterized both the CHP and DP eras.

On the other hand, the crucial political role of the military was for the first time constitutionally recognized and institutionalized through the establishment of the National Security Council (*Milli Guvenlik Kurulu*—MGK). In the perennial conflict between the

Turkish center and periphery, the periphery had made relative gains during the DP era, which the 1960 coup attempted to limit. Through the 1961 Constitution, the Turkish center tried to set institutional guarantees for the continuation of its dominant position in the Turkish state and society. As Celal Bayar claimed, "the difference between the Turkish Constitution of 1924 and the new constitution adopted after the revolution of 1960 amounted to the constitutional legitimization of the bureaucracy and the intellectuals as one source of sovereignty in addition to the 'Turkish people,' who had earlier figured as the only source of sovereignty in the Kemalist ideology."[38]

The handover of political power to civilians signaled the beginning of intense political debates in Turkish society, in which liberal political ideas were also advocated. Nonetheless, political activism was often followed by political extremism. Clashes between ultraleftist and ultrarightist groups soon became frequent, threatening public order and stability. The growth of political radicalism and violence served as justification for more military coups.

The Coups of 1971 and 1980

The second military coup "by memorandum" took place on March 12, 1971, and marked a turning point. The increasing influence of liberalism in Turkish politics of the 1960s was reversed in the 1970s. The 1961 Constitution was amended in December 1971 so as to limit the scope of political freedoms and protect state interests more effectively. Curtailment of constitutionally protected civil liberties by law became possible, while press freedom and university and media autonomy were curbed. Yet the amended constitution did not succeed in preventing political deadlock and violence. Clashes between militant leftist and state-tolerated rightist groups became widespread, especially in the late 1970s, while civilian governments seemed to be unable to control the situation.[39] Deteriorating political conditions set the scene for another military coup. On September 12, 1980, the army took over political power, dissolving the parliament and the cabinet and suspending political parties, trade unions, and newspapers. The new Constitution, as approved by referendum on November 7, 1982, brought about severe restrictions of the human rights and liberties recognized by the 1961 Constitution. The constitutional protection of fundamental human, political, and social rights was made conditional, as these could be annulled, suspended, or limited on alleged grounds of national interest, public order, national security, or danger to the republican order. The end of military rule in 1983 and the rise to power of Turgut Ozal and the Motherland Party (*Anavatan Partisi*—ANAP) led to an unprecedented drive toward economic liberalization. Nonetheless, these steps, which reshaped the Turkish economy, were not followed by analogous steps in the field of political liberalization. The established role of the military in politics and the escalation of the Kurdish conflict in southeastern Turkey did not favor any developments that could have a liberalizing effect on political culture.

EU-TURKEY RELATIONS IN THE 1990S

The Transformation of the European Union

The debate on Turkish political culture was heavily influenced by the rise of the European Union as a supranational organization.[40] During the 1990s, the European Union underwent a radical transformation: It ceased to be a predominantly economic organization regulating a free trade zone with minimal political ambitions and became an organization whose economic character was complemented through the gradual establishment of common foreign, security, and home affairs policies. This pivotal switch in the character of the European Union led to the articulation of the Copenhagen Criteria for prospective EU member states and the rise of the European federal debate. The Copenhagen Criteria, adopted at the June 1993 EU Council Summit, required the following conditions from prospective EU member states:

> The stability of institutions guaranteeing democracy, the rule of law, human rights, and respect for and protection of minorities

> The existence of a functioning market economy, as well as the capacity to cope with competitive pressure and market forces within the European Union

> The ability to take on the obligations of membership, including adherence to the aims of political, economic and monetary union[41]

Within the European federal debate, two opinion groups were soon formed. Euro-federalists maintained that the European Union should only be an intermediate stage toward the development of a supranational European federal state.[42] To facilitate this process, political and cultural elements that constituted the common European heritage, should form the basis of a new, overarching common European identity. Political liberalism would unequivocally be among the basic components of that identity, while the inclusion of religious elements was heavily contested. On the other hand, opponents of Euro-federalism contended that the transformation of the European Economic Community into the European Union should be the final stage of convergence among EU member states and that the European Union should retain a heavily economic character; they saw the debate on a common European identity as both chimerical and redundant. The influence of Euro-federalist views within the European Union, however, meant that—apart from the observance of the Copenhagen Criteria—Turkey's EU membership application could also be judged on its compatibility with the common European identity project. Some Euro-federalists, who considered Europe's Greco-Roman and Judeo-Christian heritage to be the foundations of European identity, vehemently opposed the prospect of Turkey's membership. Others, in whose view Europe's identity should not have religion-specific content but be based on liberal political values, strongly supported the accession of a liberal democratic Turkey, as this would signal the inclusive, tolerant character of a Union whose identity was based not on religion but on universal human values.

The debate on European identity was not exhausted by the Copenhagen Criteria and had a constant bearing on EU-Turkey relations and Turkey's concomitant political liberalization process. Although the decision of the Helsinki EU Council Summit in 1999 to grant Turkey the status of a candidate EU member state implied a positive answer to the question of Turkey's European identity, the question whether Turkey could be considered European continued to be debated and affected European views of Turkey and itself.[43]

Apart from the European identity debate, Turkey's decision to join the European Union and the measures taken in pursuit of that goal challenged Turkey's dominant subject political culture by hastening the introduction of participant elements. Turkey's full and effective compliance with the Copenhagen Criteria would mean the start of the transformation process of Turkish political culture: Citizens and state would have to modify their view of each other as well as their role in society. Moreover, the unitary model of national identity would be challenged, as well as the militant secularist separation of religion from the public sphere.

The Domestic Debate

Turkey's approach to the European Union also resuscitated domestic debate, which showed signals of change in Turkish political culture. Despite the predominance of official views, dissident ideological groups—which until then had had to remain latent, fearing state repression—could articulate their divergent views more easily. With respect to Turkish identity, Islamist intellectuals started debating the role of Islam in the formation of Turkish nation and identity, in contrast with official Kemalist views. The role of Islam as an indispensable element of Turkish identity came again to the fore, while the role of Islam as a factor in political mobilization was also demonstrated. The debate on Islamic Turkish identity became intertwined with the debate on Turkey's relations with the West and its Islamic neighbors in the Middle East, the Caucasus, and Central Asia.[44] Minority groups also claimed their own distinct identity within or outside the scope of Turkish national identity. Kurds, Alevis, and members of other national, ethnic, and religious minorities contested the amalgamation of their respective identities with the dominant Turkish identity. Although the escalation of the war between the Turkish military forces and the Kurdistan Workers' Party (*Partiya Karkaren Kurdistan*—PKK) during the 1990s hindered calm discussion of national identity and minority rights, the abandonment of official denial and the reconsideration of policies toward ethnic and religious groups became contested topics. Turkish liberals also found the chance to introduce ways of redefining state-society relations and the role of the citizen. The development of a novel civic Turkish identity that could accommodate all existing ethnic and religious groups attracted the interest of liberal intellectuals. In the same spirit, the lifting of illiberal limitations on religious freedom was advocated, while a liberal version of secularism was supported. The gradual emergence of civil society institutions to political significance in the 1990s also contributed to the dissemination of liberal ideas in Turkish society. Relations between citizens and the state and citizens' views of the state could be renegotiated more easily.[45] Both Islamists and minority groups came to understand that political liberalization would mean less state interference in society and improved protection of human rights. Hence, they both became active proponents of measures that favored the liberalization of political culture.

Strategic Implications of Turkey's EU Membership

The strategic implications of Turkey's EU membership were felt at the domestic level and also involved the United States as well as the debate on the future of Europe.[46] The possibility of Turkey's political liberalization and curtailment of national sovereignty as a result of Turkey's approach toward the European Union met with the suspicion and opposition of a substantial part of the Kemalist military and bureaucratic elite.[47] According to this argument, the price of liberal reform and the restriction of national sovereignty would be the disintegration of Turkish national ideology and—possibly—Turkey itself. The whole nation-building project, as conceived by Turkish nationalist leaders in the last years of the Ottoman Empire and implemented by Ataturk in the early republican years, would be endangered. In what is called the *Tanzimat* Syndrome it was feared that, as in the case of the *Tanzimat*, liberal reform would not strengthen the state but lead to further weakening and partition. Existing national minorities might then claim self-determination and independence, while latent ethnic divisions within the Turkish people could reemerge and threaten Turkish national unity. The resuscitation of the "Eastern Question," the question of the partition of the Ottoman Empire, which dominated European politics in the nineteenth century and briefly materialized in 1920 with the Treaty of Sevres, has haunted the political thought of Turkish Euro-skeptics, who also doubted the European identity of Turkey.[48]

On the other hand, there is no other visible political orientation as favorable for Turkey as its full participation in the European Union. Membership in the European Union is also still seen as part of the "Kemalist imperative" of identification with—implicitly Western— modernity. The European Union is viewed as an international organization that could guarantee Turkey's economic development and political stability. Meanwhile, current political and economic conditions in the Middle East, the Caucasus, and Central Asia offer no serious strategic alternatives to Turkey's option to pursue membership in the European Union.[49] A further deepening of Turkey's strategic relationship with the United States and its primary regional ally, Israel, could not constitute a substitute for Turkey's EU vocation. The EU member states are by far Turkey's biggest trade partner, while Turkey's willingness to blindly serve U.S. foreign policy objectives is far from given.

The U.S. Factor

While an increasing strategic rift is thought to threaten long-term relations between the United States and the European Union, the United States has been one of the biggest proponents of Turkey's EU accession.[50] Paradoxically, the improvement of EU-Turkey relations and Turkey's eventual incorporation into the European Union are viewed as extremely favorable for U.S. strategic interests in Europe and the Middle East. Turkey's membership in the European Union is seen as the best guarantee for the consolidation of Turkey's secular, pro-Western political system and globalized economy. Turkey could thus serve U.S. regional strategic interests in the Middle East, the Caucasus, and Central Asia by providing the paradigm of a Muslim democratic state, fully integrated within the Western political and economic institutions.

Open U.S. support for Turkey's EU membership[51] has led to widespread suspicion within EU circles that the United States favored Turkey's EU accession as a part of its effort to subvert the transformation of the European Union into a federal state that would have the potential to challenge U.S. global hegemony. EU suspicion of the U.S. role peaked in December 2002, when the open intervention of the U.S. President George W. Bush in support of Turkey during the Copenhagen European Council backfired.[52] This effect was exacerbated by European—mainly French and German—opposition to the U.S. campaign against Iraq in 2002–3. The technical difficulties of Turkey's EU membership were not fictitious: Its relatively large population and weak economy would disturb sensitive political power balances inside the EU institutions and strain EU economic and financial capacity. At the political level, Turkey's accession was seen as strengthening the antifederalist and Atlanticist blocs inside the European Union. It was argued that steps toward the empowerment of European political institutions would become even more difficult, while the deployment of a European security structure independent of NATO and U.S. influence would be shelved, and a common foreign policy would be harder to achieve. Turkey would thus play the role of a U.S.-sponsored Trojan horse inside the European Union.[53]

The weak point of this argument was the assumption that the strategic interests of the United States and Turkey were identical. In the aftermath of the Cold War and the demise of the Soviet Union, Turkey has been no more in need of full identification with U.S. regional strategic interests. Efforts to create a U.S.-Turkey-Israel strategic partnership had only partial success, while the rise to power

of Islamic-oriented parties, which were more sensitive to the plight
of the Palestinian people, made the alliance even more precarious.
The new U.S. strategic doctrine promulgated after the September
11, 2001, terrorist attacks also alienated Turkey to the extent that it
implied that the United States could act unilaterally. The gap grew
even wider in view of the Turkish Parliament's refusal on March 1,
2003 to allow U.S. forces to attack Iraq via Turkish territory. Hence,
the U.S. invasion and occupation of Iraq marked a watershed in
U.S.-Turkey relations, making it clear that U.S. and Turkish regional
strategic interests might even come into conflict.[54] Anti-American-
ism rose to unforeseen levels and seemed to turn into a strong feature of Turkish public opinion.[55] Even the traditionally pro-United
States and initially circumspect Turkish military eventually coincided
with this. U.S. policies in Iraq were criticized by both proponents
of Turkey's strategic cooperation with the European Union as well
as staunchly nationalist officers.[56] The United States' unwillingness
to address Turkey's security concerns by eliminating the remaining
PKK forces in northern Iraq, its ambivalent position regarding the
future of northern Iraq and the role of the Iraqi Kurds and, finally, its
unconditional support for Israeli policies in the Middle East served
as reasons for different parts of Turkish public opinion to support a

Figure 2.1   EU Eastern Enlargement and Turkey's Accession Prospects (courtesy of
David Schrank, published in the *Economist*, December 20, 2002)

shift in attitudes toward the United States. Nevertheless, the strategic partnership between the United States and Turkey could no more be considered as a given, especially if a credible alternative EU strategic vision were to emerge, which could appeal to Turkish strategic and security concerns more effectively.

THE EUROPEAN VISION

Turkey's potential EU accession sparked a serious debate inside the European Union. Although the strategic, political and economic dimensions of Turkey's EU membership have been anything but insignificant, Turkey's EU membership debate has also been used as a proxy for debates on what the European Union is or should become. Differing approaches on the issue of Turkey's EU membership have showed divergent visions of the present and future of the European Union project. Supporters and opponents of Turkey's EU membership have also been internally divided, as they have based their position on different grounds. As different definitions of European identity and visions of Europe coexist, the same factors may be used for and against Turkey's EU membership, thus making the picture even more complex.

Turkey's Islamic religious and cultural identity can—for example—be viewed as a reason either to accept or reject Turkey's EU membership application. This mirrors the fact that in the debate on the essential elements of a future European identity no consensus has been reached—even at the elite level—on how to deal with the issue of religion.[57] Advocates of multiculturalism and supranationalism, who argue that the EU identity should be based on liberal democratic values and cultural diversity, firmly support Turkey's EU prospective membership. In their view, Europe's diversity is its strength rather than weakness; it needs to be protected and celebrated, as the European Union provides an alternative way for people to coexist: "not to reproduce a national model at the level of the continent but to shape another way for people to live together and share a common project," as Nicolaidis puts it.[58] The admission of a Muslim country into the European Union would comprise the most effective guarantee of its secular, inclusive and multicultural character and provide a powerful paradigm to the rest of the world. On the other hand, Turkey's Islamic character becomes the most powerful argument against Turkey's EU membership, according to many European conservatives, who focus on the religious and cultural aspects of a European identity. Further steps toward European integration can only be made if the European

Union forges an identity on its common roots, its Judeo-Christian religious and Greco-Roman political heritage. The fact that Turkey lacks this heritage makes it unsuitable for EU membership, although a "special relationship" between the European Union and Turkey would be desirable for strategic and economic reasons.[59] Turkey's geographical position, demographic size, and level of economic development are also used as arguments for and against Turkey's EU membership. This echoes persisting divisions within the European Union between those who favor widening over deepening and prefer to view Europe as a huge integrated market and those who favor Europe's deepening and have a clear federal vision for Europe. Supporters of Turkey's EU candidacy point to the increase of the EU strategic role in the Middle East, the Caucasus, and Central Asia. Proximity to some of the most volatile and strategically crucial regions would increase the global strategic role of the European Union. Turkey's demographic size and dynamism could also be seen as an advantage for Turkey's EU membership, as it could help alleviate the emerging serious European labor shortage and contribution deficits in EU social security systems. Turkey's relatively low level of economic development, combined with its young population, also has a positive side, as these features make Turkey a large market that has by far not reached a saturation point. Nonetheless, opponents of Turkey's EU membership argued that Turkey's geostrategic position could drag the European Union into unnecessary adventures and that what is crucial is the establishment of a deeper political union among existing member states. Without this, any efforts to claim a major European regional role would be futile. This political union would be seriously complicated and eventually compromised in favor of a wider and more lax economic union if Turkey joined the European Union. The discrepancy between Turkey's population size and economic capacity[60] would upset the balance of European policy-making, seriously strain its economy, and result in massive migration of Turkish workers[61] to the prosperous EU member states, which would have unpredictable socioeconomic consequences. In this view, at a time when the deepening of European institutions has met with serious objections, undertaking the burden of Turkey's EU membership would be suicidal for the European federal project.[62]

A Brief Chronology of EU-Turkey Relations

The prospect of Turkey's accession to the European Union has posed the latest and probably most critical challenge in the course of two-hundred-year Ottoman and Turkish efforts to adopt the European

political, economic, and cultural paradigm.[63] Westernization of the
Ottoman state, society, and culture was the primary goal of the *Tanzimat* reforms in the mid-nineteenth century, while the same goal
was later adopted by Young Turks and implemented by Ataturk, who
believed that the formation of a solid Turkish nation and state were pre-
requisites of Westernization.[64] Turkey has pursued close relations with
the European Economic Community (EEC)[65] since the late 1950s.
An Association Agreement between Turkey and the Community was
signed in 1963, while an Additional Protocol was signed in November
1970, in which the rules for Turkey's prospective customs union with
the European Economic Community were outlined.[66] Nonetheless,
political developments in the 1970s and early 1980s hampered relations between Turkey and the EEC. The "coup by memorandum"
in 1971 was the first negative step. The situation deteriorated with
the subsequent radicalization of Turkish politics and rise of leftist and
rightist nationalist views, which viewed the EEC as a capitalist and
imperialist trust eager to exploit Turkey's natural resources. The final
blow against Turkey's prospective EEC membership came with the
1980 coup, which politically alienated Turkey from Western Europe.
Turkey became again interested in EEC membership during the Ozal
administration in the mid-1980s, and a formal application was filed
in 1987. Yet crucial time had been wasted, and the situation was
then much less favorable for Turkey inside the Community.[67] Despite
the rejection of Turkey's application in 1989, the improvement of
EEC-Turkey relations was still pursued. A customs union agreement
between Turkey and the European Union was signed in 1995 and
became effective in 1996. Turkey was once again disillusioned when
the EU Luxembourg Summit in 1997 refused to award it the status of
an EU candidate state, although this was awarded to ten states of Central Europe, Eastern Europe, and the Mediterranean. This brought
EU-Turkey relations to their lowest point.[68] Turkey finally became an
EU candidate state at the Helsinki EU Summit in 1999. The Helsinki
Summit also marked the shift of Greece's position from opposition
to support for Turkey's EU membership; Greece's obstructive stance
had hampered EU-Turkey relations ever since Greece joined what
was then the European Community in 1981. The start of EU-Turkey
accession negotiations would depend on Turkey's compliance with
the Copenhagen Criteria, and several political reform packages were
proposed to bring that about. Constitutional amendments were aimed
at altering the illiberal character of the 1982 Constitution. While the
Constitution was amended eight times between 1995 and 2004, the
most far-reaching amendment was made in October 2001.[69] Turkey's

political liberalization seemed to proceed at an unforeseen pace as the critical EU Copenhagen Summit of December 2002 was approaching. The EU Copenhagen Summit in December 2002 decided, however, to defer the decision on the commencement of EU-Turkey accession negotiations until the EU Summit of December 2004. Despite Turkey's disillusionment, reform efforts aiming at Turkey's full political liberalization continued and were rewarded on December 17, 2004, when October 3, 2005, was set as the start date of EU-Turkey accession negotiations. In the course of five years, the prospect of Turkey's accession to the European Union had caused the most significant political transformation the Republic of Turkey had experienced since the introduction of multiparty politics in 1946.

CHAPTER 3

CIVIL SOCIETY

WHAT IS CIVIL SOCIETY?

Definitions of civil society have historically varied,[1] the main point of contention being whether civil society can only be defined in a liberal democratic framework.[2] Most scholars accept the essentially liberal character of the term. Hall defines civil society as "the self-organization of strong and autonomous groups that balance the state."[3] Civil society is perceived as the counterweight that effectively checks the state. According to Diamond, civil society is "the realm of organized social life that is voluntary, self-generating, (largely) self-supporting, autonomous from the state, and bound by a legal order or a set of shared values."[4]

Diamond remains loyal to the tradition linking civil society with a liberal democratic political system. Gellner expands the definition so it can include the counterbalancing function of civil society against the dominant social role of the state and its arbitrative role against competing social interests. According to him, civil society is "that set of diverse nongovernmental institutions which is strong enough to counterbalance the state, and, whilst not preventing the state fulfilling its role of keeper of the peace and arbitrator between major interests, can nevertheless prevent the state from dominating and atomizing the rest of society."[5]

Other scholars, however, attempt to disengage the concept of civil society from a liberal democratic context. According to this view, state and society should be viewed as products of a common political order in which conflicts occur within the state and the civil society rather than between them. Because of this, civil society could exist and thrive in nondemocratic environments without necessarily promoting political liberalization. Thus, one could conceptualize "patriarchal, Islamic, communist and fascist civil societies."[6]

The question whether civil society can be understood as "uncivil" lies in the heart of this discourse. In this study, "civility" is understood as tolerance to opposing views, ideologies, and cultures and viewed as an essential element of civil society. Hence, social formations that are not characterized by civility cannot be characterized as components of a civil society. Civil society has been taken as one of the most accurate indicators of the existence of a substantive, participatory democracy. A high degree of citizen participation in civil society associations is positively correlated with a flourishing liberal democratic system. The proliferation of horizontal citizen networks increases the levels of social capital and reduces the influence of nonegalitarian vertical networks.

The crucial role that civil society could play in promoting democratization resulted in the active support of civil society organizations in states in a transition stage toward democracy. Western states and international organizations provided financial and moral support for the development of strong civil society institutions. The European Union was especially active in the post-communist Central and East European states that had aspired to become EU members. As EU-Turkey relations were improving in the 1990s and the prospect of Turkey's EU membership became increasingly realistic, EU interest in Turkish civil society rose. The lack of a vibrant civil society in Turkey was viewed as one of the main reasons for Turkey's weak democratic consolidation and evidence of its illiberal political culture. In this chapter, the past and present of Turkish civil society will be explored, and the role of the European Union in influencing developments will be assessed. The role of selected social actors in the rise of Turkish civil society, as well as the incidence of social learning, will also be considered. Finally, tentative conclusions on the applicability of path dependence, historical institutionalism, and two-level game models in studying the EU impact on Turkish civil society will be attempted.

CIVIL SOCIETY IN TURKEY

The Ottoman Legacy

The rise of a vibrant Turkish civil society since the 1990s has been one of the most hotly debated issues in Turkish politics. Part of the debate has been focused on the question whether the deficiencies of Turkish civil society could be attributed to an unfavorable historical legacy. Many scholars have argued that the main reason for that deficiency was historical in nature. Ottoman history lacked any equivalents to the concepts of citizenship and civil society. As Heper has suggested, "The absence of civil society in Turkey was an inheritance from the Ottoman Empire, where political, economic and social power coalesced in the center. Within the upper strata, status and wealth were attached to offices, and not to lineages or families. Bureaucratic position, thus, had the greatest weight in determining policy. The elite justified its appropriation of policymaking based on its presumed cultural preeminence and superior knowledge."[7]

Apart from the Ottoman state tradition, Islam was also held responsible for the deficiencies of Turkish civil society. The compatibility of Islam with the concept of civil society has been widely debated, and Islam—or at least its scripturalist, "high" version—has been viewed to be a rival form of social order.[8] In contrast to Christianity, Islam lacks an institutional formation equivalent to the church, which has historically provided for broad nonstate social networks and counterbalanced the monopolistic role of the state even in the peak of the Middle Ages. While Sunni Islamic political tradition favored the centralization of state power,[9] the political and military success of the Ottoman Empire from the fourteenth to the sixteenth century was an additional reason for strengthening the role of central state authorities. Ottoman state bureaucracy accumulated powers unparalleled by the powers of any other contemporary medieval state. The ongoing decline of the Ottoman Empire from the seventeenth century onwards, which was first signaled by the *Celali* rebellions in Anatolia and the emergence of local notables (*ayan*) and the Janissary corps as de facto power shareholders, reversed this process. This also led to the thriving of deep-rooted institutions such as the *intisab* (connection-based clientelism) that favored the establishment of hierarchical and clientelistic social networks and rendered the development of horizontal networks even more difficult.[10]

Others argued that it would be inaccurate to claim that quasi-civil society formations were totally absent in the Ottoman Empire. Social functions similar to those of a civil society were undertaken by traditional institutions, which mediated between the state and its subjects.[11] The Islamic foundation (*vakf*) performed a variety of social welfare functions that substituted for the absence of similar state activities. As its property was exempt from state confiscation, the *vakf* also served as a vehicle for the protection of the economic interests of state officials, and especially the emerging *ayan* class in the eighteenth century. Besides this, the activities of religious orders (*tarikat*), guilds (*esnaf*) and professional religious fraternities (*ahi*) also checked the dominant role of the state and gave the Ottoman society a more plural character. Mardin argues that a tacit social contract existed in the Ottoman context, which incorporated the Janissaries, the *ayan*, the "civilian" merchant population, and the men of religion (*ulema*) and served as justification for a series of Janissary rebellions.[12] Additionally, Ottoman non-Muslim minorities under the *millet* system developed an advanced network of social organizations, as well as religious, educational, and charity foundations and associations.

The situation changed dramatically during the *Tanzimat*. The elimination of the *ayan* class was one of the first tasks on the agenda of the early Ottoman state modernizers, while the drastic limitation of the power that the *tarikat*s, the *esnaf*s and the *ahi*s wielded followed suit. Following the model of the Western European centralized state, the Ottoman statesmen attempted to achieve maximum power concentration in their effort to make the state the agent of social modernization and also introduce elements of political liberalism. Non-Muslim minorities, which were disproportionately represented in the emerging Ottoman bourgeoisie, thrived under the more tolerant *Tanzimat* environment. Efforts were made to develop secular civil society structures across the *millet* divisions. The centralization campaign, however, had a countervailing effect on the development of an Ottoman civil society. The *intisab* networks were disproportionately strengthened, as members of the emerging bureaucratic class monopolized state power and organized their own clientelistic networks. The centralization program reached the peak of its success in the Hamidian era[13] and left its enduring legacy in the Young Turk regime and republican Turkey. The triumph of clientelism meant that horizontal social networks remained weak. The unity of the state and the presumed indivisibility of the people were principles that restrained the development of a civil society.

CIVIL SOCIETY FROM 1923 TO THE 1990S

The state-centric ideology of the Ottoman officials crucially affected the founding cadre of republican Turkey and left little free space for the development of a Turkish civil society.[14] The corporatist vision of Ziya Gokalp, the most prominent ideologue of the Turkish Republic, prescribed the absolute dominance of collective interest over individualistic ones and the concentration of all powers in the state and its functionaries.[15] Turkey's Westernization was a gigantic project requiring the coordination of all social actors. Thus, any civil society movement was viewed with suspicion as prioritizing individual interests over the general good. This choice became embedded in republican politics with the promulgation of the 1924 Constitution. Freedom of association was formally recognized, yet, in practice, the unrestrained ability of the state to limit it for the sake of alleged public interest meant that this recognition was meaningless.[16] Early reactions against Ataturk's secularization and national homogenization campaigns enhanced his determination to silence nonstate social actors. *Tarikats* and opposition political parties were banned, while the CHP claimed to be a bridge between the Turkish state and society. The number of nongovernmental associations (NGOs) remained low, and their activities were strictly nonpolitical. There was even an attempt to develop a substitute civil society consisting of public or quasi-private associations that undertook to further a state-defined political and social agenda. The role of chambers of commerce, professional associations, trades unions,[17] and other state-controlled civil society organizations (e.g. the Turkish Aviation Foundation—*Turk Hava Kurumu Vakfi*) are primary examples of the strong influence of corporatist models in the early republican years.[18] With the advent of multiparty politics, state and military elites were concerned about what they saw as a shift toward particularistic interests at the expense of the general good and attempted to "regulate" Turkish democracy through a series of military coups.[19] Developments were temporarily halted by the 1960 coup. However, the 1961 Constitution provided the legal framework for the rise of a civil society movement in Turkey. Despite the pitfalls of extreme polarization and violent activism in the 1960s, Turkish society underwent a politicization process. Politics were not simply left to "expert" state bureaucrats; each citizen claimed the right to express his political views and try to influence others. The nascent Turkish civil society suffered a blow in 1971, when a military coup enforced a constitutional amendment that limited basic freedoms. Worse was to come with the 1980 coup. The high degree of politicization of Turkish civil society and its alleged identification with leftist and minority movements sealed its fate. While the military regime lasted (September 1980–November 1983), all political activities were banned, and the 1982 Constitution imposed even further restrictions on basic freedoms. Changes in the Law on Associations completed the dramatic limitation of the operating space of civil society.[20]

The end of military rule in 1983 and the victory of the ANAP in the November 1983 elections signaled a series of social transformations that had a significant effect on Turkish civil society.[21] Turkey's economic liberalization and the shift from import substitution to an export-oriented economic model reshaped the Turkish economy. Changes in the economy necessarily affected Turkish society, although the effects were less rapid. Turkish civil society was still weak in terms of its membership and the scope of its activities, while the legislative framework was anything but conducive to its expansion. Public opinion was still unfavorable, as the view that civil society associations have divisive impact, and therefore constitute a threat to the general good, still dominated. Even the word used in Turkish for the term "organization [*örgüt*]" reinforced these views, as it was linked with criminal or separatist groups aiming to harm the unity of the people or the territorial integrity of the state. Nonetheless, the ongoing transformation of the Turkish economy and society in the 1980s would set one of the conditions for the growth of civil society in the 1990s.

CIVIL SOCIETY SINCE THE 1990S

The 1990s became a watershed for the development of a Turkish civil society. The number of civil society organizations boomed, the spectrum of their activities was widened, and citizen participation grew. There are several reasons for this phenomenon that need to be treated separately. Global and domestic factors were influential. Last, but not least, the European Union had a crucial role in accelerating the growth of civil society in Turkey.

The Impact of Global Actors

Several global events affected the rise of Turkish civil society. The fall of the Berlin Wall and the end of the Cold War had profound consequences for the political and ideological structure of Europe. The collapse of communist regimes in Central and Eastern Europe sparked new ideological explorations, which resulted in the reshaping of the political spectrum on more liberal lines. While Marxism had expressed a deep suspicion of civil society, leftist youth in the aftermath of the Cold War sought ways to change their communities, their societies, and the world by limiting state power and "[opening] the political space for civic participation."[22] Involvement in civil society activities provided an alternative mode of social engagement. Despite fierce state persecution in the past, the Turkish left remained a potential political power that was particularly popular among the younger generation. Turkish leftist youth formed a substantial part of Turkish civil society activists, shaping its distinctively political character.

The emergence of a global civil society also assisted the rise of Turkish civil society.[23] Interest in global issues such as the environment and human rights attracted the interest of like-minded people across the world. Associations like Greenpeace, Human Rights Watch, and Amnesty International grew in size and international appeal, which allowed them to intensify and diversify their worldwide activities. Under the influence of international environmental NGOs, local environmental NGOs like the Turkish Foundation for Erosion Fighting, Forestation and Protection of the National Endowment (*Turkiye Erozyonla Mucadele, Agaclandirma ve Dogal Varliklari Koruma Vakfi*—TEMA) emerged. Turkey also attracted the interest of most international NGOs focusing on human rights. As Turkey was a country in the Western bloc and, therefore, accessible with relative ease, severe human rights violations could not escape the attention of international human rights NGOs. Their increasing activity in Turkey attracted much suspicion from the state, yet it also offered a paradigm for the development of local civil society associations. The United Nations Conference on Human Settlements (Habitat II), which was held in Istanbul in June 1996, was a windfall for Turkish civil society. The organization of the conference brought to Turkey a number of international NGOs and afforded plenty of opportunities for cooperation with the existing civil society network. Local NGOs found a rare chance to obtain expertise as well as financial aid in the course of the conference preparations, which helped them take more courageous steps in the following years.

The transformation of the Turkish economy that continued in the 1990s had a significant impact on the development of civil society in Turkey. Turkish business capital was historically extremely dependent on the state. The emergence of a Turkish business class in the late nineteenth and early twentieth century was actively supported by the state, while the import substitution model selected in the republican years created favorable conditions for the emergence of a local business elite, whose industrial production would benefit from high import tariffs and have privileged access to the growing Turkish market.[24] Turkish business grew in size, and large business conglomerates dominated the Turkish economy. Nonetheless, economic liberalization and the shift from import substitution to an export-oriented economy model in the 1980s meant that Turkish business would have to compete on equal terms with their foreign counterparts for a share of the Turkish market and expand their economic activity outside the borders of Turkey. The challenge was anything but negligible, yet the performance of Turkish business was remarkably successful. The geographical expansion of its operations and its integration into the global economy also meant the end of its dependence on the Turkish state. While they no more identified with the state and its interests, Turkish businesspersons were influenced by contemporary debates on political liberalism and the social role of capital.[25] The idea of corporate social responsibility spread for the first time,[26] and interest in politics flourished in a group that had until recently avoided taking any political positions, fearing that this might alienate its indispensable allies, the state bureaucrats and the military. Turkish businesspersons established associations or activated preexisting ones, giving them a wide scope of activities, and gave financial support to independent associations. Associations like the formerly politically neutral Turkish Industrialists' and Businesspersons' Association (*Turk Sanayicileri ve Isadamlari Dernegi*–TUSIAD) developed a keen interest in Turkey's human rights situation and started pushing for democratic reforms.[27] Through its membership in the Union of Industrialists and Employers' Confederation of Europe (UNICE), it also actively lobbied in favor of Turkey's EU membership perspective as well as domestic political reform. The 1997 TUSIAD report on democratization[28] was a landmark document in this process.[29] In the same spirit, Turkish business started providing financial support to independent NGOs whose activities coincided with its political agenda. The globalization of Turkish business thus improved the success of NGO fundraising activities, rendering them more resilient and active.

The Impact of Domestic Politics

Domestic political developments had a catalytic role in the development of Turkish civil society. Civil society groups increased their demands for recognition of their rights by the state and addressed their problems as part of Turkey's democratization process.[30] Meanwhile, a series of incidents challenged the supremacy of the state in the public sphere and brought to the fore serious deficiencies in Turkish democracy.

The Kurdish Issue
The escalation of Turkey's Kurdish question was one of these developments. The 1980 military regime had intensified state policies aiming at the repression of Turkey's Kurdish minority. This policy shift had coincided with the rise of interest among the Kurds of Turkey in their

distinct identity and the intensification of the activity of the PKK. In the southeastern and eastern provinces of Turkey, where most of Turkey's Kurdish population lived and most of the fighting took place, the martial law regime remained intact. This resulted in severe violations of even the most basic human rights and freedoms. Extrajudicial killings, forced relocations and systematic torture were only some of the reported incidents of human rights violation, while the practices of the PKK were also atrocious. Throughout Turkey, the use of the Kurdish language was forbidden, and even the existence of a Kurdish minority in Turkey was officially denied. In the early 1990s, it became increasingly clear that state policies on the Kurdish question were unsustainable. Human rights violations attracted the interest of international human rights associations and caused international protests. Some first steps toward liberalization were made when the ban on the use of the Kurdish language was lifted in 1991, and Prime Minister Suleyman Demirel spoke in March 1992 for the need to accept the "Kurdish reality." This put an end to the denial policies of the 1980s.[31] Yet the intensification of warfare between Turkish security forces and Kurdish insurgents in the 1990s led to a rapid deterioration of the human rights situation. A massive forced relocation program of Kurdish villagers was organized and implemented, while the number of extrajudicial killings and torture cases peaked. The work of local and international human rights associations was obstructed by local officials, as the view that human rights NGOs were themselves a "bunch of terrorists" was widespread. This emerging humanitarian crisis led, however, to the involvement in civil society associations of citizens of Turkish and Kurdish descent who were outraged by the atrocities of the Turkish security forces and the PKK and wanted to help bring an end to the ongoing slaughter and to find a peaceful and commonly acceptable solution of the problem. Civil society mobilization seemed to be the only legitimate way to claim peacefully respect for the human rights of Turkey's Kurdish population as well as the recognition of a separate Kurdish identity in Turkey. The "Saturday Mothers [*Cumartesi Anneleri*]" demonstrations were a powerful manifestation of the human rights situation in Turkey, as well as the diffusion of civil society mobilization as a way of peacefully expressing dissent.[32] The intensity of human rights violations somewhat receded after a series of successful operations by the Turkish security forces against the PKK in 1998 and the capture of the PKK leader Abdullah Ocalan in 1999. This rendered the PKK threat as a reason to evade respect for human rights even less plausible. Nonetheless, recurrent persecutions of NGOs focusing on human rights violations showed that serious problems persisted.[33] While the state seemed unwilling to acknowledge full human rights to its Kurdish population, pressure originating from a nascent local civil society was mounting.

The Rise of Political Islam

The resurgence of Islam in Turkish politics and society beginning in the 1980s also contributed to the rise of Turkish civil society. Islam had been introduced to Turkish politics during the 1980 military regime via the "Turkish-Islamic Synthesis [*Turk-Islam Sentezi*—TIS]" ideological formation. This aimed to use Islam as a cementing factor against Kurdish nationalist and leftist centrifugal social forces (see p. 130). In the Ozal era, which had also been marked by a shift toward an increasing role of Islam in the public sphere, the enhanced role of Islam was regularized. Turkish Islamic movements started using civil society associations as a legal framework for their activities. A great number of NGOs were founded with the objective of the erection and maintenance of mosques or religious vocational schools (*imam-hatip okullari*).[34] Soon political Islam found its authentic political representative in the Welfare Party (*Refah Partisi*—RP), founded by the veteran Islamist leader Necmettin Erbakan. The RP's electoral appeal steadily grew in the elections of 1987 and 1991. Its first major electoral success was scored in the 1994 municipal elections, when the party candidates were elected in Istanbul and Ankara. A great part of the RP's electoral success was due to an unprecedented and a highly efficient mobilization of grassroots Islamist activism. Islamist activism operated at the civil society level, establishing associations that were directly or indirectly linked with the RP and focused their activities in the squatter areas (*gecekondu*) of Turkish big cities. Islamist associations developed from traditional Anatolian values, such as *imece*, the traditional, community-based form of horizontal mutual support and cooperation in rural Anatolian communities, and *himaye*, the principle of protection by and loyalty to family and larger community groups.[35] Primordial ties, which had led to the formation of separate townsmen's (*hemseri*) associations, were also exploited. Benefiting from the strong collectivistic spirit among Turkey's newly urbanized populations, they expanded their activities in a broad field of social welfare and relief operations and significantly raised their public profile.

The contribution of *tarikat*s to the growth of Islamist associations was also striking. Having been forced to operate underground after their banning in the 1920s, *tarikat*s found in civil society associations a legitimate public face for their multifarious social activities. Some of the originally Islamist associations were reformed into fully fledged Western-style civil society associations, only retaining a thin Islamic underpinning. The Organization of Human Rights and Solidarity for Oppressed People (*Insan Haklari ve Mazlumlar icin Dayanisma Dernegi*—Mazlum-Der)[36] and the Independent Industrialists' and Businesspersons' Association of (*Mustakil Sanayici ve Isadamlari Dernegi*—MUSIAD) are prime examples of successful civil society associations with Islamic roots.[37] The rise of political Islam created conditions that led to the enrichment of Turkish civil society through the emergence of civil society associations that in turn were inspired by traditional solidarity and support networks. By speaking a language more familiar to the majority of the Turkish population than conventional NGOs, these associations introduced the idea of civil society to a much broader audience. The periphery of Turkish society thus found the chance to develop its own civil society associations whose leadership constituted a part of its own emerging political elite. Turkey's Islamist civil society associations were shown to be compatible with the democratic framework of Turkish politics.[38] Despite the fact that Islamist civil society activity was often value laden, Islamist civic activities were successful in raising interpersonal trust, horizontal solidarity networks, and citizenship awareness.[39] Islamist associations also became active in pinpointing the cases where religious freedom in Turkey was compromised through the application of an extreme version of secularism.

The strength of Islamist associations was proven when the Islamist parties with which they were linked, namely the RP and its successor the Virtue Party (*Fazilet Partisi*—FP), were successively shut down by the Turkish Constitutional Court in 1998 and 2001. Despite this double blow against Turkish political Islam, Islamist civil society associations maintained their diverse activities, proving that their growth was not coincidental and incumbent upon the support of political parties. When the membership of the closed FP was split into two new Islamic parties, the Felicity Party (*Saadet Partisi*—SP) and the Justice and Development Party (*Adalet ve Kalkinma Partisi*—AKP), most of them became affiliated with the moderate AKP. Their support was decisive for the stunning electoral victory of the AKP in November 2002.

The Corrosion of the State Icon

The rise of Turkish civil society was further facilitated by a series of events that damaged the image of the Turkish state.[40] The Susurluk accident, the Manisa affair, the response to the 1999 Istanbul earthquake, and the devastating economic crisis that hit Turkey from 2000 to 2001 reduced respect for the state and encouraged the growth of civil society mobilization.

The Susurluk Accident

On November 3, 1996, a car stuffed with cash and weapons crashed into a truck in the northwestern Anatolian town of Susurluk. The car's passengers included Sedat Edip Bucak, Member of the Parliament, Huseyin Kocadag, head of the Police Academy, and Abdullah Catli, a fugitive convicted for drug trafficking and linked with the Turkish far right. Catli, who was also wanted for the murder of seven leftist students in 1976, turned out to be a holder of a green passport, a privilege reserved for high-ranking civil servants. The Susurluk accident provided ample evidence of the suspected links between the government, the police, and organized crime in Turkey.[41] Under the pretext of the need to organize covert operations against leftist and Kurdish terrorist groups, segments of the state bureaucracy, collectively called the "deep state [*derin devlet*]," had developed close cooperation with rightist terrorist groups and organized crime. The accident manifested that the "deep state" had infiltrated Turkish party politics. The Turkish public was outraged at the revelations and mobilized against the government. The most characteristic of the organized demonstrations, the "One Minute of Darkness for Permanent Light [*Surekli Aydinlik icin bir Dakika Karanlik*]" campaign,[42] was a spontaneous citizens' reaction against state corruption and a clear demand for justice and full accountability. A large number of outraged citizens, who demanded a purge of the state bureaucracy of its criminal members, made it clear that they could no more remain neutral bystanders.[43]

The Manisa Affair

On December 26, 1995, sixteen teenagers were arrested in the western Anatolian town of Manisa while writing political slogans on walls. They were immediately charged on the grounds of "being members of a terrorist organization." During their ten-day police custody, the teenagers were exposed to extensive and systematic torture. Their case was brought to court, and ten police officers were charged with torture. Despite ample existing evidence, the police officers were acquitted in March 1998 for "lack of evidence." The decision was nullified by the Court of Cassations in October 1998, yet the defendants were again found not guilty in January 1999. After a second appeal, the Court of Cassations reviewed the case and found the defendants guilty in June 1999. The lower court had to follow this decision and condemned the defendants in November 2000. An appeal against this decision was upheld by the Court of Cassations in May 2001 on procedural grounds. The defendants were finally condemned in April 2003, only three months before the period within which the defendants could be prosecuted elapsed.[44]

The Manisa affair became a symbol of the abuse of state power and disrespect for the fundamental human rights of Turkish citizens. Torture had been common in Turkey since the 1980 coup. What made the Manisa affair different was the fact that the victims were juveniles and their alleged misdemeanor so petty. Moreover, the repeated acquittal of the defendants despite the existence of ample evidence and the unusual length of the criminal procedure, which almost led to the lapse of the prosecution, raised suspicions about the complicity of members of the judiciary and the police. Domestic and international civil society associations and the media concentrated their attention on the Manisa affair and demanded the delivery of justice and full accountability. The mobilization of Turkish public opinion on the issues of torture and human rights greatly benefited Turkish civil society. The Manisa affair made clear to all Turkish citizens that potential victims of torture could be not only terrorists or criminal thugs but also their own children.

The 1999 Earthquake

In the early morning of August 17, 1999, Istanbul was shattered by a huge earthquake, 7.4 on the Richter scale, whose epicenter was in the neighboring city of Izmit. More than 30,000 people perished, and whole city quarters suffered heavy damage. The tragic situation in the aftermath of this humanitarian catastrophe ironically proved favorable for the development of Turkish civil society. The urgent need for rescue and relief operations for the millions affected by the earthquake raised expectations for immediate and effective state intervention. As the Turkish state had traditionally occupied a disproportionately large part of the public sphere, Turkish citizens were used to expecting a dominant state role in the management of humanitarian crises. Nevertheless, state mechanisms proved blatantly unable to deal with the magnitude and complexity of the situation. The inability of state institutions to respond to the great humanitarian crisis paved the way for the intervention of Turkish civil society organizations.[45] The Search

Rescue Association (*Arama Kurtarma Dernegi*—AKUT) was one of the best-organized NGOs; its immediate and efficient relief work complemented and even overshadowed the activities of the official relief organization Red Crescent (*Kizilay*). AKUT soon gained overall respect and became the symbol of an emerging Turkish civil society.[46] While the state was shown to be unable to perform its basic duties, Turkish voluntary associations filled the vacuum left by state inefficiency. This boosted their image in the eyes of the Turkish public and gave them visibility, prestige, and legitimacy in their public roles and increased their self-confidence. The earthquake crisis made clear that NGOs could really make a difference. This was converted into public recognition and appreciation.

The 2000–2001 Economic Crisis

Nonetheless, it was the collapse of Turkish economy that delivered the final blow to the image of the state. In November 2000 and February 2001, Turkey experienced a double economic crisis, the worst after the end of the Second World War. Chronic economic mismanagement, hyperinflation, massive debt, and a weak, corrupt banking sector had resulted in the December 1999 stabilization program. However, the liquidity problems of a mid-size bank (*Demirbank*) had a negative spill-over effect for the whole financial system. The central bank temporarily intervened, providing liquidity to troubled banks; when it decided to stop doing so, overnight market interest rates soared to over 2,000 percent. The crisis ended on December 6, 2000, when an IMF financial aid package of more than $15 billion was announced and *Demirbank* was taken over by the Savings Deposit Insurance Fund (*Tasarruf Mevduati Sigorta Fonu*—TMSF).[47] The crisis relapsed on February 19, 2001, when the President of the Republic Ahmet Necdet Sezer and Prime Minister Bulent Ecevit argued during a meeting of the National Security Council, and Ecevit explicitly stated afterwards that Turkey was in the middle of a "political crisis." This made financial markets believe that Ecevit's government was about to resign and that the IMF stabilization program would be abandoned. A major speculative attack was launched on the Turkish lira, while the Central Bank refused this time to act as lender of last resort. The interbank payments system collapsed on February 21, and on the following day, the government announced the floatation of the Turkish lira.[48] The extent of this crisis is hard to overstate. GNP dropped by 9.4 percent in real terms during 2001, while nominal per capita income plummeted from $2,986 to $2,110. The Turkish lira was devalued by about 50 percent, and about one million people became unemployed. The crisis affected skilled and unskilled labor equally and led to a dramatic aggravation of cases of extreme poverty.[49] It also underlined the acute deficiencies of a state unable to play its regulatory role in the economy. Clientelistic ties and patronage networks had limited the ability of state mechanisms to regulate the smooth operation of the economy. The proliferation of corruption also meant that in many cases state officials had themselves become the source of inertia. The heavy economic price that Turkish citizens had to pay had a highly damaging effect on their image of the state. The fact that the consequences of the crisis were mainly overcome through informal networks of social support and the informal economy, rather than coordinated state action, resulted in a massive loss of legitimacy for the state.[50]

THE IMPACT OF THE EUROPEAN UNION

The European Union showed keen interest in the development of civil society in Turkey and the solution of its various problems. EU policies were developed in two pillars: The program of financial support aimed at providing new opportunities and healing existing deficiencies of Turkish civil society associations. Legislative reform was supported through the application of the political conditionality principle in the process of Turkey's prospective EU membership evaluations.

Financial Support

As a member state of the Euro-Mediterranean Partnership since its inception in 1995, Turkey received EU financial aid through the MEDA I program, which lasted from 1995 to 1999.[51] Turkish NGOs were among the beneficiaries of this program. Some of them that were active in promoting democracy, human rights, and civil society started receiving financial aid under various EU budget lines even before 1995. Between 1993 and 2001, Turkish NGOs received an average of 500,000 in grants per annum.[52] The 1999 Helsinki EC decision, which gave Turkey the status of EU candidate member state, was the first step toward the establishment of comprehensive EU financial aid programs for Turkey. The signing of Accession Partnership documents in 2000 and 2003 also paved the way for the support of structural reform. In the 2000 Accession Partnership document,[53] the Turkish government was required to strengthen "legal and constitutional guarantees of the right to freedom of association and peaceful assembly and encourage development of civil society."[54] The same commitment was reiterated in the 2003 Accession Partnership document. Turkey became eligible to participate in the Pre-Accession Assistance Program, which meant that the amount of financial aid would drastically rise, with the aim of facilitating Turkey's convergence with the EU economic, political, and social *acquis*. Six major programs were launched from 2003 to 2004 to support the development of Turkish civil society.[55] The amount of financial support reached the level of 20,008,091 in total.

While the amount of financial aid was not substantial and problems persisted with contract administration, especially for poor and inexperienced organizations, EU programs had a beneficial effect on civil society. Most Turkish NGOs made good use of EU funds for the expansion of their activities. Capacity-building programs aimed to overcome the Achilles' heel of Turkish civil society associations, that is, their relatively low organizational and operational quality. Some of the perennial structural problems of Turkish civil society—such as the high degree of politicization; the ideological, partisan nature of civil society associations; and the lack of a consensual approach to politics—were not definitely resolved; on the other hand, they were mitigated by EU financial assistance and training. It was not so much the financial assistance as the grant program itself that disciplined NGOs and made them think and develop focused proposals.

Legislative Reform

Before the Reform

Constitutional and legal restrictions on the development of civil society in Turkey were mainly a product of the military regime installed by the 1980 coup. The 1982 Constitution, as well as the relevant legislation, did not provide for effective protection of the freedom of association, which is a prerequisite for the development of a free civil society. According to Article 33 of the 1982 Constitution, associations were prohibited from pursuing political aims, engaging in political activities, receiving support from or giving support to political parties, or taking joint action with labor unions or public professional organizations or foundations. Associations could normally be dissolved by a decision of a judge or suspended by the competent (administrative) authority pending a court decision in cases where delay was deemed to endanger the "indivisible integrity of the State with its territory and nation, national security, national sovereignty, public order, the protection of the rights and freedoms of others, or the prevention of offenses." The Law on Associations, which was also promulgated under the military regime in 1983, followed the same illiberal line.[56] Founding an association for the purpose of engaging in any activity on the grounds of or in the name of any region, race, social class, religion, or sect was banned. Relations with international associations were also forbidden, and associations could not use languages other than Turkish in their official contacts. Finally, the grounds for banning an association were loosely described, so maximum state intervention was allowed.

The first amendment to Article 33 was enacted in 1995 as part of a limited reform program aiming at overcoming objections by the European Parliament to the Customs Union agreement between the European Union and Turkey negotiated in that year. The ban on the political activities of associations was abolished, and collaboration with political parties and other associations was permitted. In cases where an association was suspended from activity by the decision of the competent administrative authority, this decision had to be submitted to the approval of the competent judge within twenty-four hours. The judge was required to announce his decision within forty-eight hours; otherwise, the administrative decision automatically ceased to be effective.[57] Despite these minor reforms, constitutional and legal protection of the freedom of association was anything but satisfactory.

The regular reports prepared by the European Commission on Turkey's progress toward accession consistently cited the insufficient protection of the freedom of association as one of the main deficiencies in Turkey's progress toward the fulfillment of the Copenhagen Criteria. In 1998, the European Commission report clearly stated that the freedom of association in Turkey was "subject to certain limitations" and listed an indicative list of restrictions. Associations were not allowed to "invite foreign associations to Turkey, issue public statements or organize any activities outside their premises without obtaining the prior permission of the authorities." At the same time, however, the report noted the significant rise in the number and activities of Turkish NGOs.[58] In 1999, the Commission report briefly commented that the situation regarding the freedom of association had not changed since 1998, adding that several branches of the Turkish Human Rights Association (*Insan Haklari Dernegi*—IHD), a prominent Turkish NGO with extensive activity in the field of human and minority rights protection, had been closed, either temporarily or for an indefinite period.[59] From 2000 onwards, the Commission reports devoted much more space to the freedom of association in Turkey. As a result of the 1999 Helsinki European Council decision,

Turkey became an EU candidate state. This focused the attention of
EU officials on human rights and freedoms violations, including the
freedom of association. In 2000, the Commission report repeated
that the freedom of association was still not fully respected. The need
for official permission for common NGO activities such as confer-
ences or distribution of leaflets, the ban on establishing umbrella
institutions and arranging institutional collaboration with other international NGOs—unless permitted by a decree of the Council of Ministers—and pressure on NGOs active in the field of human rights were
among the problems cited. The situation was particularly problematic
in regions under emergency rule. The IHD branch in Diyarbakir was
closed down and re-opened several times by administrative decision
of the Governor without explanation. The Commission report concluded by stating that "major efforts are still required to guarantee
freedom of association and assembly."[60] Bureaucratic obstacles to the
establishment of an association, close state control, and restrictions
on the receipt of financial aid from abroad continued to restrict the
development of civil society.

The Reform Process
Political conditions in the aftermath of the 1999 Helsinki and the
2002 Copenhagen European Council decisions[61] were more favorable for reforms affecting the freedom of association. In principle,
the coalition government supported Turkey's bid for EU membership and declared its willingness to fulfill the Copenhagen criteria so
as to permit the start of accession negotiations between the European Union and Turkey. Nonetheless, consensus disappeared when
the reform debate touched on sensitive issues that were thought to
affect Turkey's sovereignty, territorial integrity, and security. Freedom
of association was thought to be one of these issues. As a result of this,
reforms were piecemeal and rather reluctant.

A first step was made with the amendment of Article 33 of the
Turkish Constitution on October 3, 2001,[62] which guaranteed the
freedom of association. General rules and restrictions on the right to
form associations were modified, with minor positive effects on the
freedom of association. The right to form an association was broadened, but restrictions "to the extent that the duties of civil servants so
require" were retained.[63]

Much more comprehensive amendments were made to the Law on
Associations, a remnant of the authoritarian 1980–83 military regime,
under the second "reform package [*uyum paketi*]" of March 2002.
Articles 7, 11, and 12, which restricted relations with international

associations, were removed. The freedom to establish and join associations was elaborated, while the grounds for banning an association were reduced.[64] On the other hand, countervailing reforms of the Civil Code in January 2002 maintained the possibility of state control over NGO relations with international organizations. Further reform of the Law on Associations was undertaken under the third reform package of August 2002. Limitations on civil servants' right to establish associations were lifted, as was the possibility of a ban on association activities for civil defense purposes.[65] A new body in charge of associations was created within the Ministry of the Interior, as opposed to the Directorate General of Security.[66]

Further reforms were enacted under the fourth reform package of January 2003 after the election of the AKP government in November 2002. Associations were allowed to use any language in their nonofficial correspondence, while legal persons were also allowed to become members of associations. Restrictions on making announcements or distributing publications were eased, while the obligation to forward copies of these documents to the relevant authorities prior to distribution was removed.[67] Under the seventh reform package of July 2003, restrictions on the establishment of associations by people convicted of certain crimes or former members of an association or political party closed down by a court decision were eased. Higher education students could establish associations related not only to education and recreation but also to art, culture, and science. Following the provisions of the third reform package, a Department of Associations was established in August 2003 within the Ministry of Interior.[68]

Finally, a new Law on Associations was adopted in July 2004.[69] The new law dealt with many of the shortcomings of the previous legislation,[70] although its implementation was temporarily suspended due to a presidential veto. The law was finally promulgated unchanged in November 2004,[71] although its implementation has again been partially blocked[72] after an appeal to the Constitutional Court by the CHP. Limitations on the establishment of associations on the basis of race, ethnicity, religion, sect, region, or any other minority group were lifted, as well as the requirements to seek prior permission to open branches abroad, join foreign bodies, or hold meetings with foreigners and to inform local government officials of general assembly meetings. The new law lifted all restrictions on student associations and allowed for the establishment of temporary and informal platforms or networks for all civil society organizations. Governors were now required to issue warnings prior to taking legal action against

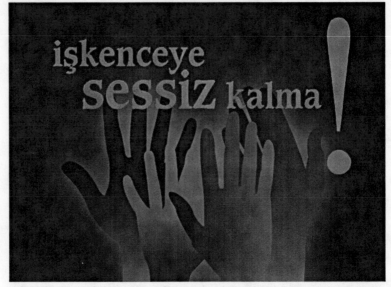

Figure 3.1 "Don't stay silent about torture!" A poster from the 2004 campaign of the Turkish Human Rights Foundation (courtesy of the Human Rights Foundation of Turkey, *Turkiye Insan Haklari Vakfi*—TIHV)

associations, while security forces were no longer allowed to enter an association's premises without a court order.

Associations were allowed to conduct joint projects and receive financial support from other associations and public institutions and no longer had to seek prior permission to receive funds from abroad. Associations acting outside the scope of their statute only received a fine and were no longer subject to dissolution.

THE STANCE OF SOCIAL ACTORS

The State Elites

It would be wrong to maintain that the whole of the state bureaucracy opposed the reform process. However, while parts of the bureaucracy seemed to be adjusting to the new political and social conditions, others remained recalcitrant opponents of liberalization. This division cut through all the branches of Turkish bureaucracy, so it would be possible to talk about reformist and reactionary factions within the judiciary, the police, the state bureaucracy and the military. The rise of an active civil society and the EU pressure to make relevant legislative steps necessary for its successful development caused fault lines to emerge between reformists and reactionaries within the bureaucracy. While some sections of the bureaucracy recognized the need for reform on instrumentalist or noninstrumentalist grounds, reform was vehemently opposed by some other bureaucratic groups. Systematic police harassment of NGOs, which were frequently cited in the human rights reports of domestic and international organizations, provided evidence of this. A series of judicial decisions that had a negative impact on the activities of NGOs corroborated the point. The annulment by the Court of Cassations in May 2005 of a lower court decision that had refused to order the closure of the Education Trades Union (*Egitim-Sen*) on the alleged grounds that its constitution defended the right of education in one's mother tongue was a clear signal that reform efforts had not affected old mindsets at the highest echelons of the judiciary.[73] The ambivalence and hesitation with which the Turkish parliament treated the issue of reform in civil society legislation as well as the piecemeal nature of adopted reforms—especially during the rule of the 1999–2002 coalition government—showed the strength of resistance. Coalition partner parties like the far-right Nationalist Action Party (*Milliyetci Hareket Partisi*—MHP) and the nationalist leftist Democratic Left Party (*Demokratik Sol Parti*—DSP) opposed reform or accepted it with the greatest reluctance only as a *sine qua non* for the success of Turkey's European bid. The AKP government showed more courage in reforming the legislation on civil society. This became clear with the promulgation of the new Law on Associations. Yet the immediate reaction of the President of the Republic Ahmet Necdet Sezer, who returned the law to parliament,[74] and the major opposition party CHP, which appealed against the law to the Constitutional Court, showed that the liberalization of civil society legislation was still not popular among parts of the highest echelons of the Turkish politics and bureaucracy.

Business Capital

The positive role of business capital in the rise of Turkish civil society cannot be ignored. Turkish business capital has been the biggest social ally as well as domestic financial supporter of Turkish NGOs and has also participated in the formation of some of the most successful NGOs. While Turkish businesspersons had historically shown no interest in politics, preferring to do lucrative business with the state, the situation changed rapidly in the 1990s. Turkish capitalists assumed the role of a pressure group for democratization and the development of civil society. A series of reports originating from the most prominent capitalist association made this point clear. The 1997 TUSIAD report on democratization stated that "not only TUSIAD, but all Turkish citizens and all institutions representing the civil society are obliged to strive towards the improvement and assimilation of democracy in this country. Our future depends on it. Turkey's future does not lie in isolating itself from the world; on the contrary, it should keep step with global developments. Barriers between the world and democracy are being raised one by one. Henceforward, economic and political relations cannot evolve independently of democracy and human rights."[75]

The rise of a consciousness of corporate social responsibility and the resulting clear defense of democratization and liberalization were unprecedented for a business association of the size and political importance of TUSIAD. TUSIAD saw itself as a member of the larger community of NGOs in Turkey, which had a special role to play in the process of Turkey's democratization:

> A broader-based democracy will certainly not result from this study, nor will it be realized by TUSIAD alone. This can only be achieved by those who adopt the perspectives put forward by this document and who are willing to come together to reach an agreement on the details. Thus, it would only be possible by the concerted effort of groups such as: non-governmental organizations, trade unions, professional bodies, industrialists and businesspersons' associations, whose struggle would be reflected in Parliament by the political parties. After all, if we decide that "now is not the right time," or "it is not our job" then we, as the true sovereigns of this land, who authorize politicians to represent us in Parliament, we as members of civil society organizations should ask ourselves this question: If not us—who?, If not now—when?[76]

Support for such statements was not unanimous inside TUSIAD. Some of its own members took a critical stance toward the report and TUSIAD's increasing interest in politics. The reaction of several nationalist, extreme leftist and conservative groups was even harsher. TUSIAD was accused of being a "Western agent."[77] Yet the argument was finally won by the reformists. Business capital thus made an important contribution to the legitimation of civil society as an independent social actor. However, the role of business capital was not exclusively moral and political, since Turkish civil society soon benefited from increasing financial support by Turkish businesspersons. Some of the most prominent NGOs, such as the Economic and Social Studies Foundation of Turkey (*Türkiye Ekonomik ve Sosyal*

Etudler Vakfı—TESEV) and the Third Sector Foundation of Turkey (*Turkiye Ucuncu Sektor Vakfı*—TUSEV), were able to support their extensive research and advocacy work through the active support of Turkish businesspersons, who had also founded their own nonprofit foundations. The Vehbi Koc Foundation (*Vehbi Koc Vakfı*), Haci Omer Sabanci Foundation (*Haci Omer Sabanci Vakfı*) and the Aydin Dogan Foundation (*Aydin Dogan Vakfı*) are characteristic well-endowed nonprofit foundations that are named after their businessman founder and perform a broad range of social activities in the fields of education, health, and culture. Although this support might have not always been even-handed, and some civil society sectors were disproportionately favored, this cannot minimize the importance of the business capital contribution in general.[78]

THE INCIDENCE OF SOCIAL LEARNING

The Europeanization of civil society in Turkey might have faced serious problems and drawbacks, yet it also initiated a process whereby views on the meaning, role, priorities, and objectives of Turkish civil society have been rethought and modified. Social learning has taken place at different levels within the ranks of several social actors. Turkey's business community was the social actor most affected by this socialization process. It was more widely agreed that civil society should be prepared to intervene in all aspects of policymaking and support Turkey's course toward democratization.[79] Similar trends were also observed within the ranks of Turkish bureaucracy, although the existence of strong opposing views showed that the socialization process was incremental and incomplete. Within civil society, self-confidence and trust in the ability of NGOs to bring about political and social change in the direction of Turkey's democratic consolidation were reinforced. A positive change was also noted in public opinion polls. Civil society was approached with less suspicion and more appreciation and interest in its activities.

The AKP government, which came to power in November 2002, has been the relatively most receptive to NGOs. When NGO delegations were invited for the first time by the government to discuss a series of political issues arising from Turkey's EU candidacy, the government made a move of major symbolic importance.[80] The degree of change in the relations between the state and civil society under the impact of improving EU-Turkey relations was clearly displayed. After the meetings, most NGOs remained disappointed by the outcome of their meetings with the government, as their views did not seem to have the expected impact on government decisions. Nonetheless, a crucial first step was accomplished: Turkish civil society was accepted by the government as a legitimate social actor and interlocutor, which was to be consulted when government decisions in the field of their expertise were pending. Support for the development of Turkish civil society was viewed no more as part of Turkey's "homework" for the fulfillment of the Copenhagen Criteria but as a strategy for the empowerment and consolidation of Turkey's democratic institutions, with its own rationale.

CONCLUSIONS

The path-dependent character of the transformation of civil society is one of the main conclusions of this chapter. The qualitative and quantitative growth of civil society resulted in the increasing empowerment of civil society actors and the formation of new social alliances. The successful engagement of Turkish civil society associations in multifarious social and political activities increased their appeal and legitimation in the eyes of public opinion. It also made clear that a vibrant civil society was not a threat but—on the contrary—a valuable asset. This made a reversion to the previous illiberal regime increasingly difficult.

The usefulness of historical institutionalism and the two-level game model as explanatory tools for the EU impact on Turkish civil society is also clearly manifested. Given that the creation of conditions conducive to the growth of civil society has been among the primary objectives of EU democratization policies, a success can be claimed in the case of Turkey. Through their generous financing of civil society activities, the identification of the areas where reform was necessary, and the careful tracking of improvements, EU institutions proved their crucial impact on the transformation of civil society in Turkey. The European Commission, in particular, exerted through its annual reports considerable pressure toward the amendment of the Constitution and the drafting of the new Law on Associations. This facilitated the work of local NGOs, liberal intellectuals, business capital, and reformist bureaucrats. While it would have been barely possible to achieve such a comprehensive reform program with their own political influence, this became possible as a result of Turkey's efforts to converge with the Copenhagen Criteria.

CHAPTER 4

THE STATE

DEFINING STATE TRADITION

One of the basic functions of a state is to compromise inherently antithetical and often conflicting interests represented by different social groups. The point where this balance is struck is a function of the degree of popular participation and political tradition. In democratic political systems, the need to secure full and effective popular participation in political decision-making needs to be matched with the need to guarantee swift and effective government. Sartori described this as the horizontal and vertical dimensions of democracy. Horizontal links, which refer to popular participation and action, give a regime its essentially democratic character. As Sartori put it, "Public opinion, electoral democracy, participatory democracy, referendum democracy—all represent a horizontal implementation and diffusion of democracy. . . . For the uniqueness of democracy resides precisely in establishing, or re-establishing, the horizontal dimension of politics."[1]

Horizontal links in modern democracies are countervailed by vertical links. While vertical links between rulers and ruled exist in nondemocratic regimes, modern democratic regimes are also characterized by a vertical dimension. Apart from securing popular empowerment and participation, democracy is also a system of government that strikes a balance in the relationship between the rulers and the ruled in a democratic context.[2] A democratically elected representative leadership exercises command and control to achieve the long-term interests of the political community. Power is concentrated in the hands of the state and is employed to ensure coercion to the rulings of the representative leadership, while state bureaucracy aims at increasing the efficiency of this policy. The establishment of salient vertical links in a democratic system makes sure that democracy will not degenerate into anarchy. As Dahl argues, "everyone who is not an anarchist is likely to agree that the risks of concentration are sometimes offset by the advantages of a uniform policy. The conflict between the advantages and risks of concentration is genuine, and citizens and leaders cannot escape the force of this dilemma in any democratic country."[3]

A nexus of horizontal and vertical links coexists in democratic systems, and the balance struck between them can indicate priorities for a more participatory or more efficient government. Berki attempted to juxtapose two different prioritizations of balancing vertical and horizontal dimensions of democracy by introducing the polar terms "transcendentalism" and "instrumentalism." Transcendentalism prioritizes the vertical aspect of democracy, giving absolute priority to the state, which is conceptualized as a transcendental entity, over the individual: "Transcendentalism, then, refers to the belief that man primarily belongs to a *moral* community. . . . that the community has a paramount moralizing function and is, therefore, logically speaking 'prior' to its members. . . . The public interest does not merely delimit but also defines the proper pursuits of individuals who belong to it. . . . (Transcendentalism) connotes the high ideals of duty, service, the sublimation of energies."[4]

Instrumentalism, on the other hand, does not recognize a transcendental character to the state but rather considers it to be an instrument for the promotion of individual private aims. Instrumentalism lays its weight on the horizontal aspects of democracy and prioritizes individual over state interests: "Instrumentalism hence has an air of freedom, diversity, plurality, colorful and 'healthy' conflict about it; it is unheroic, and its dynamism is confined to that of its self-assertive members."[5]

Therefore, the quality of a democratic regime could be measured by its success in striking an optimal balance between the horizontal and vertical dimensions of democracy and taking a moderate instrumentalist approach. A democratic state tradition, therefore, refers to a balance that neither dismisses particularistic groups nor ignores the need to pursue long-term state interests.[6] Politics thus becomes the tool for the resolution of different views and interests on the basis of compromise and a mechanism to reach a "dynamic rather than static consensus" and "organic rather than mechanical solidarity."[7]

A strong state tradition has been a common theme in Ottoman and republican Turkish politics.[8] Classical Ottoman and *Tanzimat* state traditions coalesced in recognizing absolute priority to "community" interests expressed by the state over any particularistic interests. The pursuit of individual interest was dismissed as divisive and harmful for the common good. In republican years, this legacy has been instrumental in shaping politics, as well as the way the balance between the horizontal and vertical dimensions of democracy was struck. Shifting the balance point in the direction of accepting a more instrumental view of the state and increasing the relative importance of horizontal aspects of democracy has been a key element of the democratic consolidation process in Turkey.

STATE TRADITION IN TURKEY

The Ottoman Legacy

The Ottoman state tradition is a topic of critical importance in the study of Balkan and Middle Eastern politics. Ozbudun defined it as "a strong and centralized state, reasonably effective by the standards of its day, highly autonomous of societal forces, and occupying a central and highly valued place in Ottoman political culture."[9]

Although the Ottoman Empire in its classical era still belonged to the medieval world, it was the most centralized of all its contemporaries. The absence of hereditary landed gentry meant that the power of the sultan met no effective power checks. The appointment of Janissaries in all critical military and administrative positions epitomized the patrimonial character of the system[10] and prevented the development of a military and administrative aristocracy.[11] The concentration of most land in the hands of the sultan and systematic confiscations of private property proved to be an effective way of keeping sultanic power intact. Meanwhile, the gradual development of a predominantly non-Muslim urban merchant class did not have any impact on state-society relations.[12] The Islamic nature of the Ottoman state prevented the conversion of the economic power of the non-Muslim merchant elites into political power.[13] Non-Muslim Ottoman subjects could normally have no claim to a share of political power or participation in the military and administrative state apparatus.[14]

The Ottoman state tradition was shaped under the influence of two countervailing trends. On the one hand, the Ottoman Empire was influenced by the Middle Eastern patrimonial dynastic tradition, where the political and religious realms were diffused and political legitimacy rested on the person of the sultan. Sultan Mehmed the Conqueror (*Fatih*) declared his "holy warrior [*gazi*]" title to be the basis for the legitimacy of his rule.[15] Moreover, the sultan was considered personally responsible for the welfare of his subjects.[16] The personal character of sultanic rule was also manifested by the customary ratification of existing laws each time a new sultan ascended to the throne. On the other hand, political legitimacy was not exclusively based on Islam and personal rule. The sultan was bound to take measures outside the Islamic law if this was demanded by state interest. In due course, a special body of legislation (*orf-i sultani*) was accumulated that did not emanate from Islam or the sultan's whim but from reason and necessity. The sultan was then referred to not as "the shadow of God upon earth," but as a temporal, secular ruler. The traditional Middle Eastern notion of "circle of justice"[17] served as an additional justification for the shift toward reason-based rule.[18] This secular tradition was codified under the word *adab* and remained a constant determinant of Ottoman state policy, differentiating it from other Islamic states.

The first signs of Ottoman decline in the seventeenth century were followed by a decrease in the power of the central state and the *adab* tradition. The devastating results of Ottoman campaigns against the Habsburg and Russian Empires stressed the need for increased state cash revenues, which could only be possible through the abolition of the *timar*[19] system and the establishment of tax-farming. Local notables (*ayan* and *derebey*) who took over the function of tax-farming emerged as serious contenders for state power at the regional level. The "Deed of Alliance [*Sened-i Ittifak*]" of 1808 was the document that marked the apogee of the power of local notables, as well as the separation between the person of sultan and the state. It was the state and not the sultan that was mentioned as a party to the pact.[20]

Sultan Mahmud II saw the need to modernize the Ottoman state in order to forestall its disintegration. The Napoleonic expedition to Ottoman Egypt in 1798, the outbreak of the Greek Revolution in 1821, and the successful Westernization reform program of Egypt's ruler Mehmed Ali were all powerful signals of the urgent need for Ottoman reform. The brutal suppression of the Janissary Revolt in 1826 was the first successful test of the modernizing state apparatus and removed the last vestiges of a parochial institution that could perform even a minor power-check role. The abolition of traditional checks and balances in the absence of Western-based equivalents meant that the Ottoman state could grow virtually uncontrolled. The reform of military and civil bureaucracy increased state efficiency, while the introduction of Western technology increased the ability of the state to control society. In fact, the state was seen as an indispensable tool in the struggle to transform society. While the state was growing stronger domestically, its international position was increasingly precarious. Successive military defeats and territorial concessions showed the military and diplomatic incompetence of the Ottoman state, which resulted in the rise of the "eastern question." The urgent need for reform was epitomized in the question often discussed among Ottoman intellectuals of the time: "How can this state be saved [*Bu devlet nasil kurtarilabilir?*]?" Ottoman reformists thought state reform and centralization was the only answer.[21] A vision of "order-in-progress" replaced the emphasis on the durability of the established order.[22]

The 1876 Constitution was the first attempt to introduce representative institutions. However, these efforts were quickly frustrated when the new Sultan Abdulhamid II indefinitely suspended the force of the Constitution in 1878. While the previous steps toward political liberalization were swiftly undone in the Hamidian era, state modernization continued unabated. A strong Ottoman state was needed to serve the Hamidian government domestically and prevent the disintegration of the ailing Empire. The Ottoman state further developed an unmistakably authoritarian character; it was valued in its own right and remained relatively autonomous from society. Phrases like "May God not bring adversity to the State and the Nation [*Allah Devlete, Millete zevel vermesin*]," "the Sublime State [*Devlet-i Aliye*]," and "the sublime interests of the State [*Devletin ali menfaatleri*]" entered Ottoman political vocabulary and survived the demise of the Ottoman state itself.[23] The state retained its tutelary role even after the 1908 Young Turk Revolution, when the 1876 Constitution was reinstated and parliamentary elections were held. The Revolution brought an end to Hamidian rule but built upon its already strengthened state apparatus. After a brief and unsuccessful experimentation with pluralism, a military dictatorship was established shortly after the outbreak of the Balkan Wars. According to Karpat, this was inevitable for the implementation of the Young Turk agenda: "The only way out of this chaos, was, as Young Turks saw it, to strengthen the state apparatus and launch a series of cultural and economic reforms to modernize the social and political structure. . . . Thus, Young Turks ended in the dictatorship of a small group, which fully utilized the state to achieve those ends. The age-old autocratic traditions were continued on behalf of the state."[24]

The Young Turk triumvirate (Enver Pasa, Talat Pasa, and Cemal Pasa) resorted to state violence and terror to defend the Empire's interests and transform the remaining territories into a Turkish nation-state. Ferocious atrocities orchestrated by state and parastatal apparatuses tainted the last years of the Ottoman Empire but could not prevent its demise. After the Ottoman Empire surrendered by signing the Moudros Armistice of October 30, 1918, it was not the Istanbul government, but the Ankara-based nationalists who successfully claimed the mantle of Ottoman state tradition. The new Republic was a radical break from the old order, but, at the same time, continuities were too significant to ignore.

The Turkish State from 1923 to the 1990s

Despite all the cataclysmic changes in the transition from the Ottoman Empire to republican Turkey, the Ottoman state tradition showed remarkable endurance in the new era. Kemalism could also be viewed as the institutionalized republican version of the Ottoman *adab* tradition.[25] This climate was anything but conducive to the development of a free civil society.[26] In accordance with the ideological trends of the interwar years, corporatist ideas were also seriously considered.[27] Under the leadership of Recep Peker, the CHP developed in the early 1930s strong corporatist features,[28] while attempts to develop a statist but more leftist ideology were stalled.[29] While the allegiance of Kemalism to democracy remained—at best—dubious,[30] the image of the strong state remained impeccable, and its role as the agent of a forced top-down modernization was reaffirmed. As Kazancigil argued, "Kemalists, although very different from the traditional Ottoman bureaucrats, since they were trained in secular schools to become adepts of Western ideas, were heirs to the old patrimonial tradition, which assumed the dominance of state over civil society and reserved the monopoly of legitimacy and authority to state elites."[31]

Dissidence or opposition were not tolerated in this Hegelian type of state, and coercion was crucial in the implementation of the Kemalist reform program. The state elite[32] became the implementer of the Kemalist reform, given that the lack of a multiparty, democratic system meant the absence of a political elite.[33] The emergence of a competitive political elite after the introduction of a multiparty system in 1946 changed this picture, as the state elite was not willing to give up its political prerogatives.[34] A struggle between state elite and politicians has been a common theme of Turkish politics since then and has shaped republican state tradition. As Heper argued, "For a long time democracy in Turkey developed as a conflict between the state elites and political elites. The state elites tended to act basically

Figure 4.1 Anitkabir, Ataturk's Mausoleum in Ankara, a symbol of Kemalism (photo by author)

as the guardians of the long-term interests of the country and held a condescending attitude toward the particularistic interests; political elites in turn perceived themselves primarily as the defenders of the particularistic interests. The state elites' expectations of democracy and the consequent rift between them and the political elites came to have critical implications for Turkish politics."[35]

The advent of multiparty politics also gave the chance for a rapprochement between the Kemalist state elite and peripheral political forces. Nonetheless, the process of integration turned out to be highly problematic. The state failed to penetrate the periphery, of which politicians took over the leadership.[36] The struggle between the state elite and politicians was also characterized by a strong sense of repugnancy to any form of opposition.[37] Empowered by popular vote and support, politicians, represented by the DP in the 1950s, attempted to challenge the dominant role of the state elite by renegotiating the relationship between state and society, center and periphery.[38] This happened without the due respect to the democratic rights of the opposition.[39] What resulted was a vicious circle. As Heper has argued, "the state elites were sensitive to the crisis of integration and were therefore intolerant toward the periphery, whilst the periphery, mostly smothered and, therefore, overly defiant whenever it could afford to be, was prone to add fuel to and reinforce the prejudices of the state elites."[40]

The effort of the DP to reshape Turkish politics through majoritarian democracy was violently interrupted by the Turkish military. The coup of May 27, 1960, was the first clear response of the state elite to the effort made by politicians to challenge its power and promote particularistic interests against the perceived long-term state interests.[41] It also initiated a vicious circle of military coups, illustrating the deadlock that Turkey's democratization process had entered. The establishment of a multiparty democratic system by the state elite led to the election of political parties that allegedly did not show the same commitment to Kemalist principles. Such policies inevitably led to a new military coup, which, after abolishing existing democratic institutions, purifying the political space from harmful influences and reinforcing institutional guarantees for the Kemalist nature of the system, set democracy back into operation.[42]

Before handing over the power to a civilian government, the military attempted to make sure, through the promulgation of the 1961 Constitution, that bureaucratic elites would maintain formidable political power and that the restored "static order" of Kemalist orthodoxy could not be again challenged by peripheral forces.[43] On the one hand, the new constitution greatly expanded human rights protection; on the other hand, it also strengthened the institutional position of the bureaucracy vis-à-vis the government and the parliament.[44] A National Security Council (*Milli Guvenlik Kurulu*—MGK) of military-civilian composition was established to decide on national security issues with a remit, which was very widely interpreted.[45] The dominant role of the military was further established by its close involvement in the economy. The Armed Forces Mutual Assistance Fund (*Ordu Yardimlasma Kurumu*—OYAK) was founded in 1961 to manage military social security funds.[46] Soon it became one of the biggest economic actors of the country, with multifarious and lucrative business operations that improved the living standards of Turkish officers and provided them with additional power. Special links were also developed with business groups, which exchanged their protected dominant position in the domestic market with a degree of subordination to the state elite.[47] The constitutional amendments in the aftermath of the 1971 coup further strengthened the position of the military.[48] The establishment of State Security Courts (*Devlet Guvenlik Mahkemeleri*—DGM) in 1973, in line with a constitutional amendment passed in February 1972, was an additional manifestation of the accumulation of power in the hands of the bureaucracy.[49] The DGM tried cases deemed to affect national security and became instrumental in checking political dissent under the provisions of the extremely illiberal Turkish Penal Code.[50] The state elite maintained its grip over all forms of civil society. Political parties, trades unions, and business and professional organizations remained partly subordinated to the state.[51] The MGK and the DGM became the symbols of the institutionalized nature of the military's political role.[52]

The rift between politicians and the state elite was also instrumental in the rise of political patronage and clientelism in Turkey. As the state elite claimed to be the sole advocate of long-term community interests, politicians were persuaded to represent purely the particularistic interests of the periphery.[53] This strengthened existing local patronage and clientelistic links and led to a bifurcation of the state, which was "double-faced," strong in some respects and weak in others.[54] The expression "father state [*devlet baba*]" was not coined in the republican era; in fact, its roots can be traced to the Ottoman times.[55] The Ottoman state had maintained a strong paternalistic character. It acquired a fatherly image; it—in theory—cared for the welfare of its citizens but never allowed individual freedom.[56] However, this expression became a more accurate representation of societal perceptions of the state after the introduction of multiparty democracy. Suleyman Demirel, one of the most influential politicians of the second half of the twentieth century, who served long tenures as Prime Minister and President, came to personify in the eyes of many Turks a fatherly political figurehead as well as political patronage and clientelism.[57] The cognomen "Father [*Baba*]," which Demirel gained for his populist and paternalistic policies, clearly illustrated this perception.[58] Patronage politics in the 1960s and 1970s had their impact on the coherence of the bureaucratic elite. Political parties succeeded in colonizing large segments of the civil bureaucracy, so it was only the military that remained insulated from party infiltration and fragmentation and maintained a clear autonomy and conscience of its vanguard and tutelary mission.[59] Politicians were dismissed as sectarian, selfish, and inefficient.[60] This included the CHP, the party of the Kemalist elite, which had lost its elitist bureaucratic credentials. It was suggested that its role came to be de facto played by the military. The rise of patronage politics coincided with a period of serious political violence and anarchy, which ended with the military coup of 1980.

The 1980–83 military regime took drastic measures to restore the dominance of the state and the tutelary role of the bureaucracy, besides reinterpreting Kemalism in a more conservative way. The promulgation of a new constitution was one of its most important restoration tools. In the Preamble of the 1982 Constitution, the exaltation of the state came almost to the point of sanctification, the state being referred to as "sacred" [*kutsal Turk Devleti*].[61] State interests took increased priority,[62] and the position of the military was also significantly strengthened.[63] In the aftermath of the 1980 coup, the grip of bureaucratic elites over academia was tightened with the establishment of the Higher Education Council (*Yuksek Ogretim Kurulu*— YOK), which was entrusted with the inspection of Turkish higher education institutions and their faculty. The YOK became very active in suppressing dissident voices among Turkish academics, thus imposing an authoritarian aura in the academic world. Although the end of political violence, as a result of the 1980 military coup, was met with relief by most Turks, an exorbitant price was paid for this. The weakness and immaturity of the Turkish democratic system became once more clear. It was reasonably argued that the rigid suppression of political dissent was not the only alternative to political anarchy and that democracy consisted not merely of an elected government but also the right to express dissident opinions.[64] The clearly illiberal character of the regime also led to a reaction by European states, which had been less critical of military coups in the past. The emphasis on national security also meant that programs for welfare and social services had little priority.[65]

In the aftermath of the 1980–83 military regime, the wave of economic liberalization initiated by the Motherland Party (*Anavatan Partisi*—ANAP) governments reshaped economic and social conditions and questioned the dominance of the state elite. The ideological fragmentation of civil bureaucracy was allowed to continue, while the dramatic growth of the private sector lowered the status and prestige of the civil service.[66] This facilitated the autonomization of politicians from the tutelage of the bureaucracy. A new generation of politicians emerged, led by Prime Minister Turgut Ozal, which had a technocratic rather than ideological approach to politics and was markedly closer to public sentiment.[67] The debureaucratization of the state was resumed through politicization, a personalistic style of government, and closer government control over the bureaucracy.[68] In 1987, Ozal came to the point of openly challenging the military by appointing to the position of the Chief of General Staff not the Commander of the Land Forces General Necdet Oztorun, who was earmarked by military custom, but his preferred candidate General Necip Torumtay. This was seen as a violation of the military-enforced principle that governments should not influence appointments at the top the armed services. Ozal's insistence on having the political initiative in security and foreign policy issues led to the early resignation of Torumtay following their disagreement on Turkey's position during the first Gulf crisis in 1990–91.[69] This was, however, a crucial first test pointing to the gradual civilianization of the regime.[70]

The Turkish State since the 1990s

The Impact of Global Actors

State-society relations in Turkey were also affected by global developments in the aftermath of the Cold War. A new strategic and security environment emerged in Turkey's region. The collapse of the Soviet Union resulted in the establishment of eight new states in the Caucasus and Central Asia, many of which shared cultural and linguistic links with Turkey. The first Gulf war brought the Middle East into the center of international and U.S. interests and reshuffled regional strategic balances. Under these circumstances, the loss of strategic importance, which the end of the Cold War meant for Turkey, was counterbalanced by its new strategic role in the volatile regions of the Middle East, the Caucasus, and Central Asia. Aiming to use Turkey as a strategic ally for their regional policy, the United States—especially its security establishment—planned a special relationship with the Turkish military, thus de facto recognizing its extrainstitutional political role. This tacit support for the dominant role of the military in Turkish politics was based on the United States will to ensure stability and a pro-Western regime in Turkey. The Turkish military was seen as the strongest and most reliable domestic interlocutor and ally and a guarantee for the continuation of a pro-U.S. regime in Turkey. While the United States clearly favored the predominant role of the state elite, the impact of globalization was countervailing. Access to private and international media weakened the information monopoly of the state elite and spread understanding of Western European, liberal ways of dealing with state-society relations. The spread of liberal democracy in Eastern Europe after the fall of the Berlin Wall showed that democratic consolidation was not an impossible task and left Turkey's tutelary democracy more exposed to criticism. In Europe, demands to subordinate military forces to democratic control gained general support, while the significance and status of the military, in the aftermath of the Cold War, was reduced.[71] Meanwhile, there was a shift from "hard" security issues to "soft" issues like regime type, civil disorder, and terrorism. This new security agenda influenced the role of the

Turkish military, which became increasingly preoccupied with issues of "soft" security.[72] Nonetheless, globalization only marginally challenged the dominant position of the state elite. In fact, the state elite grew stronger in some cases as a result of domestic developments.

The Impact of Domestic Politics
The struggle between transcendental and liberal perceptions of the state continued in the 1990s.[73] Two issues that dominated the political agenda, the escalation of the Kurdish conflict and the rise of political Islam, were used as pretexts for reinstating a powerful role for the state elite. The sudden death of Ozal in 1993 further facilitated this development, as there was no other politician with sufficient popular authority to balance bureaucratic power. In due course, the military attempted to develop a concept of national security that legitimized and perpetuated its involvement in almost every aspect of domestic politics.[74]

The PKK insurgency took the dimensions of a full-scale war in several provinces of eastern and southeastern Turkey in the early 1990s. This allowed for the implementation of martial law in the "state of emergency" region (*Olaganustu Hal Bolgesi*—OHAL), where the military enjoyed virtually unlimited powers. The PKK threat gave the military the chance to take over extensive administrative and judicial duties in the conflict-ridden provinces and gain wide public support for its security operations. The prioritization of state over individual interests took new dimensions as severe and brutal human rights violations affecting the civilian population of eastern and southeastern Turkey, PKK members, and prisoners were justified as necessary for the protection of long-term state interests. The defeat of PKK forces in 1998 and the subsequent capture of its leader Abdullah Ocalan in February 1999 was seen a success for the military, which proved its ability to defend state sovereignty and territorial integrity.

The growth of political Islam also mobilized the secularist reflexes of the bureaucracy and the military. The rise of the RP to power in 1996 was a shock for the state elite, which mobilized to prevent its infiltration by Islamists. Their campaign culminated in the MGK meeting of February 28, 1997, which has been cited since then as a "soft" coup. The military members of the MGK presented to the civilian members—in effect, the government—an 18-point memorandum, which aimed at suppressing "reactionary Islam [*irtica*]." The most important of these points included limitation of Islamic vocational education, screening of the economic activity of Islamic groups, strict control in the recruitment of people with Islamist leanings into the bureaucracy, and prevention of acts that could be deemed antisecular through the introduction of stricter legislation for the protection of the secular character of the state.[75] After some hesitation, Prime Minister Erbakan was forced to endorse the memorandum on March 5, 1997. His coalition government came under tremendous political, social, and bureaucratic pressure through backbench defection and was finally forced to resign on June 18, 1997. This mode of military intervention was drastically different from former military coups and was coupled with the mobilization of the secular segment of civil society.[76] Although the "February 28 process" can be seen as a big setback in the process of democratic consolidation, it was significant that the military avoided an outright coup and attempted to influence political developments through the mobilization of friendly civil society forces.[77] The mode of the military intervention and the interest of the state elite in coopting civil society showed evidence of increasing legitimation of the civil society and the politicians in the eyes of the state elite.[78] While in the past the military had aimed to invoke societal indifference and fear, now it aimed to secure consent and support. The segments of the civil society that collaborated with the military did not necessarily oppose the political role of the military. On the contrary, many of them thought that "the intensity of the Islamic threat might require the suspension of democratic freedoms and limitation of representative principles and institutions."[79]

The Securitization of Turkish Domestic Politics

The securitization of Turkish domestic politics was a process that reshaped Turkish national security perceptions. The rise of the Kurdish and Islamist issues were instrumental in a military effort to redefine the concept of national security. National security was no more defined as a "hard" foreign military threat but also included issues of domestic public policy. As Cizre succinctly argued:

> The most radical implication of the post-Cold War understanding of security in Latin America, Turkey, and other similar contexts is that it is conceived of as synonymous with public policy, thus granting the military a free entry into policy making. This is made possible by letting the national security concept influence codification of laws pertaining to internal security, anti-terrorism, and maintenance of public order, criminalizing certain political activities, constraining public debate and expanding military jurisdiction over civilians. It is the translation of national security into laws, decrees and regulations that, in fact,

gives the Turkish military a wide latitude in policy making and law enforcement.[80]

The securitization of domestic politics strengthened the political role of the military and facilitated the compromise of human rights for the sake of national security.[81] This was expressed both through the operations of a powerful MGK as well as through various statements of high-ranking officers who took clear position on contested issues of domestic policy. This attitude accorded with the guardian role of the Turkish military and the shifting of attention toward the "internal enemies [*ic dusmanlar*]" of the state, in other words, the groups that were allegedly aiming to compromise Turkey's territorial integrity and sovereignty as well as the secular, unitary, monoethnic character of the Turkish state.[82] The military maintained for itself the privilege of defining what an internal or external threat to national security was.[83] On the other hand, increased military activity had also its downside, as Cizre and Cinar stressed:

> The military is more exposed to charges of partisanship and is more vulnerable to criticisms. Given the fact that the military's traditional "most trusted institution" status was based on its image of being "above politics," one could argue that by remaining in the political arena it weakens the very foundations of its own strength. The increasing intolerance of the military for any criticism or alternative views, which we can observe in the frequency with which the institution responds to what it considers counter-positions taken by public figures, reflects its increasing sense of insecurity about its status. It is perhaps for this reason that the military aims to construct its own support base by acting like a political party directly addressing the public. However, this strategy feeds back into the weakening of the military's carefully nurtured "above politics" image.[84]

Meanwhile, increased interest in "internal" enemies did not mean that "external" threats were discounted. Armenia, Greece, Iran, Syria and—occasionally—the Russian Federation were listed as states comprising "external" threats to Turkish national security. The Cyprus question also maintained its key importance in foreign policy. The often-exaggerated emphasis on the possibility of external security threats, given the comparative size of the Turkish military machine, economy, and diplomatic position, had a historical explanation. The Sevres syndrome, the atavistic fear that the Great Powers could collaborate with Turkey's neighboring states with the aim of partitioning it, following the model of the 1920 Sevres Treaty, remained a feature

of the social *habitus*[85] of the Kemalist elite.[86] The Sevres syndrome
has been a constant undercurrent of thought in the Turkish national
psyche and security thinking that proliferated in large parts of the
public opinion. Suspicion and fear of encirclement have resulted not
only in poor relations with neighboring states, exorbitant military
expenditure, and respective increase of the military's influence. It also
meant Turkey's inability to trust its own material, intellectual capacity,
and potential. Last but not least, it contradicted the military's long-
term Western orientation, as democracy was seen as causing political
instability that the "multifarious enemies of Turkey" and their local
collaborators could only benefit from. This insecurity was a lethal
threat that needed to be tackled dynamically.[87]

The MGK has had a central role in the reactivation of political
activity of bureaucratic elites and has been a focal point of the democratic consolidation debate in Turkey. Being the bulwark of military
influence into politics, its operation manifested the deficiencies of
Turkish democratic system. Despite being a democracy in the procedural sense, Turkey still lacked crucial characteristics of a substantively
democratic regime.

The National Security Council (Milli Guvenlik Kurulu—MGK)

The direct involvement of the military into politics dated back to the
late years of the Ottoman Empire, and it has been argued that Turkish politics has not been fully civilianized since then.[88] The Young
Turk movement largely consisted of military officers, and the 1908
Young Turk Revolution was essentially a military one. The coup of
1913 brought Young Turk military leadership to dictatorial power.
The Young Turk Triumvirate remained the effective ruler of the Ottoman Empire until its demise. Being a retired officer himself, Ataturk
attempted in the early republican years to bring an end to the political role of the military.[89] Although a large part of Ataturk's ruling
cadre consisted of retired officers, serving officers were banned from
politics.[90] The rule of the DP further widened the gap between the
military and politicians. However, the 1960 coup signaled the return
of the military into politics as a guardian of Turkey's Kemalist regime.
One of the main tools for the institutionalization of the military's
political role was the establishment of the MGK.[91] Article 111 of the
1961 Constitution stated,

> The MGK membership consists of the Chief of the General Staff,
> representatives of the Armed Forces and other ministers, as provided
> by law.

The President of the Republic presides over the MGK, and, in his absence, this duty is taken over by the Prime Minister.

The MGK informs the Council of Ministers about its basic views—when necessary—in order to assist decision-making on issues of national security and achieving coordination.

This article provided the basis for the institutionalization of the military's political role. The power of defining issues of national security and implementing policy measures for them was transferred from the government to the MGK.[92] The elastic definition of national security enabled policy formation within the MGK on all major issues of domestic and foreign policy. Views formed in the MGK constituted the basis of all subsequent government policies. Thus, the military obtained a crucial influence over government policy and a veto power against any possible political attempts to follow policies of which it did not approve. The state elite secured its predominant and unchallengeable role against the politicians, as well as their guardianship of the republican character of the state, whose attributes they had the monopoly to define.

The subsequent coups of March 12, 1971, and September 12, 1980, reaffirmed the leading role of the MGK, while legislation pertaining to its competence and operation widened its jurisdiction. The 1982 Constitution affirmed the conservative interpretation of Kemalism[93] and further increased the authority of the MGK. According to Article 118, the government was obliged to "give priority consideration" to the MGK decisions, in matters that "the MGK deems necessary for the preservation of the existence and independence of the state." Article 35 and Article 85§1 of the Turkish Armed Forces Internal Service Law defined the duties of the Turkish armed forces as to "protect and preserve the Turkish Republic" on the basis of the principles referred to in the Preamble of the Constitution, including territorial integrity, secularism, and republicanism. Article 35 stated that "the military is responsible for defending both the Turkish Fatherland and the Turkish Republic as defined by the Constitution." Article 85§1 stipulated that "the Turkish Armed Forces shall defend the country against the internal as well as the external threats, if necessary by force."[94] Similarly Article 2a of the National Security Council Law defined national security in such broad terms that it could—if necessary—be interpreted as covering virtually every policy area.[95] In effect, the MGK became the supreme decision-making

body of the state. Severe restrictions of human rights further embedded the absolute priority given to state over individual interests.[96]

THE IMPACT OF THE EUROPEAN UNION

Before the Reform

European Commission reports were replete with references to the
democratic deficiencies of the Turkish state structure and operations,
focusing on the military's political role and the illiberal and dysfunc-
tional judicial system. The 1999 report included references to the
judiciary and problems related to the DGM. The verdicts of the European Court of Human Rights (ECHR) against Turkey regarding the
DGM were noted. In 1998, the presence of a military judge in State
Security Court panels was deemed a violation of the European Convention of Human Rights, while the ECHR additionally concluded
in 1999 that those tried by them had been denied the right to have
their cases heard by an "independent and impartial tribunal." The
report also pointed to the major role that the MGK continued to play
in political life.[97] In the 2000 report, the lack of further progress on
the question of the DGM was noted, as well as the need for measures
that would guarantee the implementation of ECHR verdicts against
Turkey. Emphasis was given to civil-military relations. The fact that
the Chief of General Staff remained accountable to the Prime Minister
and not to the Defense Minister and that he appointed military members to the Council of Higher Education (*Yuksek Ogretim Kurulu*—
YOK) and the Higher Education Supervisory Board (*Yuksek Ogretim
Denetim Kurulu*) were cited as evidence of the exalted status of the
military and a deviation from European standards. Regarding the
MGK, the report noted that it maintained its overwhelming influence on issues related with defense, security, and the secular character
of the state and thus—in practice—drastically limited the role of the
democratically elected institutions, the government and the parliament.[98] The 2001 report stressed that little progress was made regarding the increase of civilian control over the military and reiterated the
need for measures to ensure the execution of ECHR judgments at the
domestic level.[99]

The 2002 report pointed to problems of independence and consistency in the operation of the judiciary. Lack of clarity, transparency,
and legal certainty became apparent when prosecutors were using
irrelevant articles of the Penal Code to prosecute citizens after the
abolition of the formerly used articles.[100] The public statements of

the MGK military members on the question of EU reform were mentioned, as well as their important role in domestic politics. The report commented that previous reforms did not appear to have changed the MGK's operation in practice. Although decisions were taken by majority, opinions of its military members continued to carry major weight. The report also marked the substantial degree of military autonomy in establishing the defense budget and the existence of two extrabudgetary funds available to it.[101] The defense budget and any other military expenditure was never exposed to parliamentary debate or media discussion.[102]

The 2003 report marked the ineffective or unwilling implementation of reform measures by the bureaucracy. Measures drawn up by executive bodies responsible for the implementation of specific aspects of the political reforms adopted by Parliament considerably narrowed the scope of these reforms by establishing very strict conditions. The Higher Radio-Television Board (*Radyo-Televizyon Ust Kurulu*—RTUK) and the General Directorate of Foundations (*Vakiflar Genel Mudurlugu*—VGM) were mentioned as examples. The continued autonomy of the military in dealing with the defense budget and procurement was stressed, as well as its informal—but powerful—political role. The report also pointed to problems related to the impartiality and consistency of judicial acts.[103] The 2004 report finally stressed that, apart from formal reforms to the legal and institutional framework, civilian authorities should fully exercise their supervisory functions in practice—particularly as regards the formulation of national security strategy and its implementation, relations with neighboring countries, and the control of the defense budget.[104]

The Reform Process

The reform process was admittedly long and uneasy, yet it managed in the course of five years to produce significant progress in the direction of liberalizing the Turkish state. It was argued that the extent of the EU reform on the Turkish state could only be compared with that of the *Tanzimat*. European Commission reports served again as accurate monitors of reform steps. In June 1999, the military judge was removed from the DGM.[105] The establishment of a special executive organ, the General Secretariat for the European Union (*Avrupa Birligi Genel Sekreterligi*—ABGS), attached to the Office of the Prime Minister, in June 2000, aimed to ensure the effective co-ordination of all governmental affairs related to EU-Turkey relations and facilitated the state reform process.[106] As regards the issue of civilian control over military expenditure, the Law on Public Financial Management and Control was amended in December 2003 to allow the inclusion of extrabudgetary funds in the budgets of the Defense Ministry as of January 1, 2005, and the dissolution of these funds by December 31, 2007. A military member of the YOK, appointed by the Chief of General Staff, and a member of the RTUK, appointed by the MGK Secretary General were removed as a result of legislative reform aiming to reduce the political role of the military.[107] The most important fields of reform, however, were the MGK and the judicial system.

The National Security Council (Milli Guvenlik Kurulu—MGK)

The reform of the MGK was one of the most sensitive reform issues. The political activity of a military-controlled body was repeatedly cited in European Commission reports as evidence for Turkey's serious democratic shortcomings. In October 2001, Article 118 of the Constitution concerning the role and the composition of the MGK was amended. The number of civilian members of the MGK was increased from five to nine, while the number of the military representatives remained five. In addition, the new text emphasized the advisory nature of this body, stressing that its role was limited to recommendations, which the government was required to "evaluate" instead of giving "priority consideration" to them.[108]

Further improvement was noted in the 2003 European Commission report. The advisory nature of the MGK was confirmed through an amendment to the Law on the MGK in July 2003, in which the provision that "the MGK will report to the Council of Ministers the views it has reached and its suggestions" was removed. This amendment abolished the extended executive and supervisory powers of the MGK Secretary General. In particular, the provision empowering the Secretary General to follow up, on behalf of the President and the Prime Minister, the implementation of any recommendation made by the MGK was abrogated. Other provisions authorizing unlimited access by the MGK to any civilian agency were lifted. Another amendment stated that the post of Secretary General would no longer be reserved exclusively for a military officer. Nonetheless, in August 2003, it was decided to appoint a military candidate, General Sukru Sariisik, for one last year. The frequency of the meetings of the MGK was modified, so that it would normally meet every two months instead of once a month.[109]

The most far-reaching reforms of the MGK took place in 2004. As regards the duties, functioning, and composition of the MGK, a regulation was adopted in January 2004 implementing previous legislative

changes of July 2003. The MGK Secretariat General was also transformed into a body serving the purely consultative function of the
MGK. Its role was limited to the definition of the agenda. The Secretariat was no longer able to conduct national security investigations
on its own initiative and manage directly the special funds allocated to
it, which came now under the exclusive control of the prime minister.
Further changes concerned the internal restructuring of the MGK,
with a substantial staff reduction and the abolition of some units. Legislation that came into force in December 2003 abolished the secret
status of decrees governing the activities of the MGK General Secretariat. Finally, in August 2004, a high-profile diplomat, Yigit Alpogan,
became the first civilian MGK Secretary General. This appointment
had a highly symbolic significance, as it provided one of the clearest
manifestations of the civilianization trend in Turkish politics.[110]

The Judicial System

Shortcomings in the Turkish judicial system were noted by successive European Commission reports. The State Security Courts (*Devlet Guvenlik Mahkemeleri*—DGM) and Turkey's illiberal legislation
were among the main foci of concern. Noteworthy steps were first
made in 2002 with respect to the DGM. The number of offenses falling under their jurisdiction decreased, while the right of defense for
detainees falling under their competence was improved. Limitations
on detainees' right of access to a lawyer were abolished. Detainees
prosecuted for collective offenses falling under the jurisdiction of the
DGM became legally entitled to access to a lawyer, but only after 48
hours. As regards the application of the European Convention on
Human Rights, the Constitutional Court ruled in March 2002 that
this was a source on which the Turkish courts could base decisions.
In August 2002, provisions were added to the Turkish legal system
to allow for retrial in the event of convictions that were found contrary to the Convention. Training programs for judges continued in
such fields as the prevention of torture, freedom of expression and
fair trial.[111] In 2003, the Code of Civil Procedure and the Code of
Criminal Procedure were amended to allow retrial in civil and criminal cases in which the ECHR found violations of the Convention and
its Additional Protocols. The Law on the Establishment and Trial
Procedures of Military Courts was amended aiming to end military

jurisdiction over civilians and to align the provisions of the military code of procedure with reforms adopted by previous packages concerning freedom of expression. An increasing number of judges and prosecutors attended training seminars, while a Justice Academy was created to train junior judicial officers.[112] Courts also started making concrete steps in the implementation of political reform. As the 2003 Commission report pointed out, "criminal proceedings launched against individuals on the basis of Articles 312 [incitement to class, ethnical, religious, or racial hatred] and 159 [insulting state institutions] have generally concluded with acquittals. The courts have started to review convictions of persons convicted under Article 8 of the Anti Terror law and to order their release from prison. The courts have also started to review the convictions of persons convicted under article 169 of the Turkish Penal Code, which has been amended, and in appropriate cases, to order their release."[113]

Judicial reform accelerated in 2004. Following a constitutional amendment adopted in May 2004, the DGM were abolished. Jurisdiction over most of the crimes falling within the competence of the DGM—mainly organized crime, drug trafficking, and terrorist offenses—was transferred to the newly-created regional Serious Felony Courts. The office of the Chief Public Prosecutor for the DGM was also abolished. Prosecutions before the Regional Serious Felony Court were handled by the office of the Chief Public Prosecutor. In accordance with the May 2004 constitutional amendments, Article 90 of the Constitution was revised, enshrining the principle of the supremacy of international and European treaties ratified by Turkey over domestic legislation. Where there was conflict between international agreements on human rights and national legislation, the Turkish courts would have to abide by the international agreements. A new Penal Code was adopted in September 2004, replacing the previous 80-year-old Penal Code. In general, the Code adopted modern European standards, in line with the recent developments of criminal law in many European countries. It strengthened sanctions against certain human rights violations and introduced new offenses reflecting contemporary trends in international criminal law, such as genocide and crimes against humanity, discrimination, and abuse of personal data. Some of its stipulations, however, were considered to weaken fundamental rights and freedoms, and a good deal of public reaction ensued.[114]

THE STANCE OF SOCIAL ACTORS

The State Elites

The role of civil and military bureaucracy was of critical importance for the transformation of the Turkish polity. It was the military that had three times[115] stalled attempts of political leaders to shift the balance of power toward their side. The process of EU reform affected this balance in favor of the politicians. Nonetheless, this time the empowerment of the political leadership could not lead to the imposition of a majoritarian authoritarian regime, as one could argue in the 1950s, or to anarchy and chaos, as one could argue in the 1970s. It was linked with the process of Turkey's full and effective democratic consolidation in its effort to meet the Copenhagen Criteria. Bringing Turkey closer to Europe was the foremost mission of the state elite; however, the very process of Turkey's Europeanization meant ending its tutelary political role. Military and civil bureaucracy reacted differently. The civil bureaucracy was always more prone to internal fragmentation, as the experience of the 1970s had demonstrated, even though the 1980–83 military regime was quite successful in restoring the homogeneous character of the state elite. Moreover, among the aims of the 1997 "soft" coup was also the purge of bureaucratic staff with—real or alleged—Islamist leanings. Nevertheless, the divide that appeared within the civil bureaucracy was an unprecedented one. There was a reaction against the imminent loss of status and political influence that the full implementation of the reform program would entail. Reaction sometimes became clear and explicit but in most cases remained silent and implicit. Obstructing reform programs through the swift use of procedural tools, procrastinating with the implementation of reform programs up to the latest possible point, or deliberately failing to understand and implement the spirit rather than the letter of the law were common practices among these increasingly marginalized and nationalistic bureaucrats who objected to the reform process. As Atilla Yayla commented on a speech by the President of the Constitutional Court Mustafa Bumin (see p. 118): "[The speech of Mustafa Bumin] showed us once more and in a bitter fashion the distance which separates a part of Turkey's judicial bureaucracy from commitment to the rule of law and a liberal democratic understanding."[116]

On the other hand, other bureaucrats, mainly in the Ministry of Foreign Affairs but also in other ministries, the judiciary, and public administration, showed a keen interest in promoting reform. The General Secretariat for the European Union (*Avrupa Birliği Genel*

Sekreterliği—ABGS) became a reformist bulwark, while increased interest in participation was manifested for multifarious seminars aiming to train Turkish bureaucrats on how to ensure full and effective respect of liberal democratic norms during the performance of their duties. State bureaucrats were willing to exchange their customary hard power for soft power and enjoy an improving public image.

While fragmentation in the ranks of civil bureaucracy was not a novel phenomenon, it certainly was in the case of the military. For the first time in the history of republican Turkey, a latent division emerged between the military leaders. While some objected to the diminution of the political role of the military and the abolition of its tutelary role, others saw—with more or less uneasiness—the military's withdrawal from politics as an inevitable step in the process of Turkey's Westernization and democratic consolidation. The EU reform process and the prospect of EU membership became an additional reason for the development of two countervailing trends within the body of the Turkish bureaucracy. On the one hand, traditionalists were very hesitant about a possible erosion of the predominant role of the bureaucracy as a result of the EU reform process and refused to make any reinterpretation of Kemalist principles in line with contemporary developments. As an eclectic vision of Westernization was substituted by Europeanization, which entailed political liberalization, they felt that this transformation left Turkish national interests in jeopardy.[117] General Tuncer Kilinc, Secretary General of the MGK, epitomized this stance on March 7, 2002, when he stated during a conference at the Istanbul Military Academies Directorate that he opposed Turkey's membership in the European Union and added, "Turkey absolutely needs to seek new alliances. In my opinion, the best direction would be to seek an alliance with the Russian Federation, which would include Iran, without ignoring the United States—if possible. Turkey has not received any help from the European Union. The European Union has negative approaches to the problems that concern Turkey."[118]

Such a statement by a top-ranking officer was not only a blunt verbal intervention in the ongoing debate over Turkey's EU membership and the steps Turkey had to make to fulfill the Copenhagen Criteria. It was also a radical departure from the perennial quest of the state elite to decisively direct Turkey toward the West. The fear that the culmination of Turkey's Westernization process, namely its membership in the European Union, would lead to the abolition of their undemocratic privileges and their subordination to politicians turned many bureaucrats against the prospect of EU membership.

On the other hand, a much more reserved stance was held by the majority of the Turkish military, including the Chief of the General Staff General Hilmi Ozkok, who saw Turkey's EU membership as the fulfillment of Ataturk's political program.[119] The reform programs of both the Ecevit coalition and the AKP government called for significant limitations in the power of the military and civil bureaucracy. The abolition of the DGM, the gradual civilianization of the MGK, the diminution of its competences, and the increasing governmental control of military expenditure meant the loss of privileges mostly accumulated during previous periods of military rule. The prospect of Turkey's EU membership also meant that this process was irreversible; the military could not reclaim its former prerogatives without marginalizing Turkey in the world scene. Nonetheless, the majority of the military supported the reform process, viewing it as an inevitable step in a process that Ataturk himself had initiated. Tacit support or acceptance of more liberal approaches was not limited to the desecuritization of several domestic policy issues and the abolition of the military's institutional prerogatives. Even in issues of foreign and security policy, like the Cyprus question, the military did not oppose a liberal shift of government policies that brought the Turkish position into harmony with United Nations initiatives. Although it would be exaggerating to attribute this shift to a single person, it appears that the moderate stance of the Chief of the General Staff General Hilmi Ozkok greatly facilitated the reforms. After he assumed the leadership of the Turkish armed forces in 2002, Ozkok did not object to the reforms. His circumspectly supportive stance was instrumental in silencing other top-ranking officers, who might have openly criticized the reduction of military privileges.[120] Ozkok seemed to prioritize Turkey's long-term interests over the interests of the state elite he was leading.

The Political Leadership

Turkey's political leaders became increasingly assertive in claiming the role that they reasonably thought they should play in a liberal democratic Turkey. Although there was still some support for the continuation of the status quo,[121] an increasing number of politicians, journalists and civil society figureheads stressed the need for a reconsideration of state-society relations so as to end the tutelary prerogatives of the state elite. A speech made by the leader of the ANAP and government coalition partner Mesut Yilmaz at a congress of his party in August 2001 attacked the national security taboo:[122]

Regarding the obstacles to the efforts to converge with the EU standards, there is a taboo issue, which almost everyone knows about but remains silent. . . . These are the national security exigencies. . . . Or, more accurately, the national security syndrome. . . . The time has come today to lift the curtain of this taboo issue.

National security is a concept absolutely necessary to ensure the continuity of a state. . . . However, the way this concept is currently used, produces the opposite results. The concept of national security has become an obstacle to any step that secures the future of our state. . . . Our concern is that the prevention of any initiatives under the pretext that national security is getting out of control will cause great damage to the future of our country as well as to our national security.[123]

Yilmaz clearly implied that national security was used as a tool for legitimizing the tutelary role of the military in Turkish politics and obstructing EU-inspired reforms. The protection of the secular, unitary, monolingual, monoethnic, monocultural character of the state was seen as the essence of national security. Hence, if EU-initiated liberalization steps put any of these into question, then they had to be resisted in the name of national security.[124] Yilmaz clearly stated that national security was a concept indispensable for the welfare of a state but also added that the way national security was understood in Turkey was damaging to Turkey's national security. Democratization would not mean the collapse of national security but rather its reinforcement.[125] Therefore, the desecuritization of Turkish politics would constitute a substantial step in the course of Turkey's political liberalization.

The need to eliminate the military's political role in Turkey was also expressed by a growing number of journalists and other opinion makers. It was pointed out that a large part of Turkish public opinion had become addicted to the military's political tutelage role and this had contributed to a trend of political inactivity or indifference. By thinking that the army would intervene whenever governments diverted from Kemalist orthodoxy in dealing with the issues that came under the umbrella of "national security," many Turkish citizens neglected their own civic responsibilities. As the widely read columnist Mehmet Ali Birand remarked in the aftermath of the November 2002 elections, "In the past, we have been in the habit of complaining to the army about the attitude of the politicians in the government every time we believed that the secular system was under threat or when someone whose views we did not share got into power. In such circumstances, we always appealed to the military to intervene to 'do their duty' by putting pressure on the government in our name and thus to put an end to these developments."[126]

Nonetheless, it was argued that the Turkish public should become more mature and exercise its democratic responsibility. The November 2002 elections gave a unique opportunity for the maturation of Turkish politics, since the AKP, a party with clear antiestablishment features, won an impressive victory that was publicly acknowledged by the state elite. Birand added that it was the public's responsibility to let the military retreat from politics and focus on its essential duties:

> In this new phase, the nation must give up this habit of entrusting the military with the task of protecting and guaranteeing the system, the mission of oversight and control. The essential duty of the army is to protect the country against external threats. People see the military as the "saviors to whom one turns as a last resort." For them, the army is an insurance policy. But it would be better if the army left the field of day-to-day politics. This objective could be achieved not by adopting the short cut of knocking on the doors of the military every time the country is faced with a difficulty, but by letting the population express its reactions through nongovernmental organizations. These are the bodies that should protect the system. Let us not forget that these organizations, which can lead millions of people to come down into the streets, would be much more effective than the serried ranks of the army advancing in formation. No government could resist pressure of that kind.[127]

Therefore, the development of a vibrant civil society should create a discursive space where all opinions regarding domestic and foreign policies could be democratically discussed. This would make any political intervention from the military not only illegitimate but also redundant, and the gravity center of politics would thus move from the state elite to civil society movements.[128]

THE INCIDENCE OF SOCIAL LEARNING

The change in the stance of some of the state elite toward their guardian role and the abolition of established prerogatives provided ample evidence that a process of social learning was ongoing as a result of improving EU-Turkey relations. A significant part of the civil and military bureaucracy became increasingly accustomed to a new role that required the limitation of their duties to what a liberal democratic regime would allow. The duties of the military would be limited to countering external security threats, while civil bureaucrats would prioritize the protection of human rights and liberties and consider them the basis of state interest.[129] The prosecution of the retired Admiral Ilhami Erdil on corruption charges in December 2004 was indicative of a dramatic shift in military practices regarding accountability and the rule of law. Until then, accusations of corruption within the military were never brought to court. Bureaucratic solidarity and the fear that the impeccable and uncorrupted image of the Turkish military would suffer heavy damage were supposed to justify this practice. Nonetheless, the Erdil case was the first occasion—since the 1930s—in which a high-ranking military officer was prosecuted on corruption charges. This provided evidence that the military—and Ozkok personally—responded positively to public pressure and the need to address questions of integrity and rule of law.[130] Similarly, political leaders staunchly supported political liberalism as the new ideological basis of state-society relations and increased protection of individual interests against long-term state interests. Politicians, journalists and civil society activists claimed a more assertive role in the process of liberalization. The need to reconsider the social role of the state was also addressed. It was argued that the establishment of a liberal democracy should not mean weakening of the development of a social welfare system.[131]

On the other hand, it should be noted that the process of social learning was neither smooth nor complete. Several examples can be cited where the persistence of transcendentalist views of the role of the state and individual rights and interests was evident. In spite of judicial reform and the acceptance by many judges of the new liberal-minded legislation, there was also strong resistance to reform in some quarters. A decision of the Court of Cassations in a case based on Article 312 of the Penal Code stated that "the limitation of freedom of thought with the aim to protect the public order of democratic regimes does not harm but, on the contrary, strengthens pluralist democracy."[132] This argument indicated that transcendentalist visions of democracy were still popular among the Turkish judiciary. Despite stiff EU reaction, the Chief of the General Staff remained accountable to the Prime Minister and not the Defense Minister.[133] This resistance showed the persistent refusal of the state elite to accept its full subordination to politicians, even at the symbolic level.

Even more serious was the relapse of leading reformist figures within the military elite into practices reminiscent of previous military interventions in politics. In a ninety-minute speech at the Military Academy on April 20, 2005, the Chief of General Staff General Hilmi Ozkok broke a long-held silence and addressed all issues of Turkish domestic and foreign policy. The Kurdish question and the PKK, the Armenian question, Cyprus and disputes with Greece, relations with the European Union, the United States and Iraq, the economy, political Islam, and democratization were all addressed in Ozkok's speech, which spared only fifteen minutes to talk about military issues.[134] The publication of this speech allowed many Europeans to question the sincerity of the military retreat from politics.[135] Nonetheless, this time reaction was also sparked within Turkey. In two opinion pieces written as a response to Ozkok's speech, Mehmet Ali Birand outlined the dilemmas the Turkish military faced. He argued that although Ozkok supported Turkey's EU membership, other commanders did not show the same sensitivity on questions of civil-military relations. Nonetheless, the Turkish military had to abide by the rules of democracy and the Copenhagen Criteria; otherwise, Turkey should give up its EU objective. Birand added:

> There will be some who will denounce this discussion as "anti-military" or "anti-secularism/separatism.". . . [However,] support for the EU and abiding by its rules come together. All senior commanders, especially the Chief of General Staff, repeatedly state their support for Turkey's European Union membership. Those with a minimal knowledge of strategy would realize that they don't have any other option. The strange thing is [that] the same commanders who say they support the EU seem determined not to abide by one of the most fundamental principles of the organization. The EU Copenhagen Criteria stipulates that the military needs to be subservient to the civilian authority. In other words, military officers cannot interfere in politics and cannot put pressure on civilian authority. [In liberal democratic countries] the Office of the Chief of Staff is an institution subordinate to the Defense Ministry and is responsible for formulating military strategies in line with the choices made by the civil authority. It is obvious that the way things work in Turkey needs to be changed dramatically.[136]

Birand also speculated that Ozkok's intervention might have been a result of pressure from lower-ranking generals and commented on the political activities of the Deputy Chief of Staff General Ilker Basbug and the Commander of the Land Forces General Yasar Buyukanit. He then chastised their usual response to such critiques: "We are executing our duty as stipulated in the Constitution and our service laws. It is our job to protect and preserve the country."[137]

Birand concluded his first piece by warning the military of the disastrous consequences of a possible reaffirmation of its political role and a collapse of Turkey's EU membership perspective as a result. In his second piece, he raised the issue of the responsibility of politicians in democratizing and civilianizing the state to achieve EU membership. Politicians had to become more trustworthy and thus make the public stop looking at the military whenever things wrong. He advised politicians and media as follows:

> Our politicians need to be principled, hard-working, serious individuals who know when they are spurned by the people and have to protect the people they represent. Unless they fulfill these criteria, the public will continue to look to the military for leadership. . . . The media needs to make up its mind. We need a certain degree of clarity to replace the confused picture we now face. If Turkey is to become European, the media needs to stop asking the generals, "Where are you?" The tendency to praise the generals at receptions, before dismissing them as "useless," should end. The media needs to stop making statements by a general headline news, while trying to teach the people how democracy works.[138]

Birand's opinion pieces skillfully pointed to the shortcomings of the EU-initiated political liberalization process on the issues of civil-military relations. Nevertheless, these shortcomings should not occlude the progress made in a number of significant fields. While Ozkok could reasonably be accused of interfering in politics, due to his speech of April 20, 2005, this should not fully discount his previous stance throughout the long and arduous political reform process. Although still lagging behind EU standards, the civilianization of Turkish politics made substantial steps. Last, but not least, the very fact that the need to fully civilianize and debureaucratize Turkish politics was openly discussed was indicative of a significant liberal shift within Turkish society and a step in the process of democratic consolidation.

CONCLUSIONS

The value of path dependence theory in explaining the gradual liberalization of Turkish state tradition is explicit. It could be convincingly argued that the reform process remained unfinished and that serious deviations from European standards persisted. Yet the major steps made in the cases of the MGK and the DGM showed the extent and nature of the accomplished progress. The reform of these institutions did not occur at once but was the result of long deliberations and negotiations. However, as the need for reform became clear, further developments could only take the form of more comprehensive reform: there could be no going back. As the decision to give Turkey a date for the start of accession negotiations was pending, the opponents of reform could only object to its details but had no power to reverse it.

The role of EU institutions was also crucial in bringing about reform. Pressure from the European Commission was exerted in the repeated inclusion of criticisms on the issues of civil-military relations and the judicial system in Turkey. Significant pressure also came from the European Parliament,[139] whose reports and resolutions often stressed the problems arising from the tutelary functions of the state elites. The timing of the reform steps provided ample evidence that it was the impact of the EU institutions that dictated them. The two-level game approach helps to clarify this process. Pressure imposed at the international level (Level II) alleviated the work of those members of the political elite, NGOs and intellectuals, who supported the limitation of the privileges of the state elite, its subordination to the democratically elected government, and the redefinition of the concept of national security at the domestic level (Level I).

Chapter 5

The Secularism Debate

Defining Secularism
History and Types of Secularism

The question of the relationship between political and religious authority has been a recurrent theme in Western political debates. Ever since the question was first addressed in Christianity,[1] the need to delineate the jurisdictions of the political and the religious realm has been a pressing political issue. The diffusion of the two realms became a reality with the dominant political role of the Papacy and the Catholic Church in medieval Western Europe. The Pope was the undisputed religious leader and one of the most influential political figures in Europe. His dominance would only be effectively challenged with the rise of the Protestant Reformation movement in the sixteenth century. The ensuing ferocious fights and massacres of Catholics and Protestants, which left Europe in rubble, led to the limitation of papal political and religious domination of Europe and the opening of a new debate on the relationship between religion and politics. The protection of religious minorities, who had become the main victims of atrocities during the religious wars of the Reformation, became one of the major issues in the political agenda of liberal thought. John Locke considered freedom of religious belief to be one of the fundamental human rights whose protection formed the basis of state legitimacy. The question of state-church relations was stressed at the European level during the Enlightenment. Voltaire was the intellectual who linked his name with the advocacy of secularism, the full separation of the political and religious realms. His ideas came close to realization with the 1789 French Revolution. France became the first Western European state where secularization policies were applied. The secularization of the French state continued to be debated throughout the nineteenth century and was finally firmly established in 1905 with the promulgation of a law that broke the remaining links between the church and the state. Other European states followed the French example with varying degrees of reservation. Germany also adopted secularization measures due to the confessional division of the German people between Catholicism and Protestantism. Nonetheless, the process was not as radical as in France. The weak but existing links between the German state and churches, as well as the dominant role of the German Christian Democratic parties, have provided ample proof of this. In the case of the United Kingdom, however, the drive toward secularism did not affect the historical links between the state and the Anglican Church. While religious toleration was firmly established, the British sovereign has remained the head of the Anglican Church, and the Archbishop of Canterbury is still appointed by the British Prime Minister.

The interchangeable use of the terms "secularism" and "laicism" has also led to considerable confusion. For the purposes of this study, secularism is understood as the separation of the political and religious realm that is followed by a neutral approach of state institutions toward religion. In laicism, on the other hand, the separation of political and religious realms is followed by state will to intervene in and control religion or pursue active antireligious policies. While secularism in its varying forms has characterized most of Western European states and France since the nineteenth century, laicism prevailed in the Third French Republic (1871–1940). Any public manifestation of religious belief was banned, while state officials systematically abstained from directly or indirectly declaring any religious belief. This model had a profound impact on Young Turk intellectuals and the founding elite of the Turkish Republic.[2]

Religion and Politics in Turkey

The Ottoman Legacy

The Ottoman Empire inherited the Arab political legacy, where state formation came as a result of the rise of Islam, and religion and politics were inextricably linked. Unlike Christianity, Islam had its own state project. Therefore, the Koran simultaneously performed the roles of a holy scripture and a quasi-constitution. This meant that the state controlled religion but had at the same time an inherently religious character. State control of Islam was common in the Islamic world, as Islam lacked an independent institutional structure that would protect it from effective state domination. The crucial role of Islam in the formation of the Umayyad Empire led to its inherently Islamic character. As the Islamic world never went through the political and ideological processes that resulted in the development of secularism in Western Europe, religion and politics remained intertwined, at least at the theoretical level. As the Ottoman Sultans assumed the title of Caliph in the early sixteenth century, Islam remained a key element of the Ottoman political ideology. This however did not mean that the Ottoman state officials were not the ultimate power holders. As Mardin put it, paraphrasing Orwell, "religion and the state are twins. . . . but in the Ottoman Empire one of the twins could often become more equal."[3]

The relationship between Islam and politics remained a key issue in the process of Ottoman modernization. Young Ottomans argued that the corruption of Islam in recent centuries was the reason for the continuing decline of the Ottoman Empire and that the return to the pure Islam of the first four Caliphs was a condition for a new Islamic Era of Felicity (*Asr-i Saadet*). Despite hesitant secularization steps in the field of law in the Tanzimat era, the political role of Islam did not diminish; on the contrary, its political significance dramatically rose when Sultan Abdulhamid II attempted to use Islam as a geopolitical tool.[4] The reassertion of the Caliphate was intended to increase Ottoman influence in all the regions of Asia and Africa where European colonial rule had been established. It was hoped this would counterbalance European political and economic penetration. This instrumental use of Islam did not deter measures of secularization, which continued mainly in the fields of law and education.

However, the fact that Islam was inextricably linked with the failing empire meant that—in the Ottoman case—its ability to galvanize a radical reform movement was limited.[5] Western ideas were better fitted for this. Secularism soon found supporters among members of the Ottoman Turkish elite. The Young Turks were the first to advocate secular ideas in the late Ottoman Empire. Following the French positivist paradigm, religion was viewed as a vestige of the premodern era that obstructed the process of Ottoman modernization.[6] The renaissance of the Ottoman Empire required, according to them, a reform program based on scientific and rational thought in which Islam should be excluded from the public sphere. The 1908 Young

Figure 5.1   The Mevlana Shrine in Konya, an icon of Turkish Islam (photo by author)

Turk Revolution gave the opportunity for a radical secularization of the Ottoman Empire. However, the disengagement of Islam from Ottoman politics never appeared high on the Young Turks' political agenda. The alliance of nonreligious local elites and the religious establishment against any hesitant secularization steps made reform extremely difficult.[7] Political considerations and expediency indefinitely postponed the implementation of the Young Turks' secularist ideas. Islam was used as a mobilizing factor in the wars that the Empire waged against its Christian Balkan neighbors and the Entente forces. The question of secularism was not raised during the Turkish War of Independence, as Ataturk did not want to alienate a substantial part of the Ottoman Turkish population, which still considered Islam to be inseparable from the state. Radical steps toward secularization were only made in the aftermath of the war, when Ataturk felt powerful enough to pursue his own agenda.

Religion and Politics from 1923 to the 1990s

The separation of religion and politics was implemented by a series of severe measures in the early years of republican Turkey.[8] On November 17, 1922, the last Ottoman Sultan, Mehmed VI Vahdettin, was forced into exile. On October 29, 1923, the Republic of Turkey was proclaimed, and the Caliphate was officially abolished on March 3, 1924. Strict measures were taken to secularize the state and the society.[9] The office of *Seyh-ul-Islam* was abolished and its functions taken over by the Directorate of Religious Affairs (*Diyanet Isleri Baskanligi*) in 1924. Religious orders (*tarikats*) were banned in 1926, while the remnants of the Islamic Law (*seriat*) were replaced by the Swiss civil and the Italian penal codes. Meanwhile, existing Islamic courts and schools were abolished, as well as religious education in public schools. At the symbolic level, a measure of crucial importance was the adoption of the Latin alphabet in 1928, which broke a strong cultural bond between the Turkish nation and Islam. The breach with the Ottoman Islamic past was finalized when the declaration of Islam as state religion in Article 2 of the 1924 Constitution and of the state as the executor of Islamic law in Article 26 were removed in 1928.[10] Severe repression of the public manifestation of the Islamic faith and the abolition of *tarikat*s were evidence of the complete subordination of Islam to the state.[11]

Kemalism followed the Young Turk positivist approach to religion, dismissing it as a remnant of the despicable Ottoman past and shaping an agnostic or atheistic approach. State secularism became a constitutional principle in 1937[12] and an indispensable element of republican Turkish politics, as the potential of Islam to serve as an alternative political project, source of common identity, and resistance to modernization was acknowledged.[13] Religion remained a taboo issue in republican politics until the first multiparty elections in 1946. The rise of the Democrat Party (*Demokrat Parti*—DP) to power in the 1950 elections was a milestone event, as dissident political forces gained access to power for the first time. The DP appealed to the rural majority of the Turkish population, which had not endorsed the Kemalist secularization reform,[14] and courted the religious vote.[15] Islam was gradually reintroduced into the public sphere, and politics also obtained an Islamic coloring.[16] Religious vocational schools (*imam-hatip okullari*)[17] were established in 1951, while the budget allocation of the Directorate of Religious Affairs for mosque construction soared. The ban on the recital of the Islamic call of prayer (*ezan*) in Arabic, introduced in 1931,[18] was lifted, and Koran readings were allowed to be broadcast on public radio.[19] Consecutive electoral victories for the DP confirmed public support for the return of Islam into politics.

The DP rule came to a violent end with the military coup of May 27, 1960. The 1960 coup was the response of the sidelined Kemalist elite, which attempted to check the Islamization of Turkish politics and reassert the dominance of state secularism by banning the DP and neutralizing its leadership.[20] The military regime attempted to minimize the threat that an Islamist-leaning party could comprise to state secularism by limiting the powers of the executive. Yet the 1961 Constitution, whose liberal stipulations were meant to serve as guarantees against a relapse into the rule of a majoritarian Islamist-leaning party rule, allowed for the growth of the first purely Islamist political movement in Turkey. The National View (*Milli Gorus*) movement was founded and led by the historic leader of Turkish political Islam, Necmettin Erbakan.[21] It was the driving force behind the first Islamist party in the history of republican Turkey, the National Order Party (*Milli Nizam Partisi*—MNP), founded on January 26, 1970. Having its political roots in the Turkish conservative right, the National View took pains in distancing its political ideology and program from mainstream political conservatism expressed by the DP and its successor, the Justice Party (*Adalet Partisi*—AP).[22] It also tried to appeal to the dispossessed rural populations of Anatolia as well as to the growing mass of urban migrants. *Tarikat*s also gave their full support for the MNP.[23]

The party's political ideology followed an Occidentalist[24] ideological blueprint and tried to develop an Islamic, non-Western version of modernity.[25] Its political agenda openly opposed the Kemalist Westernization program. The perceived political, economic, and moral decline of republican Turkey was attributed to the corrupting influence of the West. Islam was thus invited back into Turkish politics to deter further decline and bring Turkey back to prosperity and morality. The solution offered by the MNP and its successor political parties founded under the aegis of the National View was summarized in the Just Order (*Adil Duzen*) political program. The term "justice" was understood in purely Islamic terms and was contrasted with "unjust" Western civilization. The moral superiority of Islamic over Western civilization was based upon its preference for right (*hak*) over power (*kuvvet*).[26] The implementation of the Just Order program would be a transitory stage toward the Order of Felicity (*Nizam-i Saadet*), which would resemble the Era of Felicity of the early Islamic era.[27] Adopting a radical phraseology against the ruling class and business capital and conceptual schemes not very different from that of Marxists, the MNP and the subsequent political parties of the National View found in Islam the moral base for the regeneration of the Turkish state and society. The excesses of Western capitalism and individualism would be dealt with by a return to the original Islamic political and moral values, where justice would play a key role. An intensive program of heavy industrialization based on import substitution would secure Turkey's economic independence from the West.[28]

A second military coup on March 12, 1971, included among its objectives the control of Turkey's growing political Islam. The MNP was shut down by the Constitutional Court on the grounds that it had been "operating against the principles of the secular state and Ataturk's revolutionism."[29] Nonetheless, the National Movement soon registered a new political party, the National Salvation Party (*Milli Selamet Partisi*—MSP) under the same leadership and organization. Due to Erbakan's adroit political skills, the MSP participated as minor coalition partner in coalition governments alternately with the CHP and the AP throughout the 1970s. Access to political power helped the party broaden its political and social base and influence the agenda of coalition governments. In the field of domestic policy, the "restoration of Islamic morality" ranged from limitations on alcohol consumption to the improvement of the professional rights of the religious vocational school graduates and their appointment to public service positions.[30] In the field of foreign policy, opposition to Turkey's prospective membership in the European Economic Community (EEC) remained a cornerstone of MSP policy. In Erbakan's view, the EEC epitomized all the despicable characteristics of the West that had infiltrated Turkey and that the "Just Order" program aspired to remove. The slogan "We are the market, they are the common partners [*Biz pazar, onlar ortak*]" epitomized suspicion and animosity toward European Common Market project. EEC—and later EU—membership was seen as a Kemalist plot to finalize the conversion of Turkey to Western civilization and stall the growth of political Islam. In Erbakan's view, instead of aspiring to join the European Economic Community and other "Christian" Western organizations, Turkey should play a leading role in the formation of equivalent Islamic organizations, such as an Islamic Economic Community, an Islamic Defense Cooperation Organization, an Islamic United Nations Organization, an Islamic Common Currency (the *dinar*), and an Islamic Cultural Cooperation Organization.[31] Islam should, therefore, become the primary defining element of Turkish domestic and foreign policy.

The 1980–83 military regime shut down the MSP and banned Erbakan from politics. On the other hand, it undermined the secular character of the state by adopting the Turkish-Islamic Synthesis (*Turk-Islam Sentezi*—TIS) doctrine (see p. 130). The reopening of religious vocational schools and the mandatory character of religious education in primary and secondary schools were clear signals of an

Islamic shift in Turkish politics, with the clear aim of counterbalancing leftist and Kurdish nationalist influences.[33] The rise to power of the conservative Motherland Party (*Anavatan Partisi*—ANAP) in the 1980s did not prevent the recovery of political Islam. While the ANAP government was considerably influenced by Islam in its domestic and foreign policy orientations, a new party from the National View tradition emerged in 1983. The Welfare Party (*Refah Partisi*—RP), whose leadership was taken over by Erbakan as soon as he was re-allowed into politics in 1987, contested the hegemony of the ANAP on the right of the Turkish political spectrum.

The growth of the RP was also facilitated by Turkey's rapid social transformation. Turkey's economic growth facilitated the emergence of an Islamist counterelite—pious, but modern in ideology, education, and consumption patterns—that sought to secure its own political representation.[34] The rise of Islamist capital challenged the domination of the secular economic establishment and reshaped the Turkish economy and society.[35] Industrialization reinforced urban migration trends and brought millions of peasants into Turkey's big urban centers.[36] While the urban newcomers suffered from severe socioeconomic problems and underwent a process of painful cultural transformation, Turkish political Islam attempted to fill the vacuum of their political representation. An effort to compromise modernity with an Islamic identity became clear at the civil society level.[37] As the Turkish left had not yet recovered from the heavy blow that the 1980–83 military regime had dealt against it, the campaign of the RP was facilitated by the lack of an influential social democratic party that could serve as an alternative electoral option for the urban poor.[38] A series of economic scandals also boosted the electoral appeal of the RP. While corruption had become endemic, the RP vowed for the reinjection of Islamic moral values into Turkish politics. This populist and conservative rhetoric struck a chord among new urban migrants, who formed the backbone of the RP's urban electoral base.[39]

Religion and Politics since the 1990s

The Impact of Global Actors
Global political developments have influenced the debate on religion and politics in Turkey since the 1990s. The fall of the Berlin Wall in 1989 contributed to a global religious revival and a more intensive discussion on what the relationship between religion and politics should be. Leftist ideas suffered a recession in Turkey, and Islam filled part of the emerging vacuum.[40] On the other hand, as the

communist bloc had ceased to comprise an existential threat for the Western countries, some saw religion as a new potential ideological base of conflict. The spread of ethnoreligious conflict in Europe, Asia, and Africa seemed to provide evidence in support of this assertion. The supposed division of the world on the basis of civilizational divides brought religion to the center of world politics due to the often inextricable links between religion and culture. The civilization fault lines suggested by Huntington in his treatise on the "clash of civilizations" as the areas of conflict in the post–Cold War era were mostly identical with religious borders. Turkey's unique position between Europe and Asia and its secular regime naturally attracted the attention of scholars. Huntington found in the case of Turkey the archetypical "torn" country whose elite has systematically sought to substitute Western for its Middle Eastern Islamic civilization but faced persistent resistance by the bulk of its population.[41] The rise of global Islamic terrorism in the early 1990s also attracted attention to the relationship between Islam and democracy. U.S. diplomats often presented Turkey as a "model state" whose secular regime guaranteed the survival of one of the few democracies in the Muslim world. On the other hand, a blind eye was turned to the liberal shortcomings of the Turkish model of secularism.[42] U.S. support for Turkish secularism strengthened the hand of the Kemalist establishment but could not deter the increasing appeal of Turkish political Islam on the domestic political stage.

The Impact of Domestic Politics
In the 1990s, the influence of Turkish political Islam continued to rise. The fall of the ANAP from political power in the 1991 parliamentary elections coincided with a drastic increase in the RP's political power. The share of the RP's vote in the 1991 general elections rose from 7.16 percent in 1987 to 16.88 percent,[43] and the party entered the mainstream political arena. This was confirmed with the 1993 municipal elections, in which the RP assumed control of the municipalities of Istanbul, Ankara, and twenty-eight other cities. This success sent shockwaves toward the Kemalist secular establishment.[44] Benefiting from a growing pro-Islamist civil society[45] and a grassroots political mobilization network,[46] the RP became a protagonist of mainstream politics in the 1995 elections, when it became the biggest single party in parliament, with 21.38 percent of the vote. The rise of the RP to political power became a reality on July 8, 1996, when it formed a coalition government with the True Path Party (*Dogru Yol Partisi*— DYP) and its leader Necmettin Erbakan became Prime Minister.

While many feared a government led by Erbakan would form an existential threat to the Republic, such fears turned out to be exaggerated. While continuing to pay lip service to his Islamic-inspired "Just Order" political program, Erbakan followed a largely pragmatic line.[47] The Islamic underpinnings of the "Just Order" program were weakened; "Just Order" now simply meant more moral, transparent, and honest government.[48] Although he had attacked Turkey's European orientation ever since the 1960s and had explicitly opposed Turkey's Customs Union Agreement with the European Union, Erbakan did not overrule the application of the Agreement on January 1, 1996. Islamist traces could, nonetheless, be found in new foreign policy orientations.[49] Erbakan attempted to shift the balance of Turkish foreign policy from the West toward the Middle East and the Islamic world. A series of official visits to Arab and Islamic states, an expressed interest in the development of political and trade relations with them,[50] and Turkey's active role in the establishment of the D-8 Group, together with predominantly Muslim states countries such as Bangladesh, Egypt, Indonesia, Iran, Malaysia, Nigeria and Pakistan, were novel additions to Turkey's traditionally Western-looking foreign policy agenda. Yet Erbakan's Islamist diplomatic openings did not produce the expected results and occasionally even backfired, such as his disastrous official visit to Libya in October 1996.[51] On the domestic front, symbolic moves such as the plans to erect a new mosque at Taksim Square in the heart of Istanbul and efforts to strengthen the influence of political Islam in state education, administration, and economy met with a decisive reaction by the military. A blunt threat of military intervention appeared during the MGK meeting of February 28, 1997, which has been remembered since then as a "soft" coup (see p. 76). Erbakan surrendered—after some hesitation—to the military ultimatum on March 5, 1997, and swift steps toward the purge of Islamist elements and the restoration of secular order were made.

The collapse of the RP-DYP coalition government on June 18, 1997, signaled the return of secularist political parties and establishment forces to political dominance. Measures aiming at the restoration of early republican secularism were swiftly taken. These were contrary to the policies of not only the RP-DYP coalition government, but also of the post-coup "neorepublican" governments, which attempted to introduce Islamic elements into the public sphere discourse to provide "a moral basis, ideological unity, and some certainty in the face of global capitalism."[53] In January 1998, the RP was closed down following a decision of the Turkish Constitutional

Court, and its leader Necmettin Erbakan was—once more—banned
from politics for five years.[54]
Following the tradition of the National View parties, a successor
party of the RP had already been established in December 1997, before
its expected closure. The Virtue Party (*Fazilet Partisi*—FP) took the
mantle of Turkish political Islam and attempted to present a moderate face by supporting democratization, closer relations with the EU,
privatization, and a smaller economic role of the state.[55] Nonetheless,
divisions within the party about the future of political Islam in Turkey
could no longer remain latent. Traditionalist views expressed by the
banned leader Erbakan and his close disciples were challenged by a
generation of younger reformist politicians who sought to reorganize
the party along constitutional rules and reconcile Islamic and Western
European political values. In the first party conference in May 2000,
Erbakan's favored candidate, Recai Kutan, beat the reformist candidate, Abdullah Gul, but only with difficulty. Despite the defeat of the
reformist faction, the public profile of the FP was far more moderate and system-oriented than that of the RP.[56] However, when the
Constitutional Court shut down the FP in June 2001 on the grounds
that it was "a center of antisecularist activity,"[57] division in the party
ranks became official. Under Erbakan's auspices, Recai Kutan and the
traditionalists formed the Felicity Party (*Saadet Partisi*—SP), while
the reformists under the leadership of Recep Tayyip Erdogan founded
the Justice and Development Party (*Adalet ve Kalkinma Partisi*—
AKP). The split within political Islam was of crucial importance for
the development of novel approaches to the question of religion and
politics in Turkey.

Is Turkey a Secular State?

Republican Turkey is commonly considered the "only Muslim secular state," which can serve as a "model for the Middle East and the
rest of the Islamic world." Nonetheless, a closer look over the term
"secular" shows this description is not strictly accurate.[58] The meaning of the term "secular," colloquially understood as "nonreligious,"
is not limited to the separation of religious and political realms. It
entails a neutral stance toward different religious beliefs as well as the
phenomenon of religion in general. A genuinely secular state has no
preferential links with any religion and neither promotes nor obstructs
religious belief among its citizens. The Turkish state fulfils neither
of these conditions. Opposition to any religious form of expression
within a widely defined public sphere shows the hostile approach of

the Turkish state toward religion. The ban on *tarikats* and religious attire, the headscarf issue (see p. 114), and the removal of religion from the public sphere are indicative of a state that does not remain indifferent to religion but on the contrary takes active measures to put religious institutions under its firm control and promote a religion-free, "rational" society. Religion was expected to decline as a result of the enlightenment and modernization of Turkish society and the upward economic and social mobility of its citizens.[59] Nevertheless, the secular character of the Turkish state has often been compromised as a result of political expediency. This compromise was not in the direction of original secularism but rather toward championing a certain state religion, Sunni Islam of the Hanefi school.

Ideological opposition to religion did not mean lack of state interest in the instrumental use of religion for political purposes. Sunni Islam has been skillfully used since the founding years of the Republic as a cementing factor of Turkish national identity and a counterweight to the perceived divisive influence of ethnic nationalism and leftist ideas, even though this contradicts the principle of secularism. Ataturk himself had successfully used Islam to unify Anatolian Muslims under his leadership during the 1919–22 war. While Islam was purged from the public sphere in the early republican period, the state kept a firm control over it by banning the *tarikats* and establishing the Directorate of Religious Affairs (*Diyanet Isleri Baskanligi*).[60] Islam made a gradual comeback to the public sphere during the rule of the Democrat Party. This comprised one of the several reasons for the 1960 military coup. The rapid recovery of political Islam in the 1960s confirmed that the state could not afford to ignore the Islamic question. Passivity about religious developments was deemed extremely dangerous for the future of the Turkish Republic. Active intervention and control was viewed as the only means to secure the containment of the Islamist threat. This policy shift became institutionalized with the official championing of the "Turkish-Islamic Synthesis" by the 1980–83 military regime, the introduction of mandatory religious primary education, and the clauses of the 1982 Constitution that strengthened the power of Sunni Islam.[61] Hanefi Sunni Islam of the gained an absolute priority over other versions of Sunni, Shiite, and Alevi Islam, as well as other religions. The clear Sunni character of the Directorate of Religious Affairs, the mandatory instruction of Sunni Islam in state schools, and the state-funded construction of mosques throughout the country—even in Alevi villages—comprise clear manifestations of a pervasive bias in favor of Sunni Islam.[62] When it came to non-Muslims (see p. 128) and Alevis (see p. 134), the secular Turkish state suddenly became a Sunni one.[63] This mixed legacy of animosity toward religion, state control, and bias in favor of Sunni Islam forms the framework of state-society relations in republican Turkey. Turkey could, therefore, be characterized as a *sui generis* secular state in which long-term antireligious policies are matched by a short-term instrumental use of Sunni Islam. This situation created a serious obstacle to the process of Turkey's democratization and created an environment conducive to political conflict.[64]

THE IMPACT OF THE EUROPEAN UNION

Legislative Reform

Before the Reform
The European Union could not oppose secularism as such but merely its implementation in a way that violates basic civil liberties and minority rights. In that spirit, it has been often critical of the religious policies of the Turkish state. Issues related to the freedom of religious belief for Muslims and non-Muslims and state control over religion were addressed in all the European Commission reports on Turkey. In the 1998 European Commission progress report, the dissolution of the RP was noted, as was the criminal conviction and imprisonment of the then Mayor of Istanbul, Recep Tayyip Erdogan, due to a speech deemed to constitute "racial or religious provocation."[65] The obligatory character of Sunni religious education in state primary schools was stressed. While the practice of non-Sunni religionists—including Alevis—faced several bureaucratic restrictions, numerous administrative privileges were enjoyed by Sunni Islam. The report also pointed out the extrainstitutional role of the military, which excluded from its ranks persons suspect for links with Islamist organizations, as guardian of secularism.[66] In the 2000 report, the launch of legal procedures for the dissolution of the FP for violating the "principle of secularism" was noted.[67] Alevi complaints about state education and financial support for Sunni religious purposes and the sentencing of Necmettin Erbakan to one-year imprisonment for "inciting religious and ethnic hatred" under Article 312 of the Penal Code were also recorded.[68] In the 2001 report, Alevi grievances were reiterated.[69] The 2002 report shed light on the dissolution of the "Cultural Association of the Union of Alevi and *Bektasi* Institutions" (*Alevi-Bektasi Kuruluslari Birligi Kultur Dernegi*). This had been closed down under Articles 14 and 24 of the Constitution and Article 5 of the Law on Associations,

according to which founding an association by the name of Alevi or *Bektasi* contravened the principle of secularism.[70] The 2003 report, while acknowledging the considerable progress made, expressed the persistence of concerns regarding representation of non-Sunni religious communities in the Directorate of Religious Affairs and compulsory religious instruction in schools, which failed to acknowledge the Alevi identity.[71] In the 2004 report, the extrainstitutional role of the military as guardian of secularism was again stressed. The provisions of Articles 35 and 85§1 of the Turkish Armed Forces Internal Service Law, which defined the duties of the Turkish armed forces as being to "protect and preserve the Turkish Republic on the basis of the principles referred to in the Preamble of the Constitution," including secularism, were mentioned. Similarly, Article 2a of the National Security Council Law defined national security in such broad terms that it could be interpreted as covering the secular character of the state.[72] Regarding the status of Alevis, the report underlined the continuation of state discriminatory practices and reiterated the claim of most Alevis that "as a secular state Turkey should treat all religions equally and not directly support one particular religion (the Sunni Muslims) as it currently does through the Directorate of Religious Affairs."[73]

The Reform Process

Secularism has historically been one of the most sensitive political questions in the history of republican Turkey. Given that the principle of secularism found constitutional protection—most importantly in the Preamble and Article 2 of the Constitution—and that the military had repeatedly used its role as guardian of Turkey's secular model to justify its political interventions, any efforts to liberalize Turkey's secular model were hesitant and circumspect. This meant that the constitutional protection of secularism never became a part of the EU reform debate. The need to address the issues raised by the reports of the European Commission and human rights organizations, however, facilitated the reform of Turkish legislation on secularism and its protection. Article 312 of the Penal Code, which penalized "incitement to class, ethnic, religious, or racial hatred," was amended to meet liberal concerns. Not any incitement, but only incitement "in a way that may be dangerous for public order" would be punishable, according to the amended Article 312. Narrowing the scope of the Article allowed for more freedom in the public discussion of secularism and state-religion relations.[74] With respect to the judicial implementation of the reform, the number of acquittals in cases based on Article 312 increased. On the other hand, the broad use of Article 312 did not recede, despite the effort to limit the scope of the Article.[75] The reform record was also mixed when it came to ending the preferential treatment of Sunni Islam by the state. In April 2003, the previously banned Cultural Association of the Union of Alevi and *Bektasi* Institutions was granted legal status and allowed to pursue its activities.[76] In 2004, the regional office of the Directorate of Religious Affairs in Antakya established a multireligious committee aimed at developing a harmonious relationship between Muslims, Christians, and Jews.[77] Nonetheless, these steps did not signal a fundamental change in state policies toward religious groups. Sunni Islam continued to enjoy preferential treatment by the state, which became all apparent when it came to access to state funding and education.

The Transformation of Turkish Political Islam

Although the fruits of the legislative reform process were not impressive, the European Union was instrumental in assisting the transformation process of Turkish political Islam, which had a major impact on the discourse of religion and politics. The "soft" coup of February 28, 1997, and the subsequent fall of the Erbakan-led coalition government triggered a series of developments of crucial importance for the future and the shape of political Islam in Turkey. The impact of the European Union as a facilitator of these developments was anything but insignificant.

At the domestic level, it became clear that any ideas about regime change and the introduction of Islamic law were utterly unrealistic. This was due not only to the reaffirmation of the guardian role of the military in Turkish politics but also to the lack of appeal of any Islamization program to the vast majority of the people. Turkish political Islam managed to attract considerable popular support, but never appealed to the greater public because of its purely and narrowly Islamist orientation. If a party with Islamist political character could ever manage to claim a leading role in Turkish politics, this could only happen through its transformation into a conservative center-right party with Islamist leanings.[78] The mobilization of Turkish civil society organizations against any Islamist-leaning policies during the rule of the RP-DYP coalition government provided additional evidence for the unpopularity of pure Islamist policies.

At the European level, the decision of the European Court of Human Rights (ECHR) to uphold the decision of the Turkish

Constitutional Court to close the RP was a milestone event. On the one hand, Erbakan's decision to appeal to the ECHR against the closure of the RP undermined his rhetoric against European institutions and civilization. The establishment of an Islamic "Just Order" in Turkey, which had been the perennial quest of the National View movement, implied the moral supremacy of Islamic civilization over European. By appealing to the ECHR, Erbakan tacitly acknowledged that "Christian Europe" was an alternative and acceptable source of justice. The relativization of the concept of Islamic justice by the very person who had fought throughout his life for its establishment in Turkey undermined any belief in the superiority of Islamic civilization and showed that the Islamist political project in Turkey had reached its limits. The court ruled in July 2001 that, by closing the RP, the Turkish court did not violate Article 11 of the European Convention of Human Rights. The Court held that

> the sanctions imposed on the applicants could reasonably be considered to meet a pressing social need for the protection of democratic society, since, on the pretext of giving a different meaning to the principle of secularism, the leaders of the *Refah Partisi* had declared their intention to establish a plurality of legal systems based on differences in religious belief, to institute Islamic law (the *sharia*), a system of law that was in marked contrast to the values embodied in the Convention. They had also left in doubt their position regarding recourse to force in order to come to power and, more particularly, to retain power.[79]

This decision, which was made by the Third Section of the ECHR, was firmly upheld by the ECHR Grand Chamber in February 2003.[80] The ECHR decision demonstrated that Islamic extremism could not be protected by European liberal democratic institutions. Support of European political institutions for Turkish political parties under state persecution was not unconditional. Turkish political parties had to subscribe to European political values to be then able to claim European support. Like terrorism, Islamic fundamentalism could not expect support from European courts.[81] The threat that Islamic fundamentalism constituted for democratic principles and human rights was not underestimated, and the use of democratic institutions for undemocratic objectives could not be endorsed.

In the aftermath of the RP closure, ideological fermentation within the Virtue Party (*Fazilet Partisi*—FP) showed that political Islam was undergoing a radical transformation. Many of its members attempted to break the vicious circle of state suppression that had historically inflicted Islamist political parties by advocating a radical transformation of Islamist ideology. The establishment of an Islamic republic would no more be the ultimate aim. Allegiance to the secular principles of Western European democracy was adopted instead, and an amalgamation of Islamic values with Western political liberalism was attempted.[82] Crucial for the rehabilitation of the Western image was the experience of immigration to Western Europe for millions of Turkish citizens, who realized that they could more freely profess Islam in "Christian" Germany than in "Muslim" Turkey.[83] This ideological trend within the Islamist intelligentsia obtained a political vehicle with the formation of the AKP, in the aftermath of the closure of the FP. The AKP leadership took pains to dissociate the new party from its Islamist past and advertised itself as a moderate conservative party[84] loyal to secularism.[85] The ideology of the party was an amalgam of conservativism, liberalism, Islamic values, and rightist political ideas. The term "Islamist" was rejected as a description of the ideological identity of the party; the term "conservative democratic [*muhafazakar demokrat*]" was preferred.[86] The AKP was the first party from the Islamic political tradition to address the grievances of Turkey's pious Muslim population not in terms of Islamic justice or "Just Order," but on the basis of a liberal and human rights agenda. Turkish state secularism was criticized not from an Islamist but from a liberal perspective. Contested issues of major symbolic importance, like the headscarf and religious education, were now discussed as evidence of Turkey's democratic deficit. The liberal shift of the AKP was corroborated when—contrary to the tradition of the National View parties—it ardently supported Turkey's bid for EU membership.

The November 2002 elections became the big test case for the AKP political experiment: With 34.4 percent of the votes and 365 parliamentary seats, the AKP formed a single-party government, while the traditionalist SP gained only 2.5 percent and no seats. The AKP had succeeded in winning power, dominating the political agenda and ideology of Turkish political Islam and opening it to the influence of Western political ideas. The emphasis on Islamic morality as an antidote to chronic political corruption remained,[87] but the political priorities of the new government were different. After taking over power, the AKP and its leader Recep Tayyip Erdogan vowed to pursue the reform steps necessary for Turkey to qualify for the start of EU accession negotiations. The prospect of EU membership provided a vision that the vast majority of the Turkish society shared and for which many sacrifices could be tolerated. The AKP leadership realized that the European Union could be of critical help in its effort to gain political legitimacy[88] and promote the sensitive, religion-related aspects of its political agenda. By becoming an ardent supporter and promoter of Turkey's EU membership, the AKP leadership challenged the monopoly of Kemalist elites in their advocacy of Westernization. The reform of Turkey's human rights legislation would necessarily mean a redefinition of the public and private spheres in Turkish society. Many activities that would until the reform fall within the scope of the public realm would be transferred to the private realm and thus enjoy full protection under the new human rights legislation.[89] The prospect of EU membership and the EU monitoring of Turkish politics also provided a secure environment against any intervention by military and bureaucratic elites. This enabled the AKP government to implement its reformist political program, which confirmed the transformation of the AKP from an Islamist to a conservative democratic party[90] increasingly similar to the equivalent religious values–based Christian Democratic parties of Western Europe.[91]

A New Version of Secularism in the Making?

While Europe affirmed its opposition to Islamic fundamentalism and Turkish political Islam was transformed, the question of how to protect freedom of religion against secularist state practices remained open. Turkish political Islam traditionally viewed the secularist character of the Turkish state as a dire consequence of the greater Kemalist Westernization project. Europe was the historic cradle of secularism and as such responsible for the antireligious character of the Turkish Republic. Nonetheless, with the rise of the AKP, alternative Western systems of regulating state-religion relations were explored. The fact that the AKP abandoned the Islamic state project for the sake of Western liberal democratic principles did not mean that it lost its sensitivity on issues of religious freedom; its argument, however, was now based upon political liberalism. The establishment of a pluralist public sphere in Turkey was now seen as the solution for the problems related to the public visibility of Islamic identity in Turkey.[92] This could be the starting point for the reform of state-religion relations in Turkey. Turkish secularism was inspired by French *laïcité* of the Third French Republic, the most vehemently antireligious system in the Western world and hardly compatible with the principles of liberal democracy. It was, therefore, possible to argue for a reform of Turkish secularism not on the basis of restoring Islamic law but rather of introducing liberal principles.[93] This reform would aim at substituting a truly secular, religion-blind policy for the antireligious character of state policies as well as the bias in favor of Sunni Islam. This model of liberal secularism would be distanced from the French model of *laïcité* and could be closer related to the UK or German models of secularism. It would protect state and religion from mutual interventions and promote Turkish democracy without obstructing the free religious expression of the majority of the Turkish people. In a treatise that appeared on the official AKP website and could thus be considered to reflect the party's official views, Yalcin Akdogan argued

> The AKP understands secularism as an institutional stance and method that ensures that the state remains neutral and keeps an equal distance from all religions and ideas. Differences of religion and different confessions and ideologies can be professed in social peace without them turning into conflict. The party thinks that, for secularism to work as an adjudicating institution of the fundamental rights and freedoms under constitutional protection, it needs to be supported by democracy and operate in a conciliatory environment.[94]

Secularism was, therefore, accepted as "an indispensable condition of democracy and the guarantee of the freedom of religion and conscience"[95] and was linked to democracy and human rights. This position attempted to reconcile the legacy of illiberal Turkish secularism with respect for democratic principles and fundamental freedoms. Secularism should not mean the absence of religion from the public sphere, or the state control of religious institutions. The version of liberal secularism the AKP advocated did not eliminate religion from the public sphere but required the state to adopt a neutral stance on religious issues and respect the freedoms of religion and conscience of its citizens.[96] The reemergence of religion in the public sphere should therefore be seen not as a reassertion of militant political Islam but as maturation in the process of democratization and transition to a liberal version of secularism. The introduction of such a secular system would mean the simultaneous abolition of Kemalist secularism and Islamism in favor of a liberal democratic solution. This became clear in the AKP political program, where secularism was defined as an "orienting principle for the state but not for the individual," "a means to freedom and social harmony" and "a guarantee of freedom of conscience."[97]

The appeal of this redefinition of secularism was not restricted to the leading circles of the AKP. Prominent Islamist intellectuals, who had in the past supported the establishment of an Islamic state in Turkey, became proponents of Turkey's European vocation.[98] The

European Union was no more the archenemy but a de facto ally in the struggle against the Kemalist bureaucracy and its iron fist, the military. The reform of state secularism could be achieved through Turkey's democratization, which only Turkey's EU accession process could guarantee. While democracy and human rights had been despised as prime examples of Western concepts that had allegedly adulterated sound Islamic political thought,[99] they now occupied the center of Islamist political discourse,[100] offering a solution to the problem of secularism. The adoption of these principles of modernity resulted in a paradoxical situation whereby former Islamist intellectuals were defending human rights and democracy, pointing to the shortcomings of the Kemalist modernization project, which, despite professing modernity, had failed to deliver its biggest blessings.[101]

The Headscarf Issue

The same discourse was applied in a novel approach to the headscarf issue, one of the symbols of the secularist controversy in republican Turkey. The ban on headscarf use in state institutions was one of the clearest manifestations of the secularist character of republican Turkey. The rise of an Islamist counterelite in the 1980s resulted in the extreme politicization of the headscarf issue, as its members now felt able to challenge the hegemony of the established secularist elite. While retaining its original religious and traditional meaning, wearing the headscarf also obtained an explicit symbolic value. It became a political statement of a new rising and ambitious elite. Nonetheless, the argument in favor of headscarf use was still based on an Islamist discourse. The headscarf was understood as an indispensable element of female Islamic morality, and Islamic law failed to recognize the distinction between the public and the private sphere. The secularist principle of keeping religion outside the public sphere could not tolerate the most public manifestation of resistance to state secularism. The purge of the public sphere culminated in the aftermath of the "soft" coup of February 28, 1997. The response to this campaign by the short-lived FP and, most importantly, the AKP, markedly differed in its content. Reference was now made to universal human rights embodied in international human rights conventions, and Islamic law was no more seen as the sole manifestation of justice. The right to education, the principle of nondiscrimination, the freedom of religion as protected by the European Convention of Human Rights, and other international human rights treaties were quoted in defense of the right of women to wear the headscarf.

Figure 5.2 A group of headscarved women on a busy Istanbul street (photo by author)

Even the solution suggested for the problem based on a "social consensus"[102] was borrowed from Western liberal thought.[103]

This shift in the AKP discourse was not well received by everyone. Many saw the headscarf question as a litmus test for the commitment of the AKP to republican ideals. A segment of the republican elite has persistently doubted the motives of the AKP government, accusing it of having a secret agenda for the Islamization of Turkish state and society.[104] It was argued that the AKP leadership could not have jettisoned its Islamist worldview within a few years. According to that view, the AKP had actually been engaged in dissimulation (*takiyye*), a practice with strong roots in Shiite Islamic tradition, by hiding its true intentions to establish an Islamic state until the time was ripe.[105] Although such arguments seemed rather exaggerated, they were sometimes supported by clumsy attempts by the AKP to appease the Islamist part of its electoral base, of which the short-lived proposal to penalize adultery during the reform of the Turkish Penal Code in August 2004 is a prime example.

The rise of the AKP to power in November 2002 did not signal a break with past state policies on the headscarf issue. Despite the explicit expectations of its electoral base, the AKP government normally abstained from openly raising the headscarf issue in an effort to avoid polarizing the political scene and antagonizing the military and bureaucratic elite. Instead, it opted to wait for the imminent decision of the European Court of Human Rights decision on the issue, by which it hoped to relieve the government of the political cost of reforming the headscarf legislation. The decision of the ECHR, however, in the case *Leyla Sahin vs. Turkey* did not help these plans. The Court ruled that there was no violation of Article 9 (freedom of thought, conscience, and religion) of the European Convention of Human Rights when the applicant was denied access to university examination and enrolment because she wore a headscarf.[106] Although the Court's decision did not help resolve the headscarf issue in Turkey, this had no impact on the liberal basis of the AKP public discourse.[107]

The Directorate of Religious Affairs (Diyanet Isleri Baskanligi)

On the other hand, the AKP showed less zeal in applying the same liberal discourse in the case of the Directorate of Religious Affairs. The exponential growth of the activity of the Directorate since the 1980s has been one of the clearest indicators of the Islamic social and political resurgence. Its budget in 2000 was 11 times that of the Ministry of Labor and Social Security, 1.5 times that of the Ministry of Foreign Affairs, and 1.2 times that of the Ministry of Interior.[108] Its personnel grew from 25,236 in 1970 to over 74,114 in 2004, while the number of mosques soared from 42,744 in 1971 to 76,445 in 2004.[109] The expanding activity of the Directorate undermined the secular character of the state, given that it exclusively promoted Sunni Islam. Alevi associations and other religious minority representatives repeatedly addressed their grievances about the Sunni bias of the Directorate and the absence of any funding programs for Alevi religious houses of worship (*cemevi*). The reform of the Directorate was suggested as a necessary step for the establishment of genuine secularism. Two possible solutions were suggested. The state should either cede control of the Directorate to the religious communities themselves or maintain control of the Directorate but guarantee the proportional representation of all religious groups in it as well as their proportionate access to the Directorate's budget.[110]

The prospect of Turkey's EU membership brought the Directorate issue to public attention, as European Commission reports had repeatedly noted how it undermined the principle of secularism. During the ensuing discussions on necessary reforms, some suggested the transformation of the Directorate into an autonomous state authority, following the example of the Higher Education Council (*Yuksek Ogretim Kurulu*—YOK). Others suggested the abolition of the Directorate and the takeover of its activities by the religious communities. The equal access of non-Sunni Muslims to the Directorate and its services was also underlined.[111] While all these proposals could contribute to the elimination of the Sunni bias of the Directorate, the AKP government did not display the initiative it had shown in advocating the free profession of the Islamic faith in public space. Occasional statements by AKP officials—including Erdogan himself—on Alevi grievances regarding the Directorate did not convey the expected level of sensitivity and loyalty to liberal principles when it came to recognizing Alevis as a separate religious group and not just as a branch of Sunni Islam. Age-old Sunni prejudices of Alevi Islam survived in the AKP. A statement of Prime Minister Recep Tayyip Erdogan spoke volumes about the level of intolerance on the Alevi issue among Sunni Muslims. When asked during a television interview on his opinion on the Alevi question, he replied that Alevism is not a religion and added, "If Alevism means to love Ali and follow his path, I am also Alevi. I am one of those who struggle to live like Ali. I am more Alevi than they are."[112]

It seems that the Sunni background of the AKP leadership has obstructed a liberal approach of the Directorate question and cast doubt on the depth of its liberal convictions. Nonetheless, the existence of a persistent debate on how to bring the Directorate's role and functions in line with liberal and secular ideas provides evidence that, although the AKP has failed in this case to play the role of a catalyst, the introduction of a liberal version of secularism has had considerable social support.[113]

THE STANCE OF SOCIAL ACTORS

The State Elites

Turkey's military and civil bureaucracy has viewed the protection of the republican secular model as one of its primary missions. Throughout the history of republican Turkey, the protection of this model has become the legitimizing ground for numerous military interventions into politics. The military coups of 1960, 1971, and 1980 were all—at least partially—justified as inevitable for the protection of state secularism against the threat of political Islam. The military undertook a guardian role of state secularism, which was institutionalized with the establishment of the MGK under the 1961 Constitution and outlined in the National Security Council Law and the Turkish Armed Forces Internal Service Law. The "soft" coup of 1997 reaffirmed the keen interest of the military in the defense of state secularism. Given this recent historic precedent, the AKP experimentations with a novel, more tolerant type of secularism were bound to provoke reaction by the military. Despite the new political environment created by the prospect of EU membership and political reform, the headscarf issue served again as a reaffirmation of the civil and military bureaucracy's commitment to the protection of the republican secular model and its unwillingness to negotiate any relaxation of the tough restrictions to the public manifestations of Islam. During his annual evaluation speech in the Directorate of War Academies on April 20, 2005, the Chief of the General Staff General Hilmi Ozkok defended the Turkish model of secularism by stating that "Turkey is neither an Islamic state nor an Islamic country. The principle of secularism is the cornerstone of all the values that form the Republic of Turkey."[114]

Five days later, the President of the Constitutional Court Mustafa Bumin added,

> The decisions of the Constitutional Court and the European Court of Human Rights have reached a consensus on the headscarf issue. At this point, some print and electronic media try to keep this topic on the political agenda, while some political party officials state that they would make legal arrangements in order to have the right of education with headscarf acknowledged. This is a type of behavior aiming at securing political advantages through the use of religious sentiment, unless it stems from lack of knowledge about the court jurisdictions. As long as the secular clauses remain in the Constitution, all legal arrangements that would enable the entrance of women wearing headscarves to higher education institutions as students and after their graduation to public offices of civil servants will be against the Constitution. Even if such a clause is added to the Constitution, this new constitutional clause will be contrary [sic] to the European Convention of Human Rights.[115]

This statement was legally unfounded and met with the reaction of many liberal columnists;[116] yet, it showed that no support for any liberal openings in the issue of secularism could be expected from top-level military and civil bureaucrats. Civil and military bureaucracy remained steadfast in their uncompromising defense of state secularism.

The Intelligentsia

The liberal and post-Islamist intelligentsia has strongly supported the reform of state secularism. The social forces that brought the AKP to power expected the new government to promote full respect of their religious freedom. The headscarf issue gained a symbolic significance in this respect, as it was one of the most visible and publicized manifestations of the extremities of state secularism. However, this was expressed not in an Islamist vocabulary but in the language of political liberalism, multiculturalism, and tolerance. In a response to the previously quoted speech by the president of the Constitutional Court, the president of the AKP Parliamentary Group, Irfan Gunduz, pointed out that "the headscarf issue should be dealt with within the framework of fundamental human rights and freedoms. . . . You can force someone to cover or uncover her head; both are coercive. This is not the business of the state, the state needs to leave it to personal taste and choice.[117]

Bumin's comments also sparked a discussion about the true meaning of secularism. Liberal secularism was dissociated from state secularism and defined on the basis of tolerance and lack of state interference into religious affairs. The Turkish version of secularism was seen as a deviation that turned the public against its very principles. Instead of being a means of suppression, liberal secularism should promote freedom and democracy. In the view of the columnist Atilla Yayla,

> the words and behaviors of Bumin and those who share his mentality greatly harm secularism. This is an understanding of secularism that is against the freedom of religion and conscience, has become a religion itself, and aims at eradicating from social life other religions (especially the religion of the majority). This understanding shakes social belief and trust for secularism and becomes the reason why according to most people, the Turkish type of secularism is—with good reason— understood as atheist or antireligious. . . . This mentality, which violates human rights and freedoms and was lastly expressed by Bumin, is being manifested today in the headscarf issue but tomorrow could be manifested in another field. It can be reversed by the individual and collective struggle of all democrats. Thus, secularism can cease to be a coarse means of social engineering and become a servant of freedom and democracy.[118]

Other columnists pointed to the false way Bumin evaluated the ECHR decision on the headscarf issue and the possibility of a redefinition of Turkey's model of secularism. In their view, nothing obstructed a more tolerant arrangement of state-religion relations through a constitutional amendment.[119] The arguments of the intelligentsia displayed a high level of sophistication and maturity, making the case for the introduction of a genuinely secular system ever stronger.

The Incidence of Social Learning

There is a mixed record of social learning in regard to the question of the role of religion in politics and the impact of improving EU-Turkey relations. The adamant stance of the military and the judiciary on the preservation of the secularist character of the Turkish state clearly showed that little was learned by them during the reform process. Steps made toward political liberalization due to the need to meet the Copenhagen Criteria failed to change the way the Turkish bureaucracy viewed the relationship between religion and the state. Religion was seen as a retrograde, destabilizing factor that needed to be put under firm control through the implementation of an extreme—even by European standards—understanding of secularism.[120] It was argued that this disregarded the fundamental rights and freedoms of the majority of Turkey's population and misunderstood its intentions. A similar error was made by traditional Islamist political parties, which also misinterpreted the religiosity of a large part of the Turkish population as support for an illiberal, nondemocratic, Islamic state. As a survey by Carkoglu and Toprak clearly showed, however, Turkish public opinion professed much more secular views than one might expect. Although the majority of Turkish population are observing Muslims, their religiosity is not translated into support for an Islamist political project. While only 19.8 percent of the sample population expressed its support for an "Islamic law order [*seriat duzeni*],"[121] this support evaporated when it came to questions on specific applications of the Islamic law such as in family and inheritance affairs. Only 10.7 percent agreed with the implementation of the Islamic prescription of polygamy, 14 percent approved of the Islamic divorce rules, while 13.9 percent expressed their preference for Islamic inheritance rules.[122] On the question of secularism, 60.6 percent agreed that there should be no party whose politics were based on religion.[123] This showed the success of the Kemalist secularization program, as well as its limits.

While the views of the Kemalist state elite remained largely unaffected by the EU-initiated liberalization drive, Turkey's Islamist intelligentsia was profoundly affected. As the utopian nature of the Islamist political project became clear, the European Union ceased to be the archenemy and became a source of emulation and inspiration.[124] Old problems of Turkish politics like the question of secularism were now addressed in the language of political liberalism and human rights. State secularism was now opposed in the name of Anglo-American liberal secularism and pluralism,[125] and calls for a pluralist and partici-patory democracy, real secularism, and human rights in the Western or European sense have become the cornerstones of the Islamists' resis-tance to the further narrowing of Turkish political space.[126] Given that the European project was identified with the aforementioned values, it was the AKP and post-Islamist forces rather than the CHP and the Kemalist elite that brought Turkey closer to Europe. Through their successful management of the EU process, the AKP gained politi-cal legitimacy at the expense of the old secularist elites, whose role as agents of Europe and modernity was severely undermined.[127] The intensity and depth of learning within the AKP led to discussions on what remained from the Islamist political tradition. Without ignoring the impact of domestic politics,[128] it was mainly the prospect of EU membership and the need to fulfill the Copenhagen Criteria that cre-ated a political environment conducive to this transformation. The prospect of Turkey's EU membership minimized state leverage over the AKP, while the Copenhagen Criteria became the yardstick against which religious freedom and state-religion relations were measured. The position of the AKP on the headscarf issue and a series of other topics related to secularizing the state (with the exception of the Directorate of Religious Affairs) suggested that the AKP had become the primary agent of Europeanization in Turkey. Although the depth and sincerity of the AKP transformation was put into question by its stance on a number of issues, including opposition to reform of the Directorate of Religious Affairs, this should not be seen as outweigh-ing the contribution of the AKP administration to the redefinition of secularism as part of an overall political liberalization process.

CONCLUSIONS

The rather limited nature of legislative reform on the issue of secular-ism helps us to approach path dependence theory from an alternative perspective. The domestic balance of power between secularist, Isla-mist, and liberal forces, as well as the unwillingness of the European Union to push for liberalization in this field, did not allow for sig-nificant improvements. If there could not be any liberalization, there could only be a stalemate and no reversal toward radical illiberal solutions. Steps toward Islamization could not be promoted, both because of the constitutional limitations and the vehement reaction that such a move would cause from the European Union. This became more than clear with the harsh EU reaction against the proposal to penalize adultery in August 2004. On the other hand, a further radicalization of state secularism seemed improbable, given Turkey's need to comply with the principles of a liberal democracy.

CHAPTER 6

TURKISH NATIONAL IDENTITY

TERRITORIAL VS. ETHNIC NATIONALISM

There have been a number of typologies of nationalism, yet the most useful for this study, which will be briefly explored here, is the division between territorial and ethnic nationalism. France and Germany are the most-known examples of territorial and ethnic nationalism, respectively. French nationalism was shaped under the influence of the work of Rousseau. The civic-territorial concept of the nation was further developed during the French Revolution. All the members of the nation were citizens, equal before the law, while the members of the *ancien regime* did not even qualify as parts of the nation.[1] Civic-territorial nationalism was carried to its extremes by the Jacobins. The nation was defined in even narrower terms. The opponents of the Jacobin reform program were confronting the general will of the nation, it proclaimed, and could not be members of it; they were consequently fiercely prosecuted. Emphasis on the historic civilizing mission of the nation, national homogenization through mass education, the lack of any tolerance for minorities, militancy, and missionary zeal also characterized Jacobin nationalism.[2] The civic-territorial model of nationalism outlasted the rule of Jacobins, shaped French national identity, and became popular across Western Europe. On the other hand, German nationalism was influenced by Romanticism and the German unification movement. Culture, language, and common ethnic descent became the foci of nationhood. In contrast to the French case, where the state formed the nation, the German nation predated its own state and had to struggle for its formation. German unification was realized in 1871 under the leadership of Prussia, and the German paradigm spread over Central and Eastern Europe. Numerous ethnic and linguistic communities aspired to imitate the German nationalist project and form nation-states hosting ethnic kinsmen. Ethnic nationalism soon led to ethnic strife and massacres, as the European continent was too small and diverse to accommodate the plans of all ethnic nationalisms. German ethnic nationalism remained exceptionally strong and was among the reasons for the German involvement in both World Wars. Although discredited in the aftermath of the wars, ethnic nationalism is still a crucial shaping factor of national identity in Germany and many nation-states in Central and Eastern Europe.

DEFINING TURKISH NATIONAL IDENTITY
The Ottoman Legacy

The seeds of nationalism, spread from its Western European cradle, found fertile soil in the Ottoman Empire. In a region where multiethnic, multicultural empires had prevailed since antiquity, identities and affiliations had been developed on nonnational lines. Religion and locality remained the determining factors in the formation of collective identities. The role of religion as identity badge in the Ottoman Empire was institutionalized by the *millet* system. Although the term *millet* is usually used to refer to the non-Muslim communities of the Ottoman Empire, it is true that the term referred to Muslims as well, anchoring the decisive role of religious affiliation in determining one's identity.[3] The identification of the Turkish nation with Islam was facilitated by the leading role of the Ottoman Empire in the Islamic world[4] and its contribution to the expansion of Islam in Anatolia and Southeastern Europe. Conversion to Islam was not only an act of personal belief or expedience, but also a shift of identity, voluntary participation in the Islamic community of believers (*ummah*), and identification with the Ottoman political ideology and culture. Nationalism was the intellectual force that challenged existing allegiances, identities, and states, resulting in a radical reinterpretation of the "self" and the "other" and the transformation of religious communal into national identities.

Turkish nationalism was among the last to rise in the declining Ottoman Empire of the late nineteenth century. The preponderance of Islamic identity and the privileged position that Sunni Muslims[5] enjoyed had initially deterred the proliferation of nationalist ideas that could undermine the cohesion of the multiethnic and multireligious Empire. Nonetheless, the rapid rise of nationalism within Ottoman Christians, the formation of nation-states in former Ottoman provinces, and the imminent existential threat that these developments represented for the ailing Empire resulted in the development of Turkish nationalism. Defensive in nature, Turkish nationalism soon succeeded in striking a chord among Ottoman Turkish intellectual and military elites. Exposed to Western European intellectual debates, they found in nationalism—as did so many Europeans at the same time—the panacea for the shortcomings of the Ottoman state. The rise of the Young Turk political movement became a turning point for the success of the Turkish nationalist project. Its political agenda was also shared by a small but disproportionately influential number of Russia-born Turkic intellectuals who had been influenced by pan-Slavism before migrating to the Ottoman Empire.[6] In their view, the nation had to be freed from all the obstacles that obstructed its political autonomy and empowerment. Nonetheless, a commonly accepted definition of the nation was hardly given. The basis of the new nation was under debate. Yusuf Akcura, an immigrant intellectual from the Russian Empire, addressed in his seminal treatise "*Uc Tarz-i Siyaset*" the dilemmas of Turkish nationalism at the beginning of the twentieth century.[7] Ottomanism, the hammering of an *ethnie-* and religion-blind territorial identity for all Ottoman subjects was rejected as a chimera, given that none of the Ottoman ethnic and religious communities was willing to substitute Ottomanism for its own identity. Pan-Islamism was dismissed as unrealistic, given the reaction it would cause from the Western powers who ruled over large numbers of Muslim subjects. Pan-Turkism would antagonize the Russian Empire, which ruled over the Caucasus and Central Asia, yet Akcura seemed eventually to lean toward it. The question was not definitely answered even after the 1908 Young Turk Revolution, which marked the end of Hamidian despotism and brought Turkish nationalists to power.

An era of ambivalence and deliberation ended with the Balkan Wars, which sharply reduced the Empire's territory in the Balkans and caused a large refugee wave into the remaining parts of the Empire. The Young Turk triumvirate, which took over power in 1913 in the midst of the Balkan Wars, implemented a political program aiming at the transformation of the Ottoman Empire into a Turkish nation-state. Turkey's entry into the First World War facilitated the application of discriminative measures against non-Turkish Muslim minorities and even harsher steps against "nonassimilable" Christian minorities. Ottoman Armenians, Greeks, and Assyrians often faced exile, deportation, and even death.[8] Pan-Turkism briefly gained momentum in the last years of the Ottoman Empire, when the outbreak of the October Revolution and the collapse of the Russian Empire raised hopes for expansion toward the Caucasus and Central Asia. Nonetheless, these hopes were soon dashed by the ensuing Ottoman capitulation. In the aftermath of the First World War, the feasibility of the Turkish nationalist project was put into question,[9] yet the leadership skills of Mustafa Kemal [Ataturk] in the crucial years 1919–23 guaranteed the establishment of a Turkish nation-state in Anatolia. The 1923 Lausanne Treaty signaled the end of a long series of wars that left Anatolia ruined but under Turkish sovereignty and with an unprecedented Muslim preponderance. While non-Muslims represented 20 percent of the Anatolian population before the First World War, only 2.5 percent of the population of the new Turkish Republic was non-Muslim.[10]

Turkish National Identity from 1923 to the 1990s

The formation of a Turkish national identity in the republican years was inevitably affected by the cataclysmic political developments that led to the foundation of the Republic of Turkey. The rise of a strong Soviet state from the ashes of the Russian Empire rendered any pan-Turkist ambitions unrealistic. The near elimination of non-Muslim populations meant that Islam could cease being the defining element of Turkish national identity. In the aftermath of the Lausanne Treaty Ataturk denounced all religious and pan-Turkist ideals, focusing on the formation of a civic-territorial Turkish national identity rooted in Anatolia. Despite this clear preference, however, elements of ethnic and religious nationalism survived in state policies and formed an interesting amalgamation with the dominant model.[11] This was a clear influence emanating from Gokalp's nationalist ideas, which comprised a fusion of French and German nationalism.[12]

Territorial Nationalism

The application of the territorial nationalism model in Turkey was inextricably linked with the program of radical Westernization that Ataturk put forward in his effort to overcome Turkish political, economic, and cultural underdevelopment. To move Turkey toward convergence with "contemporary civilization [*muasir medeniyet*],"[13] lessons were drawn from the decline and dismemberment of the Ottoman Empire.[14] Both pan-Islamist and pan-Turkist ideologies had to be abandoned, and a territory-based model of national identity developed. The territorial version of Turkish nationalism that Ataturk espoused fell short of both pan-Islamism and pan-Turkism in that it had a much more pragmatic perspective: defending Anatolia and establishing a Turkish nation-state were within the military and political capabilities of Turkish nationalists, and all efforts were focused on this project. In his famous address to the Turkish Assembly from October 15–20, 1927 (*Nutuk*), Ataturk displayed his realist vision and elaborated on his effort to establish a territorial Turkish national identity: "I am neither a believer in a league of all the nations of Islam, nor even in a league of Turkish people. Each of us here has the right to hold his ideals, but the government must be stable with a fixed policy, grounded in facts, and with one view and one alone: to safeguard the life and independence of the nation within its natural frontiers. Neither sentiment nor illusion must influence our policy. Away with dreams and shadows! They have cost us dear in the past!"[15]

The French Jacobin model of republican territorial nationalism became the source of inspiration: Anatolia constituted the Turkish "fatherland," the indivisible territorial unit that would form the geographical basis of Turkish nationhood.[16] Citizenship and common culture were crucial elements in the development of territorial Turkish national identity. Equal citizen rights for all inhabitants of Anatolia would nurture "a sense of solidarity and fraternity through active social and political participation,"[17] which would become the building blocks of Turkish national identity. Warfare, massacres, and population exchanges in the first quarter of the twentieth century had altered the multireligious character of Anatolia. An undisputed Muslim preponderance was established, which made nation-building easier but by no means straightforward. Although the formerly strong Christian communities had disappeared,[18] Anatolia was still an ethnic mosaic,[19] while a significant Alevi minority challenged the Sunni majority. While Turkish national identity was not embedded in all the Muslim populations of Anatolia, these populations were deemed suitable citizens of the Turkish Republic, provided they opted for a subordination of their distinct ethnic and cultural features to the state-promoted Turkish territorial identity.[20] There was little room for minority rights in the new Republic of Turkey; even the small non-Muslim minorities of Istanbul were suspected.[21] Everybody was expected to assimilate to the state-espoused national identity model.[22] A massive education campaign was launched along with the secularization and Westernization campaign, which aimed to facilitate the establishment of a territorial-civic Turkish national identity in all the citizens of the Republic. Emphasis on territorial nationalism, however, did not mean that ethnicity and religion ceased being a factor in defining Turkish national identity. Ethnic and religious elements maintained their importance in defining Turkishness.

Ethnic Nationalism
The model of ethnic nationalism found considerable resonance among Turkish nationalists in the late years of the Ottoman Empire. The Turkish nation was seen as a single unit, stretching from the Adriatic Sea to the borders of China, whose political unification should be furthered. The spread of ethnic nationalism was boosted by the immigration of Russia-born Turkic intellectuals influenced by pan-Slavism.[23] The consolidation of the Soviet Union in the aftermath of the October Revolution, the alliance of the Soviet Union with the Kemalist forces, and the failure of the former Young Turk leader Enver Pasa to establish a Turkic state in Central Asia meant that pan-Turkism would be indefinitely shelved. Despite the official adoption of territorial nationalism, state policies demonstrated that ethnic nationalism had left its imprint on official state nationalism. Discriminatory policies against population groups on the basis of their ethnicity were a continuation of measures taken in the last years of the Ottoman Empire and aimed at the same direction, namely minority assimilation or emigration.[24] The 1934 Resettlement Law (*Iskan Kanunu*)[25] and the 1942 Property Tax Law (*Varlik Vergisi Kanunu*)[26] exemplified these policies. The importance of ethnic nationalism was also attested by the exaltation of the Turkish nation[27] and language. Systematic efforts were made to dissociate the ethnonym "Turk" from any demeaning connotations it had carried throughout Ottoman history[28] and turn it into a source of national pride. Additionally, the Sun Language Theory (*Gunes Dil Teorisi*), coined by the Turkish Language Society (*Turk Dil Kurumu*) in 1935, attempted to prove that Turkish was the most ancient, accurate, and beautiful language in the world and all the languages originated from it. The Turkish Language Reform Program aimed at purifying Turkish from its Arabic and Persian influences.[29] Antiminority campaigns in the language field continued in 1937 with the launch of the "Citizen, Speak Turkish [*Vatandas Turkce Konus*]" campaign for the exclusive use of Turkish in public.[30]

Tolerance toward minorities did not characterize republican Turkish politics.[31] Despite being recognized and protected by the Lausanne Treaty, the Armenian, Greek, and Jewish minorities of Turkey faced persistent discrimination. Non-Muslim minority foundations were not recognized as juridical persons and were denied the right to acquire immovable property. Any property acquired despite the ban was confiscated.[32] Restrictions in the freedom of religion and education were equally significant. The Orthodox Seminary on the island of Heybeliada (Chalki) was closed down in 1971, which made the education of Orthodox priests in Turkey impossible. The Armenian and Jewish communities also faced analogous problems. The ecumenical ecclesiastical status of the Orthodox Patriarchate was persistently rejected, and the Orthodox Patriarchate was only recognized as the religious directorate of the shrinking Greek Orthodox minority in Istanbul. Minority education was protected by Article 40 of the Lausanne Treaty, yet in practice, state intervention seriously hampered the educational rights of the minorities.

Despite discrimination against non-Muslim minorities, ethnic nationalism never became an ideological monopoly. Non-Muslim minorities were numerically insignificant, and a territorial national identity model was championed for all Anatolian Muslims. Despite this, ethnic nationalism had a significant influence on the formation of state national ideology. In the 1960s, Turkish ethnic nationalism also found its political representative in the person of Alparslan Turkes and the Nationalist Action Party (*Milliyetci Hareket Partisi*—MHP). Since then, the Cyprus and Nagorno Karabagh conflicts, as well as the Balkan crisis in the 1990s, have attracted interest in ethnic nationalism, while the demise of the Soviet Union, which briefly raised hopes for close cooperation of ex-Soviet Turkic republics under Turkey's leadership, also mobilized some solidarity.[33] Nonetheless, the realization that the Turkic republics were not willing to accept a "big brother" role for Turkey cooled down ethnic nationalist fervor.[34] It was through its covert impact on the official version of nationalism rather than through its political representatives that ethnic nationalism influenced Turkish national identity.

The Role of Islam
Early Turkish nationalists in the mid-nineteenth century identified Islam as one of the basic elements of Turkish identity and considered it compatible with Westernization. However, more radical views appeared soon, blaming Islam for Turkish underdevelopment and championing secularization of the state and society according to the French positivist model. The most influential Young Turk thinker, Ziya Gokalp, attempted to integrate Turkish nationalism into modernity and Islam by differentiating between civilization (*medeniyet*), culture (*hars*), and religion *(din)*. He defined civilization in technological and political terms. Culture was the set of values and beliefs

that defined a people and restricted religion into its essential content. The Turkish nation should adopt Western civilization and rediscover its own Turkish culture, which had faded under the influence of Arab culture.[35] Islam had to be dissociated from Arab culture and restricted to the private sphere.[36]

Many Young Turks did not see Islam as an essential element of Turkish identity but rather as an impediment for the progress of the Turkish nation. However, political conditions did not allow them to implement anti-Islamic policies. On the contrary, Islam was used as a political tool and mobilizing force in the wars against Western powers and neighboring Christian states. Ataturk followed the same policy in the years of armed struggle (1919–22) but disclosed his true intentions as soon as he was powerful enough to do so. Official secularization policies tried to dissociate Turkish national identity from Islam; their success, however, was only limited. At the elite level, Islam ceased to be an essential element of Turkish identity; at the grassroots level, however, the role of Islam as symbol of Turkish national identity persisted.[37] Islam was the only unifying factor of the multilingual, multiethnic populations of Anatolia and the most tangible element of their Turkish identity.[38] Intensive state efforts to inculcate territorial Turkish nationalism through the means of education and control of public and political Islam had only limited success. Islam eventually reemerged in the public sphere during the rule of the DP in the 1950s and claimed an independent active role in Turkish politics in 1970, when Necmettin Erbakan founded the MNP, the first clearly Islamist party in the history of republican Turkey. Erbakan stressed the paramount importance of Islam as an essential element of Turkish national identity, despite long state efforts to eliminate it. He also cultivated a nationalistic nostalgia for the Ottoman imperial past.[39] In this context, he defended Islamic interstate cooperation through the formation of an "Islamic Union" in which Turkey would have a leading role (see p. 101). His argument was adopted by a group of conservative Kemalist intellectuals, the "Hearth of the Enlightened [Aydinlar Ocagi]," which argued for an Islamic revival as a means of strengthening Turkish nationalism against growing minority nationalist and leftist dissidence. These positions were elaborated into an ideological construction named the "Turkish-Islamic Synthesis [Turk-Islam Sentezi]."[40] Pre-Islamic Turkish heritage and Islamic culture were recognized as the cornerstones of Turkish national identity and fully compatible with each other.[41] Islam was thus seen not as a fully fledged political ideology, as it was by Erbakan, but as an element that could revitalize Turkish nationalism.[42] The emphasis given to Islam and Turkish ethnicity was a clear shift away from the main elements of Ataturk's nationalism.[43] This shift was also in line with the U.S. policy of containing the spread of Soviet influence in the Middle East through the support of Islamism.

The military coup of September 12, 1980, acted as catalyst for the infusion of Islamic elements into official Turkish national ideology. Extreme secularist policies were held to be one of the reasons for the proliferation of radical leftist and rightist as well as Kurdish nationalist ideas, which resulted in civil strife and detrimental effects on Turkey's stability. Besides, state abstention from religious education had resulted in the increasing influence of legal and underground religious groups. In accordance with the views expressed by the "Hearth of the Enlightened," religious instruction in Turkish primary and secondary schools became compulsory under Article 24 of the 1982 Constitution. The "Turkish-Islamic Synthesis"[44] constituted the ideological core of the new school curriculum.[45] The special relation between the Turkish nation and Islam was stressed, and similarities between pre-Islamic Turkish and Islamic civilizations and values were emphasized.[46] All school textbooks were revised in 1986 to conform to the new historical doctrine.[47] Meanwhile, state funding of religious education and foundations increased exponentially. Islam was regarded as an essential element of Turkish national identity, and its public manifestation was tolerated to the extent that it respected the principles of republicanism and secularism. The rise of an Islamist economic counterelite in the 1980s made consumption patterns an additional level of identity debate between secularists and Islamists. The return of Necmettin Erbakan into politics as leader of the RP polarized the debate on Turkish political Islam but did not disturb the balance set by the 1980 military regime.

Turkish National Identity since the 1990s

The debate on Turkish national identity gained new dimensions in the 1990s under the influence of international and domestic factors. In the field of domestic politics, the escalation of the Kurdish conflict, the emergence of the Alevi question, and the rise of political Islam to power challenged dominant perceptions of existing national identity. At the international level, the end of the Cold War was followed by increased interest in identity questions and a rise of nationalism. These brought the question of national identity into the center of academic and popular interest.

The Impact of Global Actors

Interest in minority rights and identity discourses rose in the aftermath of the Cold War. This was a response to the increasing global growth of nationalism and its concomitant threats. As the appeal of Marxist ideas shrank and the demise of communist regimes in Eastern Europe resulted in a power vacuum, nationalism became in many cases a substitute ideology that reshaped borders, caused humanitarian catastrophes, and brought the issue of minority protection to the fore. The plight of minorities in the wars of the former Yugoslavia, Rwanda, Iraq, and the former Soviet Union made clear that the international community should be mobilized in the direction of better minority rights protection. At the European level, the Council of Europe addressed the problem through the preparation of two international treaties, the European Charter for Regional or Minority Languages[48] and the Framework Convention for the Protection of National Minorities,[49] which aimed at improving the level of minority rights protection within the member states of the Council.[50] At the global level, the organization of *ad hoc* international criminal courts for the wars of the former Yugoslavia and Rwanda and the campaign to establish a permanent International Criminal Court in the framework of the United Nations were significant steps.[51] Nonetheless, this discourse had a minor influence on minority rights discourses and practices in Turkey.[52] Turkey expressed its concern about the condition of Turkish and other Muslim minorities throughout the Balkans and the Caucasus but failed to sign either of the two Council of Europe treaties on minority rights protection. Minority policies remained generally unaffected. It was only through Turkey's recognition of the right of individual appeal to the European Court of Human Rights in 1990 and the increasing number of condemnatory judgments from 1995 onwards that a certain degree of pressure was exerted in the direction of improving protection of minority rights.

The Impact of Domestic Politics
The Kurdish Issue

Kurdish nationalism far preceded the 1990s. Nonetheless, it was then that the Kurdish issue came to occupy a central position in Turkey's political agenda. The PKK intensified its operations against Turkish armed forces in the eastern and southeastern provinces of Turkey and terrorist attacks against civilian targets throughout the country. The Turkish armed forces responded with the deployment of an increasing number of troops and the brutal forced evacuation of thousands of villages and migration. A state of emergency (*Olaganustu*

Hal—OHAL) was declared in the eastern and southeastern provinces, according to Article 122 of the Constitution. This meant that severe restrictions of fundamental rights and freedoms—already weakly protected under the 1982 Constitution—were at the discretionary power of the Council of Ministers and regional governors. Throughout the PKK insurgency, from 1984 to 2000, 4,049 civilians, 5,121 military personnel and 17,248 insurgents were killed, while 3,200 villages were destroyed, 380,000 people were forced to relocate in the region and another 3,000,000 to migrate to Turkey's big cities and Western Europe.[53] This situation, which did not fall short of a normal war, polarized Turkish society and sharpened ethnic divisions.

Kurdish—and any other ethnic—descent had not previously been an issue in Turkish politics, provided one fully adopted Kemalist civic nationalism. The highest ranks of Turkish politics,[54] bureaucracy, and military were open to Turkish citizens of Kurdish descent, but only under the condition that they jettisoned their Kurdish identity. As Kymlicka accurately observed, "The problem is not that Turkey refuses to accept Kurds as Turkish citizens. The problem is precisely its attempt to force Kurds to see themselves as Turks."[55]

While assimilation policies were not tolerated by most Kurds, atavistic fears for the future of Turkish nationalism reemerged with the rise of the Kurdish question. Ethnicity started gaining importance and dividing Turkish society. When it became impossible to deny the existence of a Kurdish minority in Turkey, Turkish nationalists attempted to "otherize" the Kurdish nationalist movement.[56] The Sevres syndrome (see p. 78) reappeared and hardened the position of the public opinion on the Kurdish issue. The military activities of the PKK further strengthened this suspicion. Although it has been argued that the PKK should be credited with increasing international sympathy for the plight of Turkey's Kurds, in fact it often worsened it. The PKK's military operations and terrorist attacks gave a pretext for devastating reprisals by the Turkish armed forces and reduced the scope for a political solution of the Kurdish minority by sidelining voices advocating a nonviolent solution to the Kurdish question.[57] As long as the Kurdish question was approached as a national security issue, there could be no hope of democratic reform that could improve the position of Turkey's Kurds. State persecution measures were not limited to PKK members but also included most nonviolent Kurdish political activists. The closure of the People's Labor Party (*Halkin Emek Partisi*—HEP) and its successors the Democratic Labor Party (*Demokrasi Partisi*—DEP) and the People's Democratic Party (*Halkin Demokrasi Partisi*—HADEP) and the imprisonment of the leading figures Leyla Zana, Hatip Dicle, Orhan Dogan, and Selim Sadak further limited the possibility of a peaceful resolution.[58] The situation improved only after the Turkish armed forces succeeded in significantly limiting the operational capacity of the PKK in the late 1990s. The PKK leader Abdullah Ocalan was forced to flee his refuge in Syria in October 1998 and was eventually captured in February 1999. The PKK then declared a unilateral ceasefire. The de-escalation of the armed conflict was a necessary but not sufficient condition for the reconsideration of the Kurdish question as a human rights issue and part of the overall Turkey's democratization process. Nonetheless, serious violations of Kurdish minority rights persisted.[59]

The rise of the Kurdish issue succeeded in mobilizing a substantial number of Turkey's ethnic Kurdish population and had an irreversible effect on the Turkish national identity discourse. The ethnic homogeneity of the Anatolian Muslim population was openly questioned for the first time. The rise of Kurdish nationalism posed the first serious challenge to Turkish nationalism, as it manifested the failure of civic nationalism to strike roots in a significant part of the population.[60] Moreover, it contested one of the most fundamental assumptions of Turkish nationalism, namely the congruence of Islam with Turkishness in Anatolia. The majority of Turkey's Kurds did not support terrorism and political violence but claimed their fundamental human and minority rights.[61] The failure to assimilate Turkey's Kurds shook the self-confidence of Turkish nationalism[62] and spread concern that other ethnic groups might follow the same path.

The Alevi Revival

While the revival of Alevi identity could be first traced within the sociopolitical fermentations following the promulgation of the 1961 Constitution, the dynamic reappearance of Sunni Islam in Turkish politics throughout the 1980s challenged the Alevi community. Increased interest in Alevi culture, reaction against attempts to undermine the secular character of the Turkish state through the rise of Sunni Islam into a dominant position, and indecisiveness on how Alevi identity should be preserved all characterized the Alevi community.

Two events marked the rise of Alevi conscience in the 1990s. A literature conference in Sivas was organized in July 1993 on the occasion of the festival of Pir Sultan Abdal, one of the most revered Alevi religious figures. Among the participants was Aziz Nesin, a prominent secularist writer, who had commenced the translation of Salman Rushdie's controversial book *The Satanic Verses* into Turkish.

A mob of Sunni Islamist fanatics gathered outside the hotel that was the venue of the conference and set it on fire. Seventeen participants perished—although not Nesin himself. The police, who had usually been exceptionally effective in brutally suppressing all kinds of demonstrations, this time showed an unexplainable passivity and unwillingness to intervene until it was virtually too late. The Sivas incident shocked public opinion and—most of all—Alevis. It was clearly reminiscent of past massacres against Alevis in the 1970s. The passivity with which police treated the riots raised suspicion about complicity of "deep state" circles in the anti-Alevi riots.[63]

The same level of distrust against state authorities was displayed in March 1995, when unidentified gunmen assassinated an Alevi elder (*dede*) in a teahouse at Gaziosmanpasa, a poor Istanbul neighborhood with a large Alevi community. The event took a sectarian dimension, and serious riots erupted in which fifteen Alevis were killed in clashes with police forces. Opposition to state discriminatory practices further strengthened a feeling of Alevi unity.[64] At the intellectual level, the movement for the recognition of a separate Alevi identity grew stronger. Action was organized against state discrimination. Alevis insisted on the inclusion of Alevi Islam in school religious education and its recognition not as a branch of Sunni Islam, but as a different religious denomination with its own rich cultural heritage.[65]

The struggle for the recognition of a separate Alevi identity was marked by ambivalence on whether this struggle should be based on a claim for a religious minority status. Alevis hesitated to base their claim for religious and cultural rights on the recognition of their religious minority status. Republican official history celebrated Alevism as an offshoot of pre-Islamic Turkish culture that preserved the essence of Turkishness while mainstream Sunni Turkish culture had become largely Arabized.[66] These accounts struck a chord among a large part of Turkey's Alevi population. Alevi cultural diversity was not only no longer looked down upon or despised, as in the Ottoman years; on the contrary, it became the symbol of an original, unadulterated Turkish identity.[67] Moreover, the same nationalist historical accounts denigrated the term "minority," linking it with fragmentation of national unity, secessionism, and collaboration with foreign powers.

This made difficult for many Alevis to accept the term "religious minority" for their community. The case of the Istanbul non-Muslim communities, the minorities *par excellence* of the Turkish Republic, was anything but appealing. State minority policies, as well as their "suspect" patriotic credentials, did not make the prospect of recognition of a special Alevi minority appealing. It was feared that

Alevis would thus become "second-class citizens" like the non-Muslim minorities. In response to this, some Alevi representatives protested against the use of the term "minority" for Alevis in European Commission reports.[68] Claiming protection for their religious and cultural identity against the Sunni majority was an important cause,[69] but was not to be seen as compromising their Turkishness.

Early Liberalization Attempts

Turkey's ongoing economic liberalization efforts had a spillover effect on national identity debates. Turgut Ozal, the architect of Turkey's economic liberalization program in the 1980s, attempted from his new position as President of the Republic to reduce ethnic tensions, which had soared due to increasing state repression and the intensification of the PKK activity. A series of measures was taken aimed at reducing harsh freedom limitations and opening up a freer debate on national identity issues. Ozal himself was the first senior politician who openly spoke about his partially Kurdish descent, doing so while discussion on ethnic backgrounds was still a taboo issue. Under Ozal's guidance, in April 1991, the ANAP government lifted a law introduced by the 1980–83 military regime that had officially—though ineffectively—banned the use of Kurdish language in Turkey. The 1991 Gulf War and the influx of Iraqi Kurdish refugees into southeastern Turkey led the government to establish contacts with Iraqi Kurdish leaders, which was an implicit recognition of a Kurdish identity in northern Iraq. Ozal's example was followed by Prime Minister Suleyman Demirel, who visited southeastern Turkey shortly after he took over office in November 1991 and declared in a public meeting in Diyarbakir that "Turkey has recognized the Kurdish reality."[70]

Ozal's sudden death in April 1993 put an end to his political liberalization agenda, yet promising statements from politicians did not disappear. In June 1993, Turkey's new Prime Minister Tansu Ciller[71] stated that she viewed "the ethnic and regional richness of Turkey like the variation and coloration of a mosaic." In late 1994, she even came to the point of rephrasing the famous saying of Ataturk "How happy is one who says 'I am a Turk' [*Ne mutlu Turkum diyene*]" to "How happy is one who says 'I am a citizen of Turkey' [*Ne mutlu Turkiye vatandasiyim diyene*]."[72] Yet these openings turned out to be little more than ephemeral. Verbal support was not turned into institutional reform that could form a sound base for a new national identity debate. State repression of minorities continued unabated, as the armed conflict with the PKK continued. The rise of the Welfare Party into power in the mid 1990s alarmed the state elite, which then initiated a campaign to deter increasing Islamization of Turkish society. While Islam had been viewed since the 1980s as a cementing factor in a society split by ideological and ethnic divisions,[73] it once more became a threat to state security. Turkish national identity was again envisioned without its Islamic component.

The Impact of the European Union

Before the Reforms

Despite the ongoing debate on national identity, there was little change in the relevant Turkish minority legislation until the prospect of Turkey's EU membership started exerting an important influence. The Treaty of Lausanne continued to be the main document that outlined the rights of Turkey's minority groups. Article 38§1–2 stated,

> The Turkish Government undertakes to assure full and complete protection of life and liberty to all inhabitants of Turkey without distinction of birth, nationality, language, race or religion.

> All inhabitants of Turkey shall be entitled to free exercise, whether in public or private, of any creed, religion, or belief, the observance of which shall not be incompatible with public order and good morals.

Article 39 of the Treaty declared,

> Turkish nationals belonging to non-Moslem minorities will enjoy the same civil and political rights as Moslems.

> All the inhabitants of Turkey, without distinction of religion, shall be equal before the law.

> Differences of religion, creed or confession shall not prejudice any Turkish national in matters relating to the enjoyment of civil or political rights, as, for instance, admission to public employments, functions, and honors or the exercise of professions and industries.

> No restrictions shall be imposed on the free use by any Turkish national of any language in private intercourse, in commerce, in religion, in the press, or in publications of any kind or at public meetings.

> Notwithstanding the existence of the official language, adequate facilities shall be given to Turkish nationals of non-Turkish speech for the oral use of their own language before the Courts.

Article 40 added,

> Turkish nationals belonging to non-Moslem minorities shall enjoy the
> same treatment and security in law and in fact as other Turkish nation-
> als. In particular, they shall have an equal right to establish, manage,
> and control at their own expense any charitable, religious, and social
> institutions [and] any schools and other establishments for instruction
> and education, with the right to use their own language and to exercise
> their own religion freely therein.[74]

Only Armenians, Greeks, and Jews were officially recognized as
minorities under the Treaty of Lausanne, even though their aforementioned rights were not respected. Large non-Christian minority
groups, such as ethnic Kurds or Alevis, as well as Christian minorities
not mentioned in the Lausanne Treaty, such as Assyrians (*Suryani*),
Chaldeans (*Keldani*), Protestants, and Catholics, were not recognized
as having any minority rights. The lack of an effective international
system of minority rights protection meant that protection of minority rights could not be enforced from abroad. Turkey did not sign
the Framework Convention for the Protection of National Minorities
drafted by the Council of Europe; yet it was by no means alone in this
respect among European states.[75] Where Turkey lagged far behind
EU member states was in the constitutional and legislative treatment
of minority rights. The term "minority" was absent from the 1982
Constitution. Article 90§5, however, declared international agreements to which Turkey had been a signatory to have the binding force
of law. This granted the Lausanne Treaty the status of domestic law
but subordinated it to the Constitution itself. Other constitutional
stipulations put severe limits on minority rights. Article 3 declared
that the Turkish state (*Turkiye devleti*) is in indivisible integrity "with
its territory and nation" and that its language is Turkish. Article 26
forbade the use of "any language prohibited by law"—in effect Kurdish or other minority languages—"for the expression and dissemination of thought," while article 28 also forbade publications "in any
language forbidden by law." Article 42 also banned the teaching of
any language other than Turkish as a "mother tongue." This ban only
affected local minority languages and never Western European languages, which remained the language of instruction in elite schools
and universities. Article 24 made religious—in effect, Sunni—education mandatory in primary and secondary education, while Article
136 also outlined the role of the Directorate of Religious Affairs as
part of the state administration. The identification of Islam with the

Sunni Hanefi school resulted in severe violations of the rights of Turkey's non-Sunni Muslim communities.[76]

The Reform Process
Constitutional Reform

In the aftermath of the 1999 Helsinki European Council decision, Turkey's EU candidacy facilitated reform programs aiming at better protection of minority rights and a more inclusive definition of Turkish national identity.[77] The 2000 Accession Partnership document mentioned—among other issues—freedom of expression as a field where Turkey needed to strengthen constitutional and legal guarantees. Following the provisions of Turkey's 2001 National Program, significant constitutional amendments were made with the reform package of October 2001. The Preamble of the Constitution had refused protection of "thoughts or opinions" that were against "Turkish national interests; Turkish existence; state and indivisible territorial integrity, history and moral values of the Turkish nation; Ataturk's nationalism; principles; revolution; and civilization." After the reform, the term "actions" replaced the terms "thoughts or opinions," which meant that limitations in the constitutional protection of freedom of thought were lifted. Article 13 was also amended in the direction of expanding fundamental rights and freedoms. Until the reform, fundamental rights and freedoms could be restricted on grounds of the "indivisible integrity of the state with the nation and the country, national sovereignty, the Republic, national security, public order, general order, public benefit, public morals, and public health." Limitations of the fundamental human rights and freedoms could only be imposed "by law and in conformity with the reason mentioned in the relevant articles of the Constitution without infringing upon their essence." Article 14 was rephrased so that "constitutional rights and freedoms might not be used to destroy the indivisible integrity of the state with the country and the democratic and secular Republic, based upon human rights." The clause "no language that is banned by law can be used for the expression and circulation of thoughts" was removed from Article 26.[78] Similarly, the clause "no publication can be made in a language that is banned by law" was removed from Article 28. A new constitutional amendment was passed in May 2004 that aimed at bringing about convergence of the Constitution with the Copenhagen Criteria. Article 90 resolved the issue of a contradiction between an active international treaty on fundamental rights and freedoms and a subsequent domestic law in favor of the first.[79] Hence, the provisions of the Lausanne Treaty could no longer be blocked by domestic legislation. In Article 30, the clause that allowed the confiscation of publishing houses in case of conviction for crimes against "the basic principles of the Republic and national security" was removed.[80]

Legislative Reform

Major improvements in legislation affecting the minorities were made as part of the EU reform packages. In the first reform package of February 2000, Article 312 of the Penal Code was amended so that statements inciting the public "to hatred and enmity with regard to class, race, religion, religious sect, or regional differences" would only be considered as criminal acts if they were expressed "in a manner which could be dangerous for public order." A clause was also added according to which provocations that could offend "a part of the people and harm human dignity" became punishable. In the second reform package of March 2002, the ban on publications in banned languages was removed from the Law on the Press. In July 2001, the Ministry of Culture confiscated and banned the selling of an official book published in 2000 by the same ministry and containing degrading and offensive language in relation to the Turkish Roma. Similarly, the Ministry of Education issued on October 5, 2001, a circular to eliminate pejorative words used about this group in definitions in dictionaries published by the ministry.[81] In the third reform package of August 2002, limitations on teaching and broadcasting of "languages and dialects traditionally spoken by Turkish citizens" were lifted. Article 159 of the Penal Code was amended to bring freedom of expression to the European Convention of Human Rights standards. The Law on Foundations was also modified so non-Muslim foundations could acquire immovable property after a decision of the Council of Ministers. Finally, a chance to reopen closed civil and criminal cases was given.

In the fourth reform package of January 2003, the acquisition of immovable property by non-Muslim foundations simply required the approval of the Directorate. In January 2003, the review of past trials, which had led to confiscations of minority property, was finalized. Subsequently, the abolition of Article 8 of the Anti-Terror Law in July 2003 broadened freedom of expression. The definition of terrorism was also updated to include the use of violence. Broadcasting of private TV and radio stations in minority languages and dialects became possible. The deadline for non-Muslim foundations to register their immovable property was extended. The freedom to erect a place of worship regardless of religion and belief was recognized. Limitations on the names given to infants were also lifted. Turkey also made progress with regard to international conventions on human rights. In June 2003, the Parliament ratified the UN International Covenant on Civil and Political Rights and the UN International Covenant on Economic, Social and Cultural Rights, but only after adding reservations with regard to minority rights.[82] In the seventh reform package of July 2003, Article 159 of the Penal Code was amended so that punishments for "offense against Turkism, the Republic, etc." became lighter. A similar reduction was secured with the modification of Article 169, which dealt with aid toward terrorist organizations. Criminal cases concerning torture and maltreatment were reviewed with priority to avoid the possibility of lapse. Legal personalities were given the chance to establish associations. Finally, the learning by Turkish citizens of minority languages—notably Kurdish—was facilitated, and the opening of private establishments teaching minority languages was allowed. In November 2003, the state of emergency was lifted in the last two provinces of southeastern Turkey, Diyarbakir and Sirnak. In September 2004, a new Penal Code was adopted. Article 216, which largely corresponded to the former Article 312, stated that individuals could be convicted under this article only if their incitement to "enmity and hatred" constituted a "clear and close danger" to public security.[83]

Implementation of Reform

Constitutional and legislative amendments were undoubtedly significant steps toward better protection of minority rights, yet the implementation of reforms often lagged behind expectations. In the case of broadcasting in minority languages, progress was remarkable but not without obstacles. After long hesitation, in June 2003, the state broadcasting corporation (*Turkiye Radyo-Televizyon Kurumu*—TRT) announced its intention to launch programs in minority languages under certain conditions: Broadcasting would be made in national and not local channels. There would be no children's programs and no minority language teaching programs, and all programs would be subtitled or simultaneously translated into Turkish. The first Kurdish-speaking film with Turkish subtitles was broadcast by a local television channel in Diyarbakir in May 2004.[84] In June 2004, the TRT launched its own programs in minority languages.[85] A total of five hours of radio programs and four hours of television programs per week were made in Bosnian, Arabic, *Kirmanci* Kurdish, Circassian, and *Zaza* Kurdish.[86] These broadcasts had high symbolic significance, but in practice, they had little more than cosmetic value. The TRT persistently refused to organize special channels broadcasting in minority languages. As far as private media broadcasting was concerned, a new regulation was published in January 2004 that allowed private national television and radio channels to broadcast in minority languages but also set strict time limits for these broadcasts. Applications of local private television and radio broadcasters in southeastern Turkey to broadcast in Kurdish were still pending in August 2005 when Prime Minister Erdogan visited Diyarbakir (see p. 151). In the aftermath of his visit, which was marked by Erdogan's efforts to mend fences with the local Kurdish population, the Higher Radio-Television Board (*Radyo-Televizyon Ust Kurulu*—RTUK) was reported to have approved the applications of nine local television and radio channels for broadcasting in Kurdish.[87]

Finally, it should be noted that reaction against the measure also came from some minority associations themselves. The Vice President of the Bosnian-Herzegovinian Cultural Associations Federation, Cemal Senel, replied, "May our state be well [*Devletimiz sag olsun*]. However, until today we have not made such a request. Anyway, we are not Bosnians who live in Turkey; we are first-class citizens."[88] This again demonstrated that the identification of minority rights with second-class-citizen status was firmly embedded in public opinion.

As far as the teaching of minority languages was concerned, more bureaucratic resistance was noted. Although reform measures clearly acknowledged the right to open private minority-language schools, the administration found several reasons to delay this development. The names of applicant private schools, internal organization issues, building safety specifications, the qualifications of instructors, the use of the term "language [*dil*]" instead of the term "dialect [*lehce*]" were all used as pretexts to delay the opening of private Kurdish-language schools. When over 10,000 university students applied for the opening of Kurdish language courses, 446 were prosecuted for "sheltering illegal groups," 533 were arrested, 3,621 were taken into custody, and 15 were sentenced with up to three years of prison.[89] Finally, six private schools started teaching *Kirmanci* Kurdish in Van, Batman, and Urfa in April 2004, in Diyarbakir and Adana in August 2004, and in Istanbul in October 2004.[90] However, student interest was low, and in July 2005, the school at Batman had to suspend its operation.

Analogous problems were experienced in implementing reform in the case of non-Muslim minority foundations. The bureaucratic insistence on viewing these non-Muslim minorities and their foundations as "foreign" and dangerous and on stressing the principle of "international reciprocity" in acknowledging minority rights remained an obstacle. In June 2004, a Regulation on the Methods and Principles of the Boards of Non-Muslim Foundations was adopted. This regulation sought to address the problems with respect to elections to the boards of non-Muslim foundations, which could not be held regularly due to membership diminution. Yet the progress made was only limited, as discretionary powers remained in the hands of state authorities.[91]

The "Working Group on Minority and Cultural Rights" Report
The Content of the Report
While the state administration showed it was slow to adapt to the constitutional and legislative reforms, a new debate on Turkish national identity rose at the intellectual level.[92] A report prepared by the "Working Group on Minority Rights and Cultural Rights," a committee working under the Office of the Prime Minister, acted as a catalyst of this debate. This report, which became public on October 17, 2004, referred to key issues related to Turkish national identity and sparked a wide intellectual debate.[93]

The report attempted to heal the fundamental contradiction of Turkish national identity, which combined elements of territorial and ethnic nationalism, by advocating a purely civic national identity. It started with a short intellectual history of the term "minority" in the international and domestic context. It then pointed out that, following the Lausanne Treaty, Turkey recognized the existence of minorities only on a religious—and not ethnic or linguistic—basis. Turkey maintained the same defensive approach by insisting on reservations to international treaties relevant to minority rights. Nevertheless, increased interest in minority rights since the end of the Cold War meant that Turkey's approach was at odds with the dominant international view. It was argued that the existence of minority group members within states should be treated as an objective fact rather than being subject to state definitions. The international community was interested in the protection of the fundamental rights of minority members. What remained within the discretion of the state was whether minority status would be acknowledged to a group of minority members. [94]

The report then stated that the Lausanne Treaty was not fully implemented with regard to the human rights of non-Muslim minorities as well as all the Turkish citizens. For example, linguistic minority rights granted under Article 39§4 of the Lausanne Treaty (see p. 137) were not fully acknowledged to Turkish citizens of, for instance, Kurdish origin, until the adoption of the EU reform packages in 2002–3. The reasons for these restrictions were to be found in constitutional stipulations that gave absolute priority to national integrity over minority and cultural rights. The report argued that this monolithic approach to national identity denied the existence of different constitutive ethnic identities and was, therefore, essentially undemocratic. It then went on to list a number of laws and court decisions where discrimination against minorities and an ethnic understanding of Turkish national identity were clear. As reasons for the narrow and false understanding of the minority issue in Turkey, the report listed the following:

- Turkey did not follow global developments in minority definition and law and remains loyal to the 1923 regime. In fact, Turkey misinterpreted even the Treaty of Lausanne itself.
- The acceptance of a different minority identity was considered tantamount to the recognition of minority status or rights. However, the first was an objective situation, while the second was a state affair.
- "Internal self-determination," which was synonymous with democracy, was understood as "external self-determination," which was synonymous with secession. As a result of this, recognition of different identities was considered tantamount to state disintegration.
- Monism and unity were perceived to be synonymous when referring to the nation. It was not understood that national monism gradually harms national unity.
- While talking about the Turks, it was not seen that the term "Turk" was simultaneously understood as an ethnic—in fact, religious—group.[95]

The report identified a conceptual and a historic-political reason for this situation. The first had to do with the relationship between a primary state identity *(ust-kimlik)* and a secondary ethnic or religious identity *(alt-kimlik)* in republican Turkey. While state identity was "Ottoman" in the imperial era, in the republican era it became "Turkish." This state identity identified the citizen in terms of ethnicity and even religion. This allowed for ethnic kin abroad to be called "Turks," while non-Muslim minorities were called "citizens" and not "Turks." This situation alienated all those citizens who were not of Turkish ethnic origin. If there had been a state identity based on origin "from Turkey [*Turkiyeli*]," this problem would not have existed. As this identity would exclusively refer to the principle of "territory" and not "blood," it would treat all ethnic, religious, and other identities equally. In this respect, the report referred to the 1924 Constitution, which—in contrast to the 1982 Constitution—used the term "people of Turkey" in a way similar to the term *Turkiyeli*. This state identity would separate the concepts of "nation" and "citizenship" and would incorporate all ethnic or religious identities without exception.[96] The historic-political reason was what is referred to as the Sevres syndrome (see p. 78). The fear of Turkey's partition in a fashion similar to that brought about by the Sevres Treaty created anxiety and strengthened the appeal of conspiracy theories. This seriously hampered the recognition of minority and cultural rights, as any similar requests were stigmatized as attempts to partition Turkey. The report argued that the reactionary mentality of the opponents of reform was similar to the mentality of those who opposed Kemalist reforms in the 1920s and 1930s.[97]

In conclusion, the report argued that despite serious attempts to create a monocultural, homogeneous nation in Turkey, a mosaic of identities and cultures survived. It added that Ataturk's "contemporary civilization" thesis now referred to Europe of the 2000s. The European multi-identity, multicultural, democratic, liberal and plural social model had to been taken as a paradigm. In view of this, a series of rights should be recognized—notably the right to individual freedoms, the right to freely participate in economic and social activities, the right to participate in the state, and the right to cultural pluralism. To implement these principles, the following steps should be taken:

- The Constitution and the relevant legislation needed to be rewritten with a liberal, plural and democratic content and with the participation of civil society.
- The right of the citizens with a different identity and culture to protect and develop their own identities should be protected on the basis of equal rights of citizenship.
- Central and local government should become transparent and democratize on the basis of citizens' participation and control.
- International agreements and fundamental documents that contained norms of human rights and freedoms, especially the Framework Convention of the Council of Europe, should be signed and implemented without reservation. Subsequently, statements denying ethnic and religious identities in Turkey should be abandoned.

The Opposition to the Report

The publication of this report caused widespread public interest. It attracted ardent support as well as vehement opposition, since it touched upon extremely sensitive issues. Nationalist groups formed the backbone of the opposition to reform, which included members of Parliament, civil and military officials, and trade unions and other NGOs. Apart from procedural objections, the report was attacked for advocating the replacement of the Turkish by a *Turkiyeli* state identity. It was argued that a Turkish state identity incorporated all ethnic and religious identities and that reducing Turks to an ethnic group was tantamount to rewriting history and simplistic.[98] Others argued that this report sought to terminate the Lausanne Treaty. According to this view, Turkey had—like any other state—the exclusive right to name its minorities, which it had done in the Lausanne Treaty.[99] Many argued that the acceptance of such a proposal would mean the abolition of the unitary character of the Turkish Republic. The transformation of Turkey into a federal, binational state[100] would then comprise only a transitory stage toward the partition of the country on ethnic lines. Soon top-ranking state officials joined the debate, condemning the report. The President of the Republic Ahmet Necdet Sezer argued, "Promoting—apart from cultural rights—ethnic, religious, and confessional differences of communities that live together could harm national unity and disintegrate the nation-state. . . . In the unitary state, country, nation, and sovereignty are single, indivisible. The founding and real element of the Republic of Turkey is the Turkish nation."[101]

The Chief of the General Staff General Hilmi Ozkok pointed out that "Turkey is a unitary state with a monist character. By saying 'How happy is one who says 'I am a Turk,' Ataturk based the Republic on a primary identity [*ust-kimlik*] foundation that integrates religious and ethnic differences."[102]

According to these views, the term "Turk" combined the principles of state and ethnic identity.[103] A more extreme view was expressed by the Commander of the First Army General Hursit Tolon. Tolon first wondered what a minority in Turkey is. He then added that "everyone had rights as a Turkish citizen" and that "no one had rights above Turkish citizenship."[104] The government at first hesitated to take a clear position and then sided with the other state officials who expressed their disagreement with the content of the report. To sum up, the report was seen as an aberration from the Lausanne Treaty that questioned Turkey's unitary nature and territorial integrity, as the Sevres Treaty had attempted to do at the end of the First World War.

The Supporters of the Report

On the other hand, the report attracted strong support from parts of the media, NGO representatives, and the intelligentsia. The idea of being *"Turkiyeli"* was fervently supported by a by a large number of intellectuals who saw it as the best way to resolve Turkey's Kurdish question. The development of a purely civic national identity would allow the sharing of this identity by all the Republic's citizens. The most comprehensive defense of the report was given by one of its main drafters, Professor Baskin Oran. In Oran's view, the report did not aim to abolish the Lausanne Treaty and restore the Sevres Treaty. On the contrary, the report showed that Turkey did not fulfill several of its obligations under the Lausanne Treaty. Turkey's compliance with these obligations, for instance with Article 39§4, which guaranteed the freedom to use any language, would greatly improve the contemporary minority rights situation in Turkey.[105] As regards the nature of the Turkish state and its territorial integrity, Oran argued that the report advocated neither the abolition of Turkey's unitary state system, nor its partition. On the contrary, the principle of state territorial integrity was described as natural and nonnegotiable. Moreover, the introduction of a measure of voluntarism in the notion of identity, which was one of the goals of the report, would strengthen the state. With respect to accusations that the report wished to create new minorities and divide the Turkish people, Oran replied that the existence of a minority is an objective fact, independent of the eye of the beholder or his wishes. However, the term "minority" had to be relieved of the negative connotation it had accumulated since the Ottoman era.[106] It should not be synonymous with the non-Muslim minorities or being a "second-class citizen" or "secessionist."[107] Finally, Oran stressed that the suggestion to introduce the term *Turkiyeli* allowed those minorities that did not identify themselves with the Turkish ethnic group to identify themselves with the state. Despite its relative success, the Turkish primary state identity (*ust-kimlik*) failed to unite the whole population of the Turkish Republic. Since forced assimilation policies were impossible in the age of globalization and in the context of Turkey's EU membership negotiations, the Turkish state needed to accommodate itself to the existence of multiple ethnic and religious identities that could be united under a single *Turkiyeli* identity. In his view, the introduction of this term would not divide but rather unite all the citizens of the Republic regardless of ethnic or religious identity. It would also become the symbol of a liberal democratic, pluralist mentality, signs of which were already given by Ataturk in the 1920s when he preferred to use the term "people of Turkey [*Turkiye halki*]" instead of "Turkish people [*Turk halki*]."[108]

Oran's arguments enjoyed wide support from NGOs, liberal columnists, and intellectuals. Violent protests and threats against the report and its drafters, as well as the government's unwillingness to prevent them,[109] were condemned by numerous intellectuals and NGOs.[110] Several arguments were developed in support of the report. The absence of a real ethnic basis of Turkish national identity[111] demonstrated the need to overcome the myth of common ethnic descent of all Turkish citizens and to establish a civic national identity. The importance of ending all ethnic and religious discrimination and extending minority rights to all minority groups—not only to those mentioned in the Lausanne Treaty—became clear.[112] Other columnists argued that Turkish political discourse would benefit from a clarification of the term "minority" and the removal of the negative implications it had acquired in the late Ottoman and republican years.[113] Minority rights should be dissociated from the idea of partition and external self-determination.[114] Turkish officials should abandon their phobic approach to minority issues.[115] The reluctance of existing minority groups to identify themselves as such should be dealt with so that minority rights ceased to be purely a function of Turkey's Kurdish problem.[116] Others pointed out that the proposed state identity had certain similarities with the late Ottoman state identity.[117] The adoption of the term *Turkiyeli* would improve Turkey's stability, as it would have a unifying influence on the people. Non-Muslim and other minorities would no more be seen as the "other within us [*icimizdeki oteki*]" or as "local foreigners [*yerli yabancilar*]," but as full and equal citizens.[118]

The publication of this report comprised a milestone in the identity debate. The report succeeded in summarizing the basic problems of mainstream Turkish national ideology and suggesting daring redefinitions of Turkish national identity. The public debate sparked as a result of this report was both interesting and polarized. The arguments of both supporters and opponents were indicative of the intellectual discourse developing in Turkish society.

The Stance of Social Actors

The State Elites
The stance of the bureaucracy on the liberalization of the national identity discourse in Turkey was generally not constructive. The survival of an illiberal mentality meant that the implementation of these

measures would not always be wholehearted. Difficulties in implementation often led to the need for amendments to reduce the discretionary powers of the administration. In general, the military, the civil administration, the courts, and the police were not receptive to calls for raising the standards of minority protection to the European level. Parts of the judiciary also became enclaves of resistance against liberalization. While liberal intellectuals were often indicted for comments that did not abide by the official Turkish position on sensitive national issues, ultraright mobsters received an extremely soft treatment by judicial authorities. In late August 2005, Orhan Pamuk, one of the most famous Turkish writers and would-be 2007 Nobel Laureate in Literature, was indicted[119] under Article 301§1 of the Turkish Penal Code for insulting the Turkish nation.[120] A few days later, on September 6, 2005, a group of nationalists who violently interrupted a photograph exhibition to commemorate the fiftieth anniversary of the 1955 pogrom against the Istanbul minorities, were released on the following day with minor material damage charges at the clear discretion of judicial authorities, although they could have been detained or prosecuted for much heavier criminal offenses.[121] Both incidents showed that the stance of a part of the judiciary was still incompatible with a liberal approach to the issue of national identity.[122] The practices of the General Directorate of Foundations regarding the property rights of non-Muslim minority foundations, especially in the cases where legal reform gave room to its discretionary powers, were characteristic of an enduring approach. The Directorate officials still viewed non-Muslim minorities as "internal enemies [*ic dusmanlar*]" or threats to domestic security and the territorial integrity of the state on much the same lines as their predecessors. Hence, the confiscation of minority property and the subsequent weakening of the economic position of the minorities were seen as a contribution to state security. Even the renaming of Turkish fauna species to eliminate references to Turkey's minority populations was seen by Turkish bureaucrats as a measure protecting the unitary nature of the state.[123]

Similar views affected both radicals and moderates in the armed forces. In May 2003, a secret report, drafted by the Secretary General of the MGK General Tuncer Kilinc clearly opposed even the hesitant liberalization steps of minority legislation included in the sixth reform package.[124] While General Ozkok defended the unitary character of the Turkish state and the monist character of national identity in October 2004,[125] other generals went even further, warning against the consequences that the recognition of minority rights would have for Turkey's security. General Tolon disputed in November 2004 the existence of any minorities in Turkey, arguing that everyone was a first-class citizen.[126] The ambivalence in reforming legislation regarding minority-language broadcasting and education and the minimal character of the measures finally implemented showed that military views found support in the state broadcasting authority and civil administration. Similarly, the judiciary sometimes interpreted liberalizing amendments in a way that contradicted the spirit of the law.[127] Last but not least, the incidents of extrajudicial killings by security forces in southeastern Turkey were reduced in numbers but did not disappear.[128]

Nonetheless, this should not lead to the conclusion that there were no reformist minds within the ranks of the bureaucracy. The Foreign Ministry and the General Secretariat for the European Union included a number of officials who were in favor of liberalization. Their role was crucial in the drafting and implementation of reform of the legislation regarding the minorities.[129] However, they were often not powerful enough to ignore calls to compromise their reform program.

The Intelligentsia

The liberal intelligentsia played a crucial role as an advocate of the liberalization of laws affecting the minorities and the adoption of a new basis for Turkish national identity. Benefiting from the more liberal political environment in the 1990s, columnists, academics, and NGO leaders started addressing the problematic status of minority rights protection in Turkey. Despite the escalating crisis with the PKK, many intellectuals stressed the need for a peaceful resolution of the Kurdish issue and full respect for minority rights in Turkey. Their main argument was that minority rights violations did not improve Turkish security but only increased the appeal of Kurdish extremists to the mass of Turkey's Kurdish population.[130] Their requests were not always welcomed, as nationalist reactions were often powerful. Nonetheless, the public appeal of their argument rose as governments started to implement reform measures in a slow and piecemeal fashion, following increasing international and EU pressure. The boldest part of the agenda of liberal intellectuals came to the fore with the publication of the "Working Group on Minority and Cultural Rights" report. This report was a product of this intellectual fermentation and epitomized the liberal answers to the minority and national identity questions of republican Turkey. Academics like Ibrahim Kaboglu and Baskin Oran were joined by a number of the NGOs that were represented in the Working Group in advocating liberal reform. What was more pathbreaking was that the Working Group that produced this report was—albeit loosely—connected with the Office of the Prime Minister. Although the government took pains to dissociate itself from the report and its content, it was important to see that such views gained a semiofficial status for the first time. The fervent support of the report proposals by a significant number of columnists and the intense intellectual debate on the base of Turkish national identity also showed that these views were shared by a considerable part of the country's intellectual elite. This intelligentsia succeeded in familiarizing public opinion with liberal political ideas. In this effort, it was joined by liberal media and business capital, such as the newspapers *Radikal* and *Birgun*, the magazine *Birikim*, and numerous columnists and commentators in most Turkish media, as well as several business corporations that are members of TUSIAD. The dedemonization of the term "minority" was followed by proposals to reshape Turkish national identity, which would make it inclusive and tolerant of ethnic and religious differences.[131] Turkey's liberal intelligentsia succeeded in pointing out that security problems could not be solved only by military means but by engaging Turkey's minority populations, eliminating the discrimination between first- and second-class citizens and making them feel Turkey to be their own country.[132] Full recognition of minority rights would not be detrimental but rather beneficial to Turkish national security.

The Incidence of Social Learning

The liberalization of the discourse on minorities and national identity was also felt in the liberal shift of the positions of several social actors with regard to minority rights and the nature of national identity. While the bureaucracy largely remained an obstacle to liberalization and expressed deep concerns about the reconsideration of the basis of Turkish national identity, it was no more a unitary actor. Fragmentation became apparent when, in the course of EU-Turkey negotiations, a considerable number of Foreign Ministry bureaucrats joined the cause of political liberalization and attempted to reshape state policies in a more liberal fashion. Their attempts, however, were not always successful. Political liberalization was no longer something to fear but on the contrary a useful tool to pursue the national interest successfully.

The position of the AKP government was also significantly affected. Although in autumn 2004 he had carefully distanced himself from the report of the "Working Group on Minority and Cultural Rights," Prime Minister Erdogan made an impressive opening toward Turkey's

Kurds during his visit to Diyarbakir in August 2005.[133] He admitted the existence of a Kurdish problem in Turkey and argued that denying the existence of such a problem did not befit Turkey. He also linked the Kurdish question with the general problem of democratization in Turkey. He suggested that, like many other problems in Turkey, the Kurdish issue should be should be dealt within the framework of Turkey's democratization process. He also admitted that the state had made serious political and administrative mistakes in its treatment of citizens of Kurdish descent and other social groups in the past. He added, however, that no such mistakes could serve as pretext for supporting terrorism.[134]

Erdogan's statements marked a milestone in Turkish politics. For the first time a Prime Minister openly spoke about a Kurdish problem in Turkey and admitted past errors in the treatment of the Kurdish and other minorities by the state. The reactions of social actors to Erdogan's comments confirmed the existence of deep divisions within Turkish society. While Kurdish intellectuals and political leaders,[135] Turkish liberals, and associations like TUSIAD[136] fully supported his statements, Erdogan was openly criticized by the CHP leader Deniz Baykal,[137] who accused him of "flirting with the terrorists." President Ahmet Necdet Sezer and the military members of the MGK also indirectly opposed Erdogan's initiative by insisting on the conventional state policy on the Kurdish issue.[138] Despite these reactions, Erdogan's statements were a very daring step toward resetting the agenda of the minority question in Turkey. His remarks suggested that a new, more liberal approach toward the minority question was emerging in the Turkish government.

Civil society was more profoundly but unevenly affected. Although traits of illiberal thought with regard to minority rights could be traced even among members of minority associations (see p. 142), the process of EU reform made many NGOs aware of the need to protect minority rights and adopt a more inclusive basis of national identity. These NGOs, such as the Human Rights Association (*Insan Haklari Dernegi*—IHD) and the Human Rights Foundation of Turkey (*Turkiye Insan Haklari Vakfi*—TIHV), became increasingly active in collecting evidence of minority rights violations and campaigning for legal measures that would put an end to them. The ensuing debate led to a state of creative confusion where old taboos were challenged and inclusive solutions were sought. Meanwhile, citizens' interest in their own ethnic and religious heritage rose. The October 2004 "Working Group on Minority and Cultural Rights" report was drafted and approved with the support of several NGOs that were members of the Working Group. Their support included even the most sensitive point of the report, which referred to the removal of any ethnic element from Turkish national identity. A large segment of civil society proved ready to adopt the cause of political liberalization in the fields of minority rights and identity politics and to defend it.

Conclusions

Path dependence theory is helpful in better understanding the recent developments in the field of minority rights and national identity debates in Turkey. While in the 1980s the existence of a Kurdish minority in Turkey was persistently denied and the use of Kurdish language banned, the reform process launched under the pressure of convergence with the Copenhagen Criteria since 1999 led to changes whose costs of reversal became increasingly high. The reform process certainly benefited from the arrest of the PKK leader Abdullah Ocalan, the military defeat of the PKK forces, and the declaration of a unilateral ceasefire in 1999. However, when the PKK resumed its operations in 2004, a regression to past repressive legislative and administrative measures seemed to be off the agenda. The resumption of violence by the PKK in 2004 failed to have any visible negative effects in the process of liberalizing minority rights. People continued to argue in favor of Kurdish minority rights and support the idea of a civic Turkish national identity.

CHAPTER 7

CONCLUSIONS

PROSPECTS OF TURKISH POLITICAL CULTURE

THEORETICAL CONSIDERATIONS

Path Dependence and Turkish Political Culture

The study of EU-sponsored political reform in Turkey in the previous chapters made it clear that path dependence theory could help explain the process of liberalization of Turkish political culture.[1] Turkey's approach to the European Union required a series of political decisions, which entailed, among other things, a reconsideration of state-civil society relations, the civilianization of politics, and a new approach to secularism and national identity. As Turkey was making steps toward convergence with the Copenhagen Criteria, it became increasingly difficult to change direction and relapse to old policies and practices. The Helsinki European Council decision in December 1999 became a landmark event. Giving Turkey the status of an EU candidate state had a critical and enduring facilitating impact on the process of political liberalization.[2] The increasingly realistic prospect of EU membership gave Turkey a political vision, while the Copenhagen Criteria became the yardstick against which any reform steps were measured. The increasing commitment of the 1999–2002 coalition government to Turkey's EU accession process meant that it was willing to undertake daring reform measures to meet this target. The more the government invested political capital in the prospect of EU membership, the more difficult it became to reverse the process of political liberalization. The possibility of a rejection of Turkey's EU membership bid would have disastrous consequences for the electoral fate of all coalition government partners. The opposition of Turkish Euro-skeptic groups was already a "sunk cost" for the government.[3] In other words, as the government knew that it would not enjoy any support from Euro-skeptics anyway, it did not hesitate to take measures that could further alienate them. The number of choices the government was able to make was diminishing, and a precedent was emerging that no government was in a position to ignore. This observation became even more valid for the new AKP government, which was elected in November 2002. The challenged political legitimacy of the AKP and its leader Recep Tayyip Erdogan fixed the new administration even more firmly on the path of EU membership. Fearing that the bureaucratic establishment would attempt to ban the AKP—like its predecessors, the RP and the FP—and permanently exclude its leadership from active political participation, the AKP government resumed the reform process with even greater zeal and resolve.[4] As public expectations rose, the price of a policy of protecting the status quo and disengaging Turkey from the prospect of EU membership became exorbitant. Moreover, the oppositional position that part of the bureaucracy took toward the AKP government also facilitated the reform process. The opposition of the bureaucracy was an additional "sunk cost" for the AKP government. Hence, it only had a minor impact on the reform process.[5] Steps toward the legitimation of civil society, the acceptance of ethnic diversity, the civilianization of politics, and a less assertive role of the state in religious affairs created a condition that made a relapse to the status quo ante virtually impossible.

The process of liberalizing Turkey's political culture, which was launched with the series of reform packages aiming to make Turkey meet the Copenhagen Criteria created a dynamic situation, which the government could not ignore. The emergence of a more effective civil society and the social legitimation of its role was a fait accompli. Improvements in the constitutional protection of the freedom of association and the promulgation of a new, more liberal Law on Associations were decisions corresponding not only to the Copenhagen Criteria, but also to the demands of Turkish society (see p. 59). As the process of political liberalization was strengthening civil society, it became increasingly difficult for any government to reverse the process. The speed of reform might have been contingent upon issues arising, but the direction was never questioned by most Turkish opinion.

The effect on the process of civilianization of politics was similar. The role of the military and the civil bureaucracy on political decision-making was challenged by liberal intellectuals and a significant part of civil society. As the European Commission reports repeatedly noted, there was a need to curtail the powers of the MGK, reform the judicial system, and eliminate the supremacy of the bureaucracy. Hence, governments realized the necessity of liberal reform. Initial steps that entailed the removal of military judges from the DGM and the establishment of the General Secretariat for the European Union culminated with the abolition of the DGM and the appointment of a civilian in the position of the Secretary General of the MGK (see p. 83). Although these measures did not mean the end of the tutelary role of the state elite, they signaled a major change in the relations between state and society.

As regards the role of religion in politics, the European Commission reports did not pay special attention to this beyond insisting on the protection of the rights of religious minorities (see p. 137). Consequently, legal reforms were not as far reaching, although the reform of Article 312 of the Penal Code did allow for more religious manifestations in the public sphere. Nevertheless, the overall political liberalization process had a significant impact on the level of public discourse on secularism. Although the European Union did not explicitly attack the illiberal character of Kemalist secularism, but only some of its most extreme aspects that constituted violations of fundamental human rights, it sparked a domestic debate on the need to introduce a liberal version of secularism that would respect manifestations of religious belief in the public space (see p. 112). The increasing popularity of liberal ideas among Turkish Islamist intellectuals and its adoption by the AKP in its program provided ample evidence for the emergence of a liberal discourse regarding state-religion relations.

Finally, on the issue of national identity, the European Commission reports exerted considerable pressure, describing numerous human rights violations of several minority groups and stressing the need for urgent reform on this issue. Early reforms involving reluctant constitutional amendments and legal reforms were followed by much more comprehensive ones. The lifting of the ban on teaching and broadcasting minority languages was matched by the recognition of the primacy of international law over the constitution on all issues, including human and minority rights. As minorities benefited from their newly acknowledged rights, it was increasingly difficult to reverse the process. The initiated liberalization process peaked with the publication of the report of the "Working Group on Minority Rights and Cultural Rights," which daringly set the agenda of a new, inclusive national identity in Turkey. The lively debate that followed was unprecedented in the history of republican Turkey and showed that political liberalism had infiltrated large parts of the society and the state to the point that a free discussion on even the most sensitive issue of national identity could be held (see p. 151). It was now impossible to support views that claimed the absence of any minorities in Turkey, with the exception of non-Muslims, or the "Turkishness of the 'so-called Kurdish minority,'" which had been advocated by state authorities and intellectuals until the early 1990s. This created conditions for the smooth transition of Turkish political culture from an essentially subject toward an increasingly participant model. While citizens used to adopt a much more submissive and deferential position, it now became increasingly difficult for them to revert to their previous views of state-society relations and their political role as individuals.

The Applicability of Historical Institutionalism

The European Union has probably been the primary reason for the progress made toward the liberalization of Turkish political culture. This comprises additional evidence for the validity of institutionalist theories that have tried to explain the formation of the European Union. Unlike its member states, whose views and policies over EU-Turkey relations often fluctuated, the European Union, through its main institutional representative, the European Commission, followed a distinct policy line that had a significant role in the liberalization of Turkish political culture.

The European Commission
The European Commission turned out to be a crucial actor in facilitating the liberalization of Turkish political culture. Through its annual reports from 1998 onwards, the Commission provided an accurate indicator of the shortcomings of Turkish democracy and also pointed to the areas in which reform was needed. When the reports commented on the lack of an effective legal framework for civil society, the institutionalized and informal political role of the military, the excesses of Turkey's laic regime, or the violations of ethnic and religious minority rights, they defined the steps that Turkish governments were expected to take. The criticism included in the reports was generally constructive and fair and provided Turkey with valuable reform guidelines. The distinct role of the Commission regarding the transformation of Turkish political culture could be attributed to its partial autonomy and unique political horizon.

Although the European Commission had been established by the EU member states to serve the specific political goals the member states had indicated, it soon succeeded in developing new competences and authority. Despite the efforts made by the European Council to keep all powers in the hands of member states, the Commission was able to develop its own political role and powers. The Commission turned its bureaucratic privilege of agenda-setting into an influential political tool. Through its leverage in setting the discursive content of EU politics, the Commission acquired and exerted a considerable political influence. It acquired additional leverage through its role as "process manager." The implementation of European Council decisions and the drafting of complex regulations and directives was a task assigned to the Commission, which in turn gave it important leverage.[6] Its powers also grew as a result of the inertia of rotating EU presidencies. Many smaller EU member states that took over the presidency had insufficient diplomatic infrastructure to deal with the complexity of European foreign policy issues. Thus, they de facto assigned the work of their own diplomatic services to the Commission.[7] The empowerment of the Commission had a facilitative impact on Turkey's political reform process.

The different time horizons of the European Commission and the member states was a second reason for the Commission's role in leading the transformation of Turkish political culture. While decision makers of member states were interested in the short-term consequences of their political actions, the Commission enjoyed the luxury of being able to plan long-term strategies. While the prospect of imminent parliamentary elections and the fear of popular discontent frequently became the most important factor in the member states' shaping of EU policies, the Commission was exempt from such considerations. Since changes in the party composition of the governments of member states often meant changes in political positions, the Commission was characterized by a stronger sense of institutional continuity and a longer-term view of European political developments.[8] This distinction became crucial in the case of EU-Turkey relations. The initially positive approach of many member state governments toward the process of Turkey's EU engagement and eventual accession in some cases dwindled under the pressure of hostile public opinion toward the idea of Turkey's accession. The rise of far-right, anti-immigrant political movements in several countries of Western Europe that used their opposition to Turkey's EU accession process in their domestic political campaigns alarmed center-right parties throughout Europe. Fearing electoral losses to their right, these parties increasingly took circumspect, neutral, or even negative positions on Turkey's full EU membership. This happened just as Turkey seemed to be fulfilling the criteria for the start of accession negotiations, which gave its membership a realistic perspective. In contrast to the vacillating view of many member state governments, the Commission held to a steady position based on the principle of conditionality. This allowed the Commission to lead the process of EU-Turkey relations and preempt the decisions of the European Council on the issue in December 2002 and December 2004.

The European Parliament
The European Parliament has admittedly lacked the institutional powers and political clout that it should have exercised, given that it is the only popularly elected organ of the European Union. This became even clearer in the case of the Eastern enlargement, in which the Parliament was restricted to a rather passive role of following political developments and decisions made by other European bodies.[9] Nonetheless, the Parliament proved to be unusually active and influential regarding EU-Turkey relations.[10] By preparing reports and promulgating resolutions, the Parliament claimed its own distinct political role. This could be seen a part of its search for an increased role in issues of EU enlargement, foreign policy, and human rights.[11] Although its stance had been very critical during the 1990s, pointing at violations of human rights in Turkey,[12] its position shifted in view of the progress that the reform process had made. The Morillon, Lamassoure, and Oostlander reports all criticized Turkey's human rights record, emphasizing the violations of Kurdish minority rights, but also recognized the steps made through the reform process.

The latest EU Parliament report was prepared by the Dutch MEP Camiel Eurlings on the eve of the December 2004 European Council decision and recommended the start of accession negotiations with Turkey. The status of human rights in Turkey, the Kurdish question, and issues that were not explicitly raised in the Commission reports, such as the recognition of the Armenian genocide by the Turkish state, became part of heated debate during the Parliament's plenary session. On December 13, 2004, only four days before the crucial decision of the European Council, the Parliament approved the Eurlings report by secret vote and a wide margin. Although the parliamentary resolution was not binding for the European Council, it greatly facilitated its decision on the start of accession negotiations with Turkey. By setting an impeccable standard for the protection of human and minority rights and using its democratic legitimation to support the

start of accession negotiations, the European Parliament had a significant impact on the process of political reform and the liberalization of
Turkish political culture.

Two-Level Games and Political Culture

The impact of the European Union on the transformation of Turkish political culture can be better understood if negotiations between
the European Union and Turkey regarding Turkey's prospective EU
membership are conceptualized as a two-level game.[13] Negotiations
between the European Union and a candidate member state differ
from regular negotiations in that what is pursued is not a commonly
accepted median point but rather the convergence of the candidate
state to preset EU standards. Nonetheless, there is still room for negotiation on what constitutes "convergence" with the Copenhagen Criteria, which allows for the application of the two-level game model.
In the case of EU-Turkey relations, negotiations gained momentum
in the aftermath of the 1999 Helsinki European Council decision.[14] A
vicious circle of failed negotiations and reform efforts was turned into
a virtuous one.[15] In the Accession Partnership agreements of 2001 and
2003, the European Union and Turkey agreed upon a reform agenda
that was to be implemented by Turkey on its way to the start of accession negotiations. This created a framework for negotiations that had
already commenced. At the international level (Level I), the coalition
government (1999–2002) and the AKP government (2002–5) negotiated with the EU institutions, while at the domestic level (Level II),
the governments negotiated with domestic political actors—namely
civil and military bureaucracy, parliament, civil society, and public
opinion—on the implementation of the agreement. On the European
side, the European institutions negotiating Turkey's prospective EU
membership (Level I) were dealing at the same time with the governments, parliaments, and public opinions of member states (Level II).

   At the domestic level (Level II), supporters of political liberalization
have always existed in Turkey, yet their political power was limited and
insufficient to bring about any serious political change. Nonetheless,
the shift of negotiation to the international level (Level I) changed the
domestic power balance and allowed supporters of liberalization to
pursue their own conception of national interest in the international
context.[16] As the government agreed that Turkey should comply with
the Copenhagen Criteria before the start of accession negotiations,
domestic proponents of liberal reform were strengthened. The commonly accepted strategic target of Turkey's EU membership induced

the opponents of political liberalization to consent to liberal reform. While parts of the bureaucracy, civil society, and public opinion viewed Turkey's liberal openings as concessions and a part of a package deal between the European Union and Turkey, Turkish liberals were—in effect—allied with the EU position.[17] They saw liberalization measures as a long-expected and essential step in the process of Turkey's democratic consolidation.

Similarly, the need of Turkey and the European Union to arrange for the start of accession negotiations helped both sides reach agreement. According to the two-level game approach, "the lower the cost of no-agreement to constituents, the smaller the win-set."[18] In other words, if the negotiating parties can afford to end the negotiation without an agreement, then the probability of an agreement is reduced. In this case, the Turkish government was more in need of an agreement that would pave the way for accession negotiations. Given that the expectations of public opinion had already been raised, any failure to reach an agreement with the European Union would be considered a serious failure that would jeopardize the future of the incumbent government as well as political and economic stability. In this respect, Turkey's "win-set,"[19] the set of possible agreements with the European Union that could be accepted at the domestic level, was relatively big but not without limits. Some reforms that appeared to go too far were very hard to accept because of the reaction of the state elite (see p. 86). The EU institutions were interested in an agreement, as this would manifest the inclusive, liberal, secular, values–based character of the European Union and would bring a state with serious economic and social problems, but equally large potential, into the Union. On the other hand, the "win-set" of the EU institutions was limited by the need to protect the essentially liberal character of the reform process, as well as the circumspect—if not inimical—stance of the parliaments and public opinions of several member states regarding Turkey's EU membership. The final agreement reached on December 17, 2004, lay at the intersection of both win-sets. In other words, the essentially liberal character of the reform was compromised by a more tolerant approach toward democratic consolidation, which was still clearly unfinished. For example, persisting problems with regard to religious freedom, minority rights, and the role of the military in politics did not deter the 2004 Brussels European Council from giving Turkey a date for the start of accession negotiations. This allowed the liberalization process to strike deeper roots and to continue affecting political culture.

The observation that "the size of the win-set depends on the distribution of power, preferences and possible coalitions among Level II constituents"[20] was also applicable in the case of EU-Turkey relations. When the Turkish government negotiated, its leverage was also influenced by domestic factors.[21] A considerable faction within the civil and military bureaucracy in Turkey was eager to criticize any liberal reform that could be interpreted as compromising national security or sovereignty. Minority rights, secularism, civilianization of politics, and a greater emphasis on the individual rather than the "communal" interest were all issues addressed by the liberalization reform program in a fashion that upset many bureaucrats. The record of three "hard" and one "soft" coup between 1960 and 2004 provided the government with ample reasons for concern when it negotiated the process of liberal reform at the domestic level (Level II). Ironically, this strengthened the negotiating position of the government at the international level (Level I).[22] The credibility of military threat against the incumbent government that could undo any liberalization efforts and bring Turkey back to its authoritarian past increased the negotiation leverage of the government vis-à-vis the European Union.

This became even clearer when the AKP government took over power in November 2002. The weak domestic position of a government of a party whose leader had been banned from politics and risked being shut down by the Constitutional Court showed the European side that too much pressure on the AKP government to accelerate the reform process could bring about the exactly opposite results. The AKP government could be replaced—by democratic or undemocratic means—by a government that would be much less willing to pursue political liberalization.[23] This made the European Union often turn a blind eye to some of the shortcomings of the AKP reform program, especially its implementation.[24] This pragmatic approach allowed for the continuation of the liberal reform process and the transformation of political culture.

An Assessment of the EU Role

It would be unfair to argue that the liberalization of Turkish political culture could only be attributed to EU support, since domestic political and social dynamics were also crucial. Like global actors, domestic liberal political forces had—in some cases—a significant impact on the making of liberal reform. On the other hand, it would be equally inaccurate to underestimate the role that the European Union played in accelerating and consolidating the changes once the prospect of Turkey's EU membership became a realistic perspective with the 1999 Helsinki European Council decision.[25] Until 1999, the EU political arguments were barely heard in Turkey, as there was no tangible membership prospect in the near future, but the situation changed significantly thereafter.[26] The European Union provided ample political, financial, and logistic support to Turkish social forces that were committed to further a liberal democratic agenda. Some distortions did occur, such as in the field of civil society, where it could be convincingly argued that the flow of EU funds also led to a shift from voluntarism toward professionalization and a instrumentalist rather than issue-oriented approach. Nonetheless, the importance of EU financial support for political liberalism in Turkish public sphere should not be underestimated (see p. 55).

Legislative Reform

The EU role was even clearer in the case of the reform of the legislative framework. The authoritarian legacy of the 1980 military regime continued to hamper the development of liberal democratic activities throughout the 1980s and 1990s, even though a multiparty democratic system had been restored. The proponents of liberal reform encountered an established view, according to which civil society and the state were viewed in competitive terms. It was feared that the reinforcement of Turkish civil society, political elites, and the empowerment of minorities would inevitably mean the weakening of the Turkish state and the fragmentation of the Turkish people. The reform process was significantly accelerated with the rise to power of the AKP, which showed an unforeseen responsiveness to calls for reforms and willingness to implement the Copenhagen Criteria.[27] An example is the series of reform packages that aimed at the liberalization of minority rights legislation and brought about some considerable changes but failed to resolve the problem of minority rights in Turkey. Being the product of political calculation and compromise between EU requirements and domestic political pressures, reform packages were not bold and far reaching enough. Nonetheless, it was due to European pressure and the need to converge with the Copenhagen Criteria that even this limited reform was made.

The Empowerment of Liberals

The impact of the European Union was significant in another indirect but equally important way. The prospect of EU membership and its requirements empowered Turkish liberal intellectuals, whose long-neglected political agenda became the agenda of Turkey's EU membership process and legitimized their cause. While Turkish liberals lacked any strong political representation that would enable them to pursue liberal reform in minority rights legislation, the decision across the political party spectrum to support Turkey's full EU membership meant that liberal political ideas had to be incorporated into government reform programs. Although Turkish liberals argued, for example, that the reform of minority rights legislation was beneficial per se and should not be viewed as a concession to the European Union, the pace of reform was certainly accelerated because it was seen as a necessary step toward achieving Turkey's EU vocation. Turkish liberal intellectuals and NGOs were then recruited to advise government institutions on improving minority rights. The "Working Group on Minority and Cultural Rights" was only one of three state institutions formed to produce reports on improvement measures in the field of human rights.[28] The report produced by this Working Group was a typical product of liberal political thought, which attempted to tackle the thorny issue of national identity in Turkey from a liberal perspective (see p. 143). The reaction to it showed the limits of political liberalization in Turkey. Yet the publication of such a report was a landmark event. Before the prospect of Turkey's EU membership emerged, it would have been impossible to express such opinions on minority rights issues and Turkish national identity without facing criminal prosecution.[29] Ideas about minority rights protection and civic national identity were linked to the failed Ottomanist project of the late Ottoman years. Even the comments that Prime Minister Ciller had made in 1993 and 1994 pointing toward a Turkiyeli national identity met with vehement reaction and found few supporters (see p. 144). The opening of such a liberal debate within Turkey was a major result of EU influence on Turkey.

The Sense of Irreversibility

What further strengthened the liberalization reform process was the sense of its irreversibility. Liberal democratic ideas had already appeared in the 1960s and 1970s, yet their dissemination was interrupted by two military coups in 1971 and 1980 that altered the course of political developments in a radically authoritarian fashion. However, the growth of liberal democratic movements in the 1990s was protected against an authoritarian backlash. It was the European Union and Turkey's decision to pursue EU membership by complying with the Copenhagen political criteria, which this time guaranteed that any liberalization steps made could not be reversed.[30] Although the implementation of the new legislation might have sometimes lagged behind expectations, this sense of reform irreversibility improved the self-confidence of Turkish reform supporters. The European Union successfully played the role of the anchor of political reform.

THE EU LIBERALIZING EFFECT ON TURKISH POLITICAL CULTURE

European and Turkish Political Cultures Revisited

A juxtaposition of European and Turkish political cultures, before the prospect of Turkey's EU membership became a realistic possibility, would have affirmed that the incomplete liberalization of Turkey's political system had hindered a convergence between European and Turkish political cultures. Putnam's observation that "social context and history profoundly condition the effectiveness of institutions" proved its validity in the Turkish case.[31] It was the liberalizing influence of the European Union that peaked in the years 1999–2004 and allowed for the infusion of participant elements and the transformation of political culture. Citizens gradually abandoned their traditional submissive and deferential stances toward authority and the state, defended their individual rights, and adopted increasingly assertive positions when it came to issues of political participation. This did not mean that political culture underwent a thorough and fundamental transformation. Elements of continuity coexisted with evidence of change, which formed the basis for a gradual transformation of political culture.

Elements of Continuity in Political Culture

Civil Society
Significant steps toward the rehabilitation of civil society in Turkey could not fully eliminate embedded suspicion on the part of some members of the bureaucracy. Civil society was still considered an element divisive of national and communal unity that furthered egotistic individual interests against the greater communal interest. The level of cooperation between the state and civil society associations did not improve greatly, even after the more friendly approach toward civil society adopted by the AKP government. Members of the judiciary often obstructed the implementation of reform by finding pretexts

not to apply new legislation. The opposition of President Ahmet Necdet Sezer and the CHP to the liberalizing Law on Associations comprised additional evidence for the persistence of elements of a subject
political culture that clearly prioritized state over individual interests
and distrusted civil society (see p. 61).

State

The transcendental vision of the state maintained its appeal to a large
part of the state elite. The absolute prioritization of general over particularistic interests as the only way to protect long-term community
interests, a mistrust of the people and its ability to make sound decisions, and a recalcitrant defense of a tutelary role for the state elite
continued to define its perception of state-society relations and the
role of the citizen. The military's insistence on the subordination of
the Chief of General Staff not to the Minister of Defense but directly
to the Prime Minister might have looked like a "shadow battle" but
in fact spoke volumes about the way some of the military still viewed
the civilianization of politics. Political statements by the military on a
variety of domestic political issues were reduced in numbers but never
disappeared. Part of the judiciary was equally resistant to change. Pro-
crastination and indifference to liberal reform was evident in several
court decisions, while statements by high-rank judges showed a clear
lack of liberal democratic understanding. A predominantly subject
political culture continued to define the political outlook of a significant and powerful part of the bureaucratic and military leadership
(see p. 86).[32] The case of the CHP demonstrated the survival of an
allegedly Kemalist, statist, nationalist ideology that opposed Turkey's
European transformation.[33]

The Role of Religion in Politics

For many members of Turkey's state elite the protection of republican
state secularism continued to comprise one of their main missions.
The "soft" coup of February 28, 1997, had reaffirmed zero-tolerance
policies against manifestation of religious belief in the public sphere.
The closure of the RP and the FP and the hardening of state policies
on the issues of headscarf and religious vocational schools were evidence of this approach. The unwillingness of the European Union to
take a clear position on the issue of secularism facilitated this policy.
Court decisions continued to deny any manifestation of religion in the
public sphere, while the military frequently referred to its guardian
role regarding the laic character of the Republic. Meanwhile, the will
of the state elite to maintain the state grip over religion was indicated

through the lack of any reforms of the structure and operation of the Directorate of Religious Affairs, despite increasing concern from the European Union, as well as religious groups (see p. 116). Religion continued to be perceived as a parochial and potentially divisive element of the Turkish social fabric, which had to remain under firm state control. The perceived state interest again prevailed over individual freedoms of religion and expression, which confirmed the predominance of the subject political culture model.

National Identity
The opening of a wide debate on Turkish national identity and minority rights did not mean that established approaches disappeared. On the contrary, insistence on a monoethnic, monocultural, and illiberal model of national identity and opposition to full protection of minority rights characterized the stance of a large part of the civil and military bureaucracy. The practices of the General Directorate of Foundations regarding the property rights of non-Muslim minority foundations and recurring violations of the religious freedom of non-Muslim minorities comprised clear evidence of persistent suspicion and discrimination against non-Muslim populations. Fierce reaction by members of the military against any reform measures that allowed teaching and broadcasting in minority languages, as well as the hesitant and restrictive fashion with which reform laws were applied by the judiciary, showed that the roots of opposition to liberal reform in the fields of minority rights and national identity were deep. Members of the civil and military bureaucracy also formed the backbone of the reaction against the "Working Group on Minority and Cultural Rights" report, pointing out that following the policy suggestions of the report would question Turkish national unity and territorial integrity (see p.146). Laying emphasis on fear-based and essentialist arguments about the divisive role of minorities and the need to forge national unity, and the sacrifice of minority rights for the alleged interest of the nation-state manifested the persistence of a subject political culture.

Evidence of Change in Political Culture

Civil Society
The emergence of elements of a new participant political culture became clear in the transformation of civil society in Turkey. The first step for this was the demystification of the state. The formerly impeccable image of the state came under challenge, and its famed efficiency

and technical superiority were questioned. A growing number of civil society associations were getting involved in a pool of increasingly diverse and complex social activities, thus comprising a formidable counterbalance against the predominance of the state. The rise of a vibrant civil society also benefited from the increasing and unprecedented political mobilization of business capital, which clearly favored liberal political reform. The proliferation of liberal ideas also resulted in fragmentation within the state elite, a significant part of which supported the program of political reform (see p. 60). All these developments supported increased citizens' participation in politics and contributed to the liberalization of political culture.

State

An instrumentalist vision of the state became increasingly popular in the process of EU reform, signaling a shift in Turkish political culture. Liberal views about state-society relations and the role of the citizen gained impetus within a growing segment of the political elites. Politicians, journalists, and civil society leaders attacked deferential attitudes toward the state and stressed the need to renegotiate state-society relations and put the individual into the center. The mainstream view of national security in Turkey was identified as the Trojan horse of the state elite in its effort to maintain its control of the state and tutelary role over society. It was argued that a new, more restrictive definition of national security should be adhered to so the state elite would lose its say on important domestic political issues. The desecuritization of Turkish politics was seen as a precondition for the abolition of the state elites' prerogatives and the reestablishment of state-society relations on a liberal democratic basis. This upsurge of liberal ideas did not leave the state elite unaffected. Fragmentation was observed within the civil and—for the first time—the military bureaucracy, as some of those concerned came to understand that the culmination of Turkey's Westernization process could only come about through its political liberalization and EU membership (see p. 86). The active support of segments of the civil bureaucracy and the acquiescence of the military leadership toward the liberalization reform program were crucial for its continuation and indicated that a more liberal political culture was proliferating, even among representatives of the hard core of the state.

The Role of Religion in Politics

A change in the public discourse on the role of religion in politics became more than apparent under the impact of improving EU-Turkey relations. As the European Commission reports never addressed the question of secularism in Turkey, merely focusing on its most extreme applications in cases where human rights were severely violated, the opening of a debate on secularism in Turkey was an unintended consequence of the liberal reform program.[34] The debate was developed in a more accommodating fashion.[35] Civil society associations and the liberal intelligentsia clearly differentiated for the first time between illiberal laicism and liberal secularism, arguing that respect for the fundamental freedoms of religion and expression would not mean the wholesale abolition of secularism but transition from laicism to a liberal version of secularism (see p. 118). This position found support among Turkey's Islamist elites and found its political expression in the AKP. In the writings of Islamist intellectuals and the AKP program, criticism of laicism was for the first time based not on Islamic but on liberal assumptions. The state was asked to guarantee the protection of the fundamental human rights of its citizens, not by abiding by Islamic legal principles but by adopting a passive version of secularism (see p. 120) Instrumental or real, this shift was still very important and signaled a crucial change in the process of liberalization of Turkish political culture.

National Identity
An unprecedented debate on a variety of topics related to national identity and minorities came as a surprise. The European Commission reports consistently raised the problem of minority rights protection in Turkey. However, the discussion in Turkey went far further and incorporated the question of national identity. Spearheaded by the liberal intelligentsia and media, a public discussion was opened on issues that had been considered taboo ever since the founding of the Republic. The need for Turkey to respect the minority rights of its citizens, not as a concession to the European Union but because this was a basic feature of a democratic state, was clearly expressed. The debate culminated with the publication of the report by the "Working Group on Minority and Cultural Rights," which daringly set the agenda for the resolution of Turkey's minority questions (see p. 151). The publication of this report also made clear that liberal views on these issues had also been adopted by parts of the state bureaucracy. Civil society associations also joined the debate in support of the liberal reform agenda, while citizens' interest in their own ethnic and religious heritage rose. This debate showed that an open and sophisticated discussion of sensitive political issues became

possible in Turkey and that civil society and individuals could be the leaders of this debate. This comprised additional evidence for the infusion of participant elements into Turkish political culture.

A Gradual Shift toward a New Paradigm

These observations corroborate the conclusion that the process of EU-Turkey negotiations has had a distinct liberalizing impact upon Turkish political culture. There has been an ongoing process of social capital accumulation, a shift from a predominantly subject to an increasingly participant model of political culture. As Putnam puts it, "changing formal institutions can change political practice."[36] Turkish political culture has indeed changed, albeit at a slow pace.[37] While Turkey's urgent need to comply with the Copenhagen Criteria and ensure a date for the start of accession negotiations could have important effects, the hearts and minds of citizens, politicians, and bureaucrats can only change with time. As Mehmet Ali Birand puts it, "Old habits die hard. Sacrifice and determination are needed to establish a new system and overcome the network of interests that took years to form among certain groups."[38]

Nevertheless, the gradual weakening of subject and reinforcement of participant elements in Turkish political culture can be affirmed. Before the European Union became a significant actor in Turkish politics and the prospect of Turkey's EU membership a realistic one, Turkish citizens generally showed deference to any state decisions, no matter how undemocratic they were. Military coups and the tutelary role of the military in politics were tolerated as a necessary evil or even approved of. State interests were given absolute priority over individual ones. Civil society was viewed with suspicion as dividing the people and giving undue priority to particularistic over community interests. National homogenization policies were tolerated or accepted as a necessary part of Turkey's modernization, economic development, and national security policy. Tight boundaries were drawn around public expressions of religious belief. Citizens rarely claimed their right to participate in political decision-making processes. Except in elections, they usually entrusted the management of political affairs to "expert" state elites, which were allegedly able to prioritize the long-term community interest over any kind of particularistic interest. Even citizens who did not agree with state policies and practices would rarely bear the burden of responsibility of expressing their opinion publicly or engaging in political activities.

Since the 1999 Helsinki European Council decision gave Turkey tangible prospects for EU membership, Turkish political culture entered a slow but steady process of liberalization. Citizens showed increasing interest in political affairs and participation, and civil society associations grew in numbers and improved in quality. Civil society was viewed as an essential element of a participatory democratic political system. Horizontal networks of civic engagement were developed as a result of the growth of civil society and had a positive impact on the development of public trust and accumulation of social capital. Blind deference toward the state was replaced by a more critical approach, especially when state inefficiency and corruption became evident. Trust of bureaucracy weakened, and bureaucrats were no longer beyond criticism. The absolute prioritization of community over individual interests was questioned. As adherence to democratic principles became increasingly important, political interventions by the military were no more seen as a legitimate exercise of the military's guardian role but as a serious blow to democratic consolidation. Respect for human rights and fundamental freedoms, even to the detriment of state interests, became a social value, and violations of minority rights were no longer ignored. The Turkish political spectrum was also rearranged, as politicians and intellectuals were now identified by their position on political liberalization. New cross-ideology social alliances were formed on the basis of liberal reform and the support for EU membership.

A major shift was also observed in mainstream political Islam. The Islamic political project was apparently abandoned in favor of a liberal, secular, and democratic regime. This signaled a major victory of political liberalism in Turkey, since it showed that Turkey could simultaneously nurture Western European political values and its own cultural identity. It also provided ample evidence that the liberal shift of Turkish political culture had penetrated the whole of Turkish society. This became even clearer with the rise of a new liberal discursive space. The organization of an academic conference on the Armenian question in May 2005, which was intended to include the views of historians who disagree with the Turkish official view of the events, comprised a clear example of this. The conference had to be postponed under state and government pressure, demonstrating the limits of the liberalization process. It finally took place in September 2005 in spite of judicial obstacles. The resolve of these intellectuals to further their liberal agenda became clear in their subsequent statement: "We, the participants of this conference. . . . [want] to especially point out. . . . [that] 'The emergence of different, critical and alternative voices, the demonstration of how Turkey actually contains such a rich multiplicity of thoughts would be, once again, to the utmost benefit of Turkey. We believe that the holding of our conference in the very near future would be one of the most significant steps taken in our country on the path to academic freedom, in the independence of universities, and in general toward democracy.'"[39]

The organization of such a conference aptly manifested the progress made in the liberalization of Turkish political culture, as well as the remaining shortcomings. Although the impact of global and domestic actors was often considerable (see pp. 46, 75, 102, 132), this study has shown that the causal link between the liberalization process of Turkish political culture and the EU-initiated reform process is strong. What the European Union achieved by giving Turkey a membership perspective was to untangle the liberalization process by promoting and anchoring liberal reform and facilitating the process of democratic consolidation.

Turkey's EU Membership Perspective and the Euro-Mediterranean Partnership (EMP)

To determine the effects of the EU accession process on Turkey's political culture, one would ideally need to know what would have happened if Turkey had not been a candidate for EU membership. Although counterfactual history is impractical, one can arrive at useful conclusions based on the experience of the results of the EU policy toward noncandidate Mediterranean states. The success of the EU strategy regarding Turkey becomes clearer when juxtaposed with the results of the Euro-Mediterranean Partnership (EMP),[40] an EU initiative launched in November 1995, which did not offer to the participant states the prospect of full membership. Instead, it merely aimed at developing closer political, economic, and strategic relations between the EU member states and the rest of the littoral states of the Mediterranean. Its objectives were summarized as follows:

- The creation of an area of peace and stability based on the principles of human rights and democracy
- The creation of an area of shared prosperity through the progressive establishment of free trade between the EU and its Mediterranean partners and amongst the partners themselves, accompanied by substantial EU financial support for economic transition and for

helping the partners to confront the social and economic challenges created by this transition.

• The improvement of mutual understanding among the peoples of the region and the development of a free and flourishing civil society by means of exchange, development of human resources, and the support of civil societies and social development.[41]

However, the Euro-Mediterranean Partnership failed to deliver the political results that its drafters had inspired. While in the field of economy the establishment of a Euro-Mediterranean Free Trade Area by 2010 and EU financial assistance of almost 11 billion from 1995 to 2005 were events of major importance,[42] they failed to have any significant impact on the politics of the region. Despite an ambitious political agenda,[43] no noteworthy improvements occurred in the fields of regional peace and stability, democratization, or civil society development in any of the Mediterranean and Middle Eastern states that participated in the Barcelona Process.[44] The partnership offered to these states turned out to be too weak a political incentive to facilitate any steps toward democratization. In contrast to that, offering Turkey the perspective of full membership was proven to have a much more profound domestic impact. Coupled by the

Figure 7.1 Turkey's Prime Minister, Recep Tayyip Erdogan, a former football player, in probably the most difficult shot of his career (courtesy of Ingram Pinn, published in the *Financial Times*, June 30, 2005)

existence of considerable domestic political and social forces willing to support the process of political reform, the EU membership incentive gave a vision and mobilized support for political liberalization at an unprecedented level.

On the other hand, it would be too early to say that a full transformation of Turkish political culture from the subject to the participant model has occurred. The road toward the full liberalization of Turkish political culture is still long and bumpy, and as Putnam stresses, "most institutional history moves slowly."[45] Although the European Union has already had a liberalizing effect on Turkish political culture, the culmination of this process depends on the future of EU-Turkey accession negotiations. The process of Turkey's convergence with the *acquis communautaire* will have a great impact on the character of the Turkish political system.

THE FUTURE OF TURKEY'S EU ADVENTURE AND POLITICAL CULTURE

On December 17, 2004, the Brussels European Council set October 3, 2005, to be the date for the start of accession negotiations with Turkey.[46] This decision rewarded the reform efforts of two Turkish governments, although it did not mean that Turkey had been fully transformed into a liberal democracy. At the domestic European level, this decision was a great victory of those political forces, which envisioned an inclusive, political values–based and tolerant Union as opposed to those who feared the economic, social, and cultural repercussions of Turkey's prospective EU membership.[47] Nonetheless, Turkey's prospective EU accession posed very different questions from those raised by past enlargements.[48] Turkey's EU accession negotiations cannot be an easy process; problems are likely to arise not only from the Turkish but also from the European side. The European Union faces a series of serious internal challenges and contradictions that may affect the course of EU-Turkey accession negotiations. Turkey also has to give the final definite answer to the question of its identity, whether it belongs to the West or the East,[49] and to participate constructively in the intellectual, institutional, and political evolution that has characterized post-Second World War Western Europe.[50]

A View from Brussels

The problems on the EU side are economic, political and strategic. Globalization pressure makes the European Union reconsider the basic premises of its economic and social model. As China and India rise as new formidable global economic actors, it becomes increasingly difficult for the EU economy to raise its productivity, competitiveness, and economic growth rates without a deregulation of its labor rights legislation and social welfare system. The Common Agricultural Policy (CAP), one of the foundation blocks of the European Economic Community, has become exorbitantly costly, protecting a large, inefficient agricultural sector that has done little to adjust to the new world economic environment. The need to increase and better manage the EU budget so that new political, economic, and social challenges can be better addressed is dire. Moreover, there is increased speculation about the future path of the European integration process. A two-tier Union, a regression to a free-trade-zone model, or the development of a federal postnational model are all possible outcomes of the political and ideological fermentation that the Union is currently undergoing. What is already clear, though, is that—assuming that Turkey's EU accession negotiations bear fruit after ten years or more—Turkey will join a Union very different from what it is today.

The Eastern enlargement was an additional factor that posed serious problems for the economic, social and political coherence of the European Union. Despite the obvious political and strategic advantages of incorporating ten new member states in May 2004, the difficulties that the new enlarged European Union may face in decision-making often on the basis of unanimity, are likely to be intimidating. The ability of the European Union to combine the process of enlargement with its own deepening and to develop accountable, smoothly functioning, democratic institutions, is clearly of critical importance. Also crucial will be the ability of the Union to develop strong common positions and strategies in issues of foreign and security policy against the United States, China, and other global actors. The failure to ratify the EU Constitutional Treaty and the uncertain future of the Lisbon Treaty has confirmed that the institutional reform of the Union will be an extremely difficult task. The expectation that the prospective membership of Turkey, with its relatively large population and weak economy, would make institutional reform even more difficult creates an additional obstacle to Turkey's path toward full membership.[51]

Economic and political challenges at the European level have already affected domestic politics in Germany, France and other large EU member states. The rise of unemployment rates has helped xenophobic political parties to reassert their political presence. The results of the referendums on the EU Constitutional Treaty in France and the Netherlands in May and June 2005 clearly showed that public opinion in many EU member states has been alienated from the European project. The aggressive EU enlargement policy was identified as one of the main reasons for the multifarious problems of the European Union. Given that the Eastern enlargement cannot be undone and that the European Union has already committed itself to the full membership of Bulgaria and Romania, it was suggested that a moratorium should be imposed on further enlargement.[52] This could mainly affect Turkey and Croatia, currently the two EU candidate states that have started accession negotiations. Under these circumstances, Turkey runs the risk of becoming a scapegoat for the accumulated domestic EU problems. A significant number of EU commentators and politicians have already declared Turkey's EU membership to be impractical for economic, political, and cultural reasons and proposed a model of "privileged partnership" instead.[53] This opinion has become alarmingly popular among center-right political parties in France and Germany and the majority of public opinion in many EU member states. Addressing public opinion fears

Figure 7.2 The uncertain future of EU-Turkey relations is succinctly illustrated in this cartoon. (Courtesy Peter Schrank, published in the *Economist*, September 30, 2004)

regarding Turkey's prospective EU membership seems to be one of the most crucial tasks for the European Union and Turkey.

On the other hand, one should remember that the European Union is still to a large extent a law-based organization where political expediency does not play a leading role. The European Union committed itself on December 17, 2004, to the start of accession negotiations with Turkey on October 3, 2005, and cannot withdraw from that decision. Even though member states might have changed their minds about Turkey's EU membership, EU institutions will have to follow the path set by the December 2004 decision. The end of the negotiation process, however, is anything but clear. Turkey's convergence with the *acquis communautaire* will require more reform efforts and full democratic consolidation.[54] The negotiation process will definitely be affected by the debate on the future shape and identity of the European Union. Turkey needs to make a strong case that its EU membership is not a liability but an asset for an inclusive, strong, and tolerant Union and also make its own valuable contribution to the debate. It also needs to defend its interests in a way that shows understanding toward EU concerns.[55] The success of the process will mainly depend on Turkey's will to continue reform with the same zeal and commitment.[56] Accession negotiations will be a long and tedious process, with an expected duration of no less than ten years.[57] On the other hand, they will also bear precious potential rewards for Turkey, Europe, and the greater region. As Ramonet argues, "A long way still remains to be traversed as regards respect of public freedoms and basic rights. . . . But the prospect for accession to the Union has already had as principal effect the reinforcement of Turkey's democratization, its secularization, and the defense of human rights. While the large countries of the Eastern Mediterranean are threatened by violence and current obscurantists, this accession will constitute a concrete message of hope, peace, prosperity, and democracy."[58]

Therefore, the success of Turkey's EU membership adventure should show that the European Union is fully committed to democratization and can use its "soft" power potential to expand the zone of democracy. It could thus disprove the "clash of civilizations" thesis[59] by contributing to the improvement of relations between the West and the Islamic world.[60] In the words of the UK Foreign Minister Jack Straw, Turkey's EU membership is the acid test of whether Europe can defeat terrorist attempts to sow division between Islam and the West.[61]

Turkey's Democratic Consolidation and Political Culture

In the words of Przeworski, democratic consolidation means that democracy "becomes the only game in town, when no one can imagine acting outside the democratic institutions, when all the losers want to do is to try again within the same institutions under which they have just lost."[62]

In this study, democratic consolidation has been understood in its "maximalist" understanding. A democratically consolidated state is not just a state where free democratic elections prevail but also the state where democratic values have been embraced by the majority of citizens after a long socialization process.[63] This process goes along with the establishment of a civic, participant political culture. In the case of Turkey, a multiparty political system and free elections have largely been in place since 1950. Nonetheless, the transition from a procedural to a substantive form of democracy did not gain momentum until the emergence of the European Union in Turkish politics and Turkey's EU membership perspective became realistic. The European Union acted as a catalyst for the start of reconstructing the state on a democratic basis.[64] This study has focused on the steps made toward the emergence of a participant political culture. This process is anything but complete, and its final success will be affected by the course of Turkey's EU accession negotiations. It also depends on the extent to which the liberal reform cause will not just be an elite issue but will also be embraced by the vast majority of public opinion. Public support for EU membership in Turkey has been repeatedly confirmed to be strong,[65] yet the resilience of this support will be tested when the public becomes familiar with the details of what Turkey's membership in the European Union entails. Democracy should be seen no more as a luxury[66] or a means for other ends but as an end in itself.[67] The value of liberal reform should not be instrumentally measured against the successful flow of accession negotiations but against the completion of Turkey's democratic consolidation process.

The role of the AKP, with its widespread appeal to the periphery of Turkish society in popularizing the liberal reform discourse initiated by the European Union, is of critical importance for the success of the process.[68] The repeated statements by Recep Tayyip Erdogan and other AKP officials that the democratization process in Turkey has become independent from EU-Turkey relations could be seen as a very important signal. It is argued that even if Turkey's EU accession process fails, the Copenhagen Criteria will be simply renamed the "Ankara Criteria" and democratization reform will resume.[69]

As Erdogan himself put it, "We separated religion from democracy. We are walking on the way of democracy. The European Union is the best project of the twenty-first century. If you take us [Turkey] in the European Union, our membership will be beneficial for everyone who wants democracy. . . . Otherwise, we will continue on our way, calling the Copenhagen Criteria the Ankara Criteria. The European Union is a part of Turkey's civilizational project. However, we conducted these reforms to fulfill the democratic dreams of our own people. This was not just a requirement for a membership perspective."[70]

Viewing Turkey's political liberalization as beneficial per se for Turkey, rather than merely as a concession to the European Union, shows that the AKP would be willing to rise to the circumstances and support Turkey's democratization process, regardless of the outcome of Turkey's EU accession negotiations. This policy will also facilitate the rise of a participant political culture.

POSTSCRIPT

Istanbul, September 15, 2008

In the years that followed 2005, Turkey's drive towards EU accession slowed down. Despite the start of EU accession negotiations on October 3, 2005, EU-Turkey relations deteriorated. The opposition of the French President Sarkozy to Turkey's full membership, the persistence of the Cyprus question as an obstacle to Turkey's EU accession and the decreasing pace of the reform process were matched with an upsurge of nationalist feeling in public opinion. This was also strengthened by the impact of the U.S. policies in Iraq and the relapse of PKK operations in southeastern Turkey. Under these adverse circumstances, Turkey entered in 2007 a period of domestic political instability. The candidacy of Foreign Minister Abdullah Gul for the presidency of the country triggered the reaction of a large part of the country's secularist establishment. Large demonstrations "in defense of secularism" were organized, while on April 27, 2007, a statement was posted on the Web site of the Turkish Armed Forces. What was later coined as the "e-memorandum" was a clear warning that the military would not allow the alleged Islamization of the country. A few days later, the Constitutional Court stalled Gul's expected election by unexpectedly ruling that a quorum of two-thirds was required for the presidential election. This led Prime Minister Erdogan to call for early elections on July, 22, 2007. In these elections, the AKP achieved a spectacular victory. Despite being in power for almost five years, the AKP increased its vote by more than 12 percent. Gul was elected president on August 29, 2008.

Yet, political turmoil did not end with Gul's election. An AKP constitutional amendment, which allowed the wearing of headscarves in universities, was approved in early February 2008 by the parliament with a wide margin. The opposition parties CHP and DSP, however, appealed against the amendment to the Constitutional Court, which on June 5, 2008, annulled it on the grounds of its "opposition to the principle of secularism." The intervention of the judiciary had begun earlier, on March 14, 2008, when the Chief Prosecutor Abdurrahman Yalcinkaya filed a case against the AKP, requesting the closure of the party and the ban of its leadership from politics on the grounds that they had allegedly threatened secularism. On July 31, 2008, the court delivered its decision, which accepted the prosecutor's argument that the AKP had become a "focal point of antisecular activity" but spared it from closure by issuing a warning. Meanwhile, the unraveling of "Ergenekon," a gang consisting of retired officers, policemen, rogue intellectuals, and lawyers aiming to destabilize the country and precipitate a military coup through terrorist attacks shook the country. Following the arrest and detention of the first suspects in January 2008, sensation hit the highest point, on July 2, 2008, when two retired generals, Sener Eruygur and Hursit Tolon, were arrested and detained in the framework of the "Ergenekon" investigation.

The aforementioned developments have attested to the validity of the main conclusions of this study. The liberalization of Turkish political culture is far from complete but has achieved significant steps. The mounting division within the judiciary and the military provides evidence for this change. While the Constitutional Court took over the mantle of bureaucratic opposition to the AKP, when President Sezer withdrew in 2007, a judicial investigation led to the uncovering of the "Ergenekon" affair, an unprecedented blow against the Turkish "deep state," which comprised a lethal threat for Turkish democracy. In the case of the military, while the "e-memorandum" of April 27, 2007, confirmed that generals insisted on maintaining a tutelary role over Turkish politics and society, the "Ergenekon" investigation documented deep divisions between democratic and nondemocratic officers. The launch of the closure case against the AKP provided ample evidence for the shortcomings of Turkish democracy but also that path dependent changes have irreversibly altered the rules of the political game. The triumphant victory of the AKP in the elections of July 22, 2007, was the amplest manifestation that the Turkish people opposed bureaucratic tutelage and favored democratic government. In addition, the judicial survival of the AKP—unlike its predecessors RP and FP—could be interpreted as a result of the major transformations Turkey has undergone since 1999. Despite its strong prerogatives, the Constitutional Court felt unable to close a party that had collected more than 46 percent of the vote a year earlier. The EU firm opposition to the closure of the AKP also had a significant impact. Finally, the arrest and detention of two retired generals in the framework of the "Ergenekon" affair provided evidence that the inviolability of the Turkish military was over. By refusing to intervene in the judicial process, the top military command carefully distanced itself from extremism. Despite significant domestic changes, however, the influence of the European Union maintains its critical importance. The acceleration of the reform process and strong EU commitment to Turkey's full membership are essential not only for the successful completion of EU-Turkey accession negotiations but also for the emergence of a participant political culture.

Notes

Chapter 1

1. The relative ease with which Eastern European states were accepted as members of the "European family" in the process of the EU Eastern enlargement in the 1990s made a striking contrast with European circumspection in the case of Turkey. See Helene Sjursen, "Why Expand? The Question of Legitimacy and Justification in the EU's Enlargement Policy," *Journal of Common Market Studies* 40, no. 3 (2002): 503–7.
2. The Crimean War involved Great Britain, France, and the Ottoman Empire, which formed a military alliance that successfully checked the rise of Russian naval power in the Black Sea. The "Concert of Europe" was a term with little real political content. However, what was important for the Ottoman Empire was that for the first time it was accepted as a "European power." See William Hale, *Turkish Foreign Policy 1774–2000* (London: Frank Cass, 2002), 26–27.
3. The consolidation of the Ottoman Empire in European territory and its early diplomatic engagement with Western European powers did not affect these views.
4. Iver B. Neumann and Jennifer M. Welsh, "The Other in European Self-Definition: A Critical Addendum to the Literature on International Society," *Review of International Studies* 17, no. 4 (1991): 330–31.
5. Surnames in brackets were adopted after 1934, when the Family Name Law was passed.
6. The concepts of the "West" and "Europe" could be interchangeably used at that time, as the United States had not yet gained its dominant position in international politics, which entailed the introduction of a different paradigm of Westernization. The rise of the European Union as a major international actor in the late twentieth century made the distinction between the terms "Europe" and "West" even sharper.
7. "Cultural" objections in European circles to Turkey's EU vocation constitute an additional hindrance that, however, rather concerns the ongoing debate within the European Union on its identity and potential borders and not Turkey per se.
8. Thomas Risse, Maria Green Cowles, and James Caporaso, "Europeanization and Domestic Change: Introduction" in *Transforming Europe:*

Europeanization and Domestic Change, ed. Maria Green Cowles, James Caporaso, and Thomas Risse (Ithaca NY & London: Cornell University Press, 2001), 3.

9. Diez, Agnantopoulos, and Kaliber identified four different types of Europeanization, policy-related, political, societal and discursive. See Thomas Diez, Apostolos Agnantopoulos and Alper Kaliber, "Turkey, Europeanization and Civil Society: Introduction," *South European Society & Politics* 10, no. 1 (2005): 3–7.

10. Risse, Cowles, and Caporaso, "Europeanization and Domestic Change: Introduction," 2.

11. George Tsebelis, "Decision Making in Political Systems: Veto Players in Presidentialism, Parliamentarism, Multicameralism and Multipartyism," *British Journal of Political Science* 25, no. 3 (1996): 289–325

12. Risse, Cowles, and Caporaso, "Europeanization and Domestic Change: Introduction," 12.

13. Jeffrey T. Checkel, "The Europeanization of Citizenship?" in *Transforming Europe: Europeanization and Domestic Change*, ed. Maria Green Cowles, James Caporaso, and Thomas Risse (Ithaca, NY: Cornell University Press, 2001), 182.

14. Risse, Cowles, and Caporaso, "Europeanization and Domestic Change: Introduction," 4.

15. Ibid., 13–14.

16. Ernst B. Haas, *The Uniting of Europe: Political, Social, and Economic Forces, 1950–1957* (Stanford CA: Stanford University Press, 1958), xviii-xxi.

17. Ernst B. Haas, "Turbulent Fields and the Theory of Regional Integration," *International Organization* 30, no. 2 (1976): 475–76.

18. The case of the French President Charles de Gaulle and its impact on EEC policies in the 1960s is a clear example. See Ernst B. Haas, "The Uniting of Europe and the Uniting of Latin America," *Journal of Common Market Studies* 5, no. 4 (1967): 325–27.

19. Andrew Moravcsik, "Preferences and Power in the European Community: A Liberal Intergovernmentalist Approach," *Journal of Common Market Studies* 31, no. 4 (1993): 474–76.

20. Ibid., 480.

21. Meltem Muftuler-Bac and Lauren M. McLaren, "Enlargement Preferences and Policy-Making in the European Union: Impacts on Turkey," *Journal of European Integration* 25, no. 1 (2003): 19–20.

22. Andrew Moravcsik and Kalypso Nicolaidis, "Explaining the Treaty of Amsterdam: Interests, Influence, Institutions," *Journal of Common Market Studies* 37, no. 1 (1999): 61–62.

23. Ibid., 62–69.

24. Ibid., 82–83.

25. Andrew Moravcsik, *The Choice for Europe: Social Purpose and State Power from Rome to Maastricht* (Ithaca NY: Cornell University Press, 1998), 3–4.
26. Risse, Cowles and Caporaso, "Europeanization and Domestic Change: Introduction," 13–14.
27. Frank Schimmelfennig, "The Community Trap: Liberal Norms, Rhetorical Action, and the Eastern Enlargement of the European Union," *International Organization* 55, no. 1 (2001): 27–28.
28. Thomas Risse, Daniela Engelmann-Martin, Hans-Joachim Knopf, and Klaus Roscher, "To Euro or Not to Euro? The EMU and Identity Politics in the European Union," *European Journal of International Relations* 5, no. 2 (1999): 175–78.
29. Peter A. Hall and Rosemary C. R. Taylor, "Political Science and the Three New Institutionalisms," *Political Studies* 44, no. 4 (1996): 938.
30. For a concise account of historical institutionalism, see Kathleen Ann Thelen and Sven Steinmo, "Historical Institutionalism in Comparative Perspective" in *Structuring Politics: Historical Institutionalism in Comparative Analysis*, ed. Sven Steinmo, Kathleen Ann Thelen and Frank Longstreth (Cambridge: Cambridge University Press, 1992).
31. Mark A. Pollack, "The New Institutionalisms and European Integration," in *European Integration Theory*, ed. Antje Wiener and Thomas Diez (Oxford: Oxford University Press, 2004), 139.
32. Robert D. Putnam, *Making Democracy Work: Civic Traditions in Modern Italy* (Princeton, NJ: Princeton University Press, 1993), 182–85.
33. Ibid., 182.
34. While path dependence helps us understand the historical grounds of contemporary institutional performance, *social capital* is a key factor related to that performance. According to Putnam's definition, social capital refers to "features of social organization, such as trust, norms, and networks that can improve the efficiency of society by facilitating coordinated actions." See ibid., 168. Social trust is a fundamental component of social capital and can derive in modern societies from two related sources, norms of reciprocity, and networks of civic engagement. The norm of generalized reciprocity has historically been effective in reducing opportunism and resolving problems of collective action and is likely to be associated with dense horizontal networks of social exchange, linking individuals of equivalent status and power. Horizontal networks have the propensity to sustain social trust and cooperation, in contrast with vertical networks, which link individuals of unequal status and power in asymmetrical relations of hierarchy and dependence. See ibid., 173–75. High levels of social capital are essential for the appearance of virtuous circles of political and social reform, which can enable effective democratic government.

35. Paul Pierson, "Increasing Returns, Path Dependence, and the Study of Politics," *American Political Science Review* 94, no. 2 (2000): 252.
36. Margaret Levi, "A Model, a Method, and a Map: Rational Choice in Comparative and Historical Analysis," in *Comparative Politics: Rationality, Culture and Structure*, ed. Mark I. Lichbach and Alan S. Zuckerman (Cambridge: Cambridge University Press, 1997), 28.
37. Risse et al., "To Euro or Not to Euro?" 152.
38. Ibid., 153–54.
39. Douglass C. North, *Institutions, Institutional Change and Economic Performance* (New York: Cambridge University Press, 1990), 100, 40, cited in Putnam, *Making Democracy Work*, 181.
40. Robert D. Putnam, "Diplomacy and Domestic Politics: The Logic of Two-Level Games," *International Organization* 42, no. 3 (1988).
41. Ibid., 429–30.
42. Ibid., 437.
43. Ibid., 442–52.
44. Ibid., 460.
45. Risse, Cowles, and Caporaso, "Europeanization and Domestic Change: Introduction," 14.
46. Wayne Sandholz, "Membership Matters: Limits of the Functional Approach to European Institutions," *Journal of Common Market Studies* 34, no. 3 (1996): 426–27.
47. For a contrasting view on the same question, see Peter A. Hall and Rosemary C. R. Taylor, "The Potential of Historical Institutionalism: A Response to Hay and Wincott," *Political Studies* 46, no. 5 (1998).
48. Colin Hay and Daniel Wincott, "Structure Agency and Historical Institutionalism," *Political Studies* 46, no. 5 (1998): 951–55.
49. Thelen and Steinmo, "Historical Institutionalism in Comparative Perspective," 10.
50. Paul Pierson, "The Path to European Integration: A Historical Institutionalist Analysis," *Comparative Political Studies* 29, no. 2 (1996): 132–35.
51. Ibid., 139–40.
52. Risse, Cowles, and Caporaso, "Europeanization and Domestic Change: Introduction," 14–15.
53. Alexis de Tocqueville, *Democracy in America and Two Essays on America*, trans. Gerald E. Bevan (London: Penguin, 2003).
54. Ibid., 595–600.
55. Gabriel A. Almond and Sidney Verba, *The Civic Culture: Political Attitudes and Democracy in Five Nations* (Princeton NJ: Princeton University Press, 1963).
56. Lucian W. Pye, "Political Culture," in *The Encyclopaedia of Democracy*, ed. S. Lipset (London & New York: Routledge, 1995), 965.

57. Rod Hague and Martin Harrop, *Comparative Government and Politics: An Introduction* (New York: Palgrave, 2001), 78.
58. Dennis Kavanagh, *Political Culture* (London: Macmillan, 1972), 10–11.
59. Ronald Inglehart, *Culture Shift* (Princeton NJ: Princeton University Press, 1990), 19.
60. Ibid.
61. Almond and Verba, *The Civic Culture*, 22–26.
62. Ibid., 360–65.
63. Roger Eatwell, "Introduction: The Importance of the Political Culture Approach," in *European Political Cultures: Conflict or Convergence?* ed. Roger Eatwell (London: Routledge, 1997), 3.
64. Ibid.
65. Gabriel A. Almond, "Foreword: The Return to Political Culture," in *Political Culture and Democracy in Developing Countries*, ed. Larry Diamond (Boulder, CO: Lynne Rienner, 1993), x.
66. Eatwell, "Introduction: The Importance of the Political Culture Approach," 4.
67. Almond, "Foreword: The Return to Political Culture," xi.
68. Lucian W. Pye and Mary W. Pye, *Asian Power and Politics: The Cultural Dimensions of Authority* (Cambridge MA: Harvard University Press, 1990), 20.
69. Larry Diamond, "Introduction: Political Culture and Democracy," in *Political Culture and Democracy in Developing Countries*, ed. Larry Diamond (Boulder, CO: Lynne Rienner, 1993), 10–11.
70. Ronald Inglehart, "The Renaissance of Political Culture," *American Political Science Review* 82 (1988): 1228–29.
71. Sidney Verba, "On Revisiting the Civic Culture: A Personal Postscript" in *The Civic Culture Revisited*, ed. Gabriel A. Almond and Sidney Verba (Newbury Park, CA: Sage, 1980), 394–96.
72. Putnam, *Making Democracy Work*, 15–16.
73. Ibid., 121–37.
74. Robert D. Putnam, *Bowling Alone: The Collapse and Revival of American Community* (New York: Touchstone, 2000), 283–84.
75. The publication of Samuel Huntington's controversial thesis on "the clash of civilizations" sparked fierce debate on culturalist theories. See Samuel P. Huntington, "The Clash of Civilizations?" *Foreign Affairs* 72, no. 3 (1993); Samuel P. Huntington, *The Clash of Civilizations and the Remaking of World Order* (London: Touchstone, 1998).
76. Gabriel A. Almond, "The Intellectual History of the Civic Culture Concept," in *The Civic Culture Revisited*, ed. Gabriel A. Almond and Sidney Verba (Newbury Park, CA: Sage, 1980), 31–32.
77. Putnam, *Making Democracy Work*, 180.

Chapter 2

1. Alevis represents heterodox Islam in republican Turkey. Their faith is a syncretistic version of Shiite Islam enriched with plenty of local and pre-Islamic religious elements.
2. For a detailed account of Ataturk's reform program see Niyazi Berkes, *The Development of Secularism in Turkey* (Montreal: McGill University Press, 1964), 461–78.
3. Mardin argues that in the Ottoman Empire multidimensional social confrontation and integration seem to be missing, while the major confrontation was always unidimensional, a clash between the center and the periphery. This cleavage survived the demise of the Ottoman Empire and played a crucial role in republican Turkish politics. See Serif Mardin, "Center-Periphery Relations: A Key to Turkish Politics?" *Daedalus* 102, no. 1 (1973): 170.
4. Ibid., 304–5. On the republican modernization program regarding the periphery, see Murat Belge, "Cumhuriyet'in Donusum Projesi," *Radikal*, October 23, 2004.
5. Ergun Ozbudun, "Continuing Ottoman Legacy and the State Tradition in the Middle East," in *Imperial Legacy: The Ottoman Imprint on the Balkans and the Middle East*, ed. L. Carl Brown (New York: Columbia University Press, 1996), 135.
6. Mardin, "Center-Periphery Relations," 309.
7. Metin Heper, *The State Tradition in Turkey* (Walkington: Eothen Press, 1985), 7–8.
8. Ozbudun, "Continuing Ottoman Legacy," 147–48.
9. Serif Mardin, "Turkey: The Transformation of an Economic Code," in *The Political Economy of Income Distribution in Turkey*, ed. Ergun Ozbudun and Aydin Ulusan (New York: Holmes & Meier, 1980), 23–53.
10. The *millet* system is commonly supposed to be "the framework within which the Ottoman state ruled its non-Muslim subjects," as Braude put it. Yet recent historical research has linked the emergence of the *millet* system not with the classical age of the Ottoman Empire, but rather with the *Tanzimat* administrative reforms, which could be easier justified if the *millet* system was perceived as part of the Ottoman political tradition. For more information and insights on this issue, see Benjamin Braude, "Foundation Myths of the *Millet* System," in *Christians & Jews in the Ottoman Empire: The Functioning of a Plural Society*, ed. Benjamin Braude and Bernard Lewis (New York: Holmes & Meier, 1982), 69–88.
11. The character of the Sheikh Said rebellion is widely debated in historical literature. Official Turkish sources emphasize the antisecularist, "reactionary" character of the rebellion, while Kurdish nationalists stress its strongly ethnic Kurdish character.

12. On December 23, 1930, Kubilay, a Kemalist teacher who was performing his military service as a reserve officer, was brutally killed in the city of Menemen in Western Anatolia when he attempted to intervene into a conflict among the local members of the officially banned *Naksibendi tarikat.*

13. Modernization and Westernization were largely synonymous terms in the context of Ataturk's reform program. See Ziya Onis, "Turkish Modernisation and Challenges for the New Europe," *Perceptions: Journal of International Affairs* 9, no. 3 (2004): 8.

14. On the ideas of the primary representative of Ottoman liberalism, Prince Sabahaddin, see Kaan Durukan, "Turk Liberalizmin Kokenleri," in *Cumhuriyet'e Devreden Dusunce Mirasi: Tanzimat ve Mesrutiyet'in Birikimi*, ed. Mehmet O. Alkan (Istanbul: Iletisim, 2001), 154–55.

15. Ottoman liberals comprised the core of nonnationalist opposition in the late Ottoman Empire. Kamil Pasa, an advocate of Ottomanism and adversary of Turkish nationalism, was Grand Vizier (*Sadrazam*) during the disastrous First Balkan War. The Ottoman governments of Damat Ferit and Ahmet Tevfik Pasa took over power in the aftermath of the Moudros Armistice, collaborated with the Entente forces, and antagonized Ankara-based Turkish nationalist forces until the final military victory of the latter in the fall of 1922.

16. For an account of synthetic approaches of liberalism with conservativism, see Levent Koker, "Liberal Muhafazakarlik ve Turkiye" in *Muhafazakarlik*, ed. Ahmet Cigdem (Istanbul: Iletisim, 2003).

17. For a detailed account of Ahmet Agaoglu's thought, see Simten Cosar, "Turk Liberalizmin Acmazlarina Bir Giris: Ahmet Agaoglu," in *Kuresellesme, Sivil Toplum ve Islam*, ed. E. Fuat Keyman and A. Yasar Saribay (Ankara: Vadi Yayinlari, 1998).

18. On the eclipse of political liberalism in early republican Turkey, see Cengiz Aktar, "Olmayan Avrupa Dusuncesi Uzerine," in *Modernlesme ve Baticilik*, ed. Uygur Kocabasoglu (Istanbul: Iletisim, 2002), 274.

19. On the conservative leanings of the Progressive Republican Party, see Erik Jan Zurcher, "Terrakiperver Cumhuriyet Firkasi ve Siyasal Muhafazakarlik," in *Muhafazakarlik*, ed. Ahmet Cigdem (Istanbul: Iletisim, 2003), 42–53.

20. Erik Jan Zurcher, *Political Opposition in the Early Turkish Republic: The Progressive Republican Party, 1924–1925* (Leiden: E. J. Brill, 1991), 95–109.

21. The Independence Tribunals were special military courts first established by Mustafa Kemal [Ataturk] in the aftermath of the First World War in his effort to consolidate Turkish nationalist power in Anatolia. Their reinstatement against the Sheikh Said rebellion and the Progressive Republican Party was a move of political symbolism. Turkish independence was no more threatened by foreign invaders or Christian

minorities but from internal enemies, Kurdish nationalists, Islamists, and political dissidents.

22. Erik Jan Zurcher, *Turkey: A Modern History* (London: I. B. Tauris, 1998), 177–80.
23. The Izmir Conspiracy was an attempt to assassinate Ataturk during his visit to Izmir on June 15, 1926. This event served as pretext for increasing state repression against dissidents and minorities. See Zurcher, *Political Opposition in the Early Turkish Republic*, 92–93.
24. Zurcher, *Turkey: A Modern History*, 181–82.
25. Republican People's Party (*Cumhuriyet Halk Firkasi*, later renamed into *Cumhuriyet Halk Partisi*—CHP) is the party founded by Ataturk himself that ruled Turkey from the emergence of the Turkish Republic until 1950.
26. See Fethi Okyar, *Uc Devirde Bir Adam* (Istanbul: Tercuman Yayinlari, 1980), 392–93, cited in Ergun Ozbudun, *Contemporary Turkish Politics: Challenges to Democratic Consolidation* (Boulder, CO: Lynne Rienner Publishers, 2000), 22–23.
27. Zurcher, *Turkey: A Modern History*, 185–87.
28. Ahmet Hamdi Basar, *Ataturk'le Uc Ay ve 1930'dan Sonra Turkiye* (Ankara: A.I.T.I.A. Basimevi, 1981), 30, cited in Cosar, "Turk Liberalizmin Acmazlarina Bir Giris," 143.
29. Walter F. Weiker, *The Turkish Revolution 1960–1961: Aspects of Military Politics* (Washington: Brookings Institution, 1963), 5–6.
30. Since the scarcity of information on popular political culture of the time makes a fully fledged account of grassroots opposition virtually impossible, this study will focus on the elite level.
31. Heper, *The State Tradition in Turkey*, 84–91, 130–37.
32. Fareed Zakaria, "The Rise of Illiberal Democracy," *Foreign Affairs* 76, no. 6 (1997): 22–24.
33. Hale, *Turkish Foreign Policy 1774–2000*, 111–14.
34. The relative importance of domestic, security, and foreign policy considerations in Inonu's decision to launch multiparty politics in Turkey is a still heavily debated issue. See Zurcher, *Turkey: A Modern History*, 215–28.
35. Until then a system of indirect elections of rather ceremonial function was applied in which the slates of candidates for parliamentary seats could only be appointed by CHP organs. See ibid., 185.
36. Frederick W. Frey, *The Turkish Political Elite* (Cambridge, MA: MIT Press, 1965), 350.
37. William Hale, *Turkish Politics and the Military* (London: Routledge, 1994), 137–38.
38. Celal Bayar, "Basvekilim Adnan Menderes," *Hurriyet*, June 29, 1969, cited in Mardin, "Center-Periphery Relations" 308.
39. Kemal Karpat, "Military Interventions: Army-Civilian Relation in Turkey before and after 1980," in *State, Democracy and the Military:*

Turkey in the 1980s, ed. Metin Heper and Ahmet Evin (Berlin: Walter de Gruyter, 1988), 145–46.

40. Ioannis N. Grigoriadis, "Turkey's Accession to the European Union: Debating the Most Difficult Enlargement Ever," *SAIS Review of International Affairs* 26, no. 1 (2006): 149–50.

41. Desmond Dinan, *Ever Closer Union: An Introduction to European Integration*, 2nd ed. (Boulder, CO: Lynne Rienner, 1999), 191.

42. Ibid., 138–39.

43. See Paul Kubicek, "Turkey's Place in the 'New Europe,'" *Perceptions: Journal of International Affairs* 9, no. 3 (2004): 55–58.

44. On the question of Turkish identity in the aftermath of the Cold War, see Ziya Onis, "Turkey in the Post-Cold-War Era—in Search of Identity," *Middle East Journal* 49, no. 1 (1995).

45. Although the decision of the Helsinki EU Summit in December 1999 to grant Turkey EU candidate state status could be seen as a landmark in this process, it is true that the first convergence steps at the society level preceded the Helsinki decision.

46. Grigoriadis, "Turkey's Accession to the European Union," 150–53.

47. Ihsan D. Dagi, *Batililasma Korkusu* (Ankara: Liberte Yayinlari, 2003), 3.

48. Sina Aksin, "Avrupali Miyiz?" *Radikal Cumhuriyet*, October 29, 2004.

49. Several nationalist authors have opted for the development of special relations with Russia, India, or China. See Erol Manisali, "Rusya ile Iliskiler Alternatif mi, Yoksa Bir Denge Arayisi mi?" *Cumhuriyet*, December 10, 2004. A similar view was expressed by Huntington, who argued that Turkey should seek a leading position in the Islamic world. See Samuel P. Huntington, "Culture, Power, and War: What Roles for Turkey in the New Global Politics," *Zaman (English edition)*, May 26, 2005. An unaligned role for Turkey following the economic model of China has also been suggested. See Gunduz Aktan, "Turkiye'nin Gelecegi (1)," *Radikal*, June 30, 2005. This trend was not limited to the Turkish left. For a study of anti-Westernism on the right of Turkish political spectrum, see Tanil Bora, "Milliyetci-Muhafazakar ve Islamci Dusunuste Negatif Bati Imgesi" in *Modernlesme ve Baticilik*, ed. Uygur Kocabasoglu (Istanbul: Iletisim, 2002).

50. For a succinct account of the impact of Turkey's prospective EU accession on U.S.-Turkey relations, see Morton I. Abramowitz et al., *Turkey on the Threshold: Europe's Decision and U.S. Interests* (Washington DC: Atlantic Council of the United States, 2004), 22–25.

51. United States support reached its highest point in December 200,2 when U.S. President George W. Bush personally telephoned EU leaders during the EU Copenhagen Summit to convince them to adopt a decision favorable for Turkey's EU membership prospects.

52. Ziya Onis and Suhnaz Yilmaz, "The Turkey-EU-US Triangle in Perspective: Transformation or Continuity?," *Middle East Journal* 59, no. 2 (2005): 273.

53. Graham E. Fuller, "Turkey's Strategic Model: Myths and Realities," *Washington Quarterly* 27, no. 3 (2004): 57–59.

54. Sedat Ergin, "Turk-ABD Iliskileri Yokus Asagi," *Hurriyet*, December 12, 2004.

55. Soner Cagaptay, "Where Goes the U.S.-Turkish Relationship," *Middle East Quarterly* 11, no. 4 (2004): 44–46.

56. David L. Phillips, "Turkey's Dreams of Accession," *Foreign Affairs* 83, no. 5 (2004): 92–93.

57. The heated debate and final compromise on the inclusion of religion into the European Constitution is characteristic.

58. Kalypso Nicolaidis, "Turkey is European for Europe's Sake," in *Turkey and the European Union: From Association to Accession?* (The Hague: The Netherlands Ministry of Foreign Affairs, 2004).

59. The views of German Christian Democrat leading figures are characteristic of this approach. See Angela Merkel and Edmund Stoiber, "Kanzler Muß Turkei-Beitritt Stoppen," *Frankfurter Allgemeine Zeitung*, December 5, 2004; Wolfgang Schäuble, "Talking Turkey," *Foreign Affairs* 83, no. 6 (2004).

60. Michael S. Teitelbaum and Philip L. Martin, "Is Turkey Ready for Europe?" *Foreign Affairs* 82, no. 3 (2003): 106–7.

61. Wolfgang Quaisser, "Vier Millionen Zuwanderer," Interview with Martin Halusa, *Die Welt*, December 15, 2004.

62. The former French President and President of the European Convention Valéry Giscard D'Estaing has been one of the most articulate opponents of Turkey's EU membership. See Valéry Giscard d'Estaing, "Pour ou Contre l' Adhésion de la Turquie à l'Union Européenne," Interview in *Le Monde*, November 8, 2002.

63. Grigoriadis, "Turkey's Accession to the European Union," 148–49.

64. Bernard Lewis, *The Emergence of Modern Turkey*, 2nd ed. (Oxford: Oxford University Press, 1968), 106–28.

65. The European Economic Community (EEC) became referred to as European Community (EC) during the 1980s and as the European Union (EU) after the 1991 Treaty on the European Union.

66. Meltem Muftuler-Bac, "The Impact of the European Union on Turkish Politics," *East European Quarterly* 34, no. 2 (2000): 160–64.

67. Greece's EEC membership in 1981 further complicated EEC-Turkey relations, as Greece refused to consent to the improvement of EEC-Turkey relations unless Turkey made "positive" steps toward the resolution of the Cyprus and bilateral Greek-Turkish disputes.

68. Atila Eralp, "Turkey and the European Union," in *The Future of Turkish Foreign Policy*, Lenore G. Martin and Dimitris Keridis (Cambridge, MA: MIT Press, 2002), 71–75.

69. The 2001 constitutional amendment involved thirty-four articles and had the most far-reaching effects on the fundamental rights and liberties. This amendment not only changed the overall approach to the restriction of fundamental rights and liberties but also brought about improvements with respect to a great number of individual rights. For more information, see Ergun Ozbudun and Serap Yazici, *Democratization Reforms in Turkey (1993–2004)* (Istanbul: TESEV Publications, 2004), 14–15.

CHAPTER 3

1. The concept of civil society is broad, having its roots in the works of Hegel and Marx. However, a deeper examination of this intellectual debate on civil society lies beyond the scope of this study. For a succinct account of the intellectual history and debate on the term "civil society" with emphasis on the Gramscian approach of the term, see Robert W. Cox, "Civil Society at the Turn of the Millennium: Prospects for an Alternative World Order," *Review of International Studies* 25, no. 1 (1999).
2. Sefa Simsek, "The Transformation of Civil Society in Turkey: From Quantity to Quality," *Turkish Studies* 5, no. 3 (2004): 44.
3. John A. Hall, "In Search of Civil Society," in *Civil Society: Theory, History, Comparison,* ed. John A. Hall (London: Polity Press, 1996), 15.
4. Larry Diamond, "Rethinking Civil Society: Toward Democratic Consolidation," *Journal of Democracy* 5, no. 3 (1994): 5.
5. Ernest Gellner, "The Importance of Being Modular," in *Civil Society: Theory, History, Comparison,* ed. John A. Hall (London: Polity Press, 1996), 32.
6. Bjorn Beckman, "Explaining Democratisation: Notes on the Concept of Civil Society," in *Democracy, Civil Society and the Muslim World,* Elizabeth Ozdalga and Sune Persson (Istanbul: Swedish Research Institute, 1997), 2.
7. Metin Heper, "The Ottoman Legacy and Turkish Politics," *Journal of International Affairs* 54, no. 1 (2000): 78. Heper cites Joseph S. Szyliowicz, "The Ottoman Empire," in *Commoners, Climbers, and Notables: A Sampler of Studies on Social Ranking in the Middle East,* Christoffel Anthonie Olivier van Nieuwenhuijze (Leiden: E. J. Brill, 1997), 103, 07, and Serif Mardin, "Ideology and Religion in the Turkish Revolution," *International Journal of Middle Eastern Studies* 2, no. 3 (1971): 202.
8. See Ernest Gellner, *Conditions of Liberty: Civil Society and its Rivals* (London: Penguin, 1996), 15–18.
9. The importance of strong central power in Islamic political thought was already emphasized in the following saying of Ibn Hanbal, one of the most prominent Islamic jurisprudents: "Sixty years under a tyrant

are better than a single night of anarchy." See Fazlur Rahman, "The Law of Rebellion in Islam," in *Islam in the Modern World: 1983 Paine Lectures in Religion*, Jill Raitt (Columbia, MO: University of Missouri-Columbia Department of Religious Studies, 1983), 1–10.

10. Murat Belge, "Modernizasyon'da Intisab," *Radikal*, October 17, 2004.

11. Emre Erdogan, *Turk Sivil Toplum Kuruluslarinin Gelisimleri Uzerine Bazi Notlar* (Istanbul: Infakto, 2005), 1–3.

12. Serif Mardin, "Freedom in an Ottoman Perspective," in *State, Democracy and the Military: Turkey in the 1980s*, ed. Metin Heper and Ahmet Evin (Berlin: Walter de Gruyter, 1988), 30–31.

13. Sultan Abdulhamid II wielded far greater powers than any of his predecessors. See Bernard Lewis, "Why Turkey is the Only Muslim Democracy," *Middle East Quarterly* 1, no. 1 (1994).

14. Non-Muslim minorities had become numerically insignificant as a result of events that preceded the foundation of the Republic, so their role in the formation of a Turkish civil society was negligible.

15. For more details, see Taha Parla, *Ziya Gokalp, Kemalizm ve Turkiye'de Korporatizm*, ed. Ikinci Basim (Istanbul: Iletisim, 1993), cited in Aykut Kansu, "Turkiye'de Korporatist Dusunce ve Korporatizm Uygulamalari," in *Kemalizm*, ed. Ahmet Insel (Istanbul: Iletisim, 2001), 260.

16. See Articles 70, 79, and 86 of the 1924 Constitution at Edward Mead Merle, "The New Constitution of Turkey," *Political Science Quarterly* 40, no. 1 (1925): 96-98.

17. For more information on trade unions, see Ronnie Margulies and Ergin Yildizoglu, "Trade Unions and Turkey's Working Class," *MERIP Reports* (1984).

18. See Kemali Saybasili, "Chambers of Commerce & Industry, Political Parties, Governments: A Comparative Study of British and Turkish Cases," *Studies in Development* (Ankara: Middle East Technical University, 1976). Such associations are referred to in the academic literature on civil society as governmental nongovernmental organizations (GONGOs).

19. Metin Heper, "State and Society in Turkish Political Experience," in *State, Democracy and the Military: Turkey in the 1980s*, ed. Ahmet Evin and Metin Heper (Berlin: Walter de Gruyter, 1988), 6.

20. For more details, see Paul Kubicek, "The Earthquake, Europe, and Prospects for Political Change in Turkey," *Middle East Review of International Affairs (MERIA)* 5, no. 2 (2001): 36.

21. See Omer Caha, "The Inevitable Coexistence of Civil Society and Liberalism: The Case of Turkey," *Journal of Economic and Social Research* 3, no. 2 (2001): 40–44.

22. Binnaz Toprak, "Civil Society in Turkey," in *Civil Society in the Middle East*, Augustus Richard Norton (Leiden: E. J. Brill, 1996), 95–96.

23. E. Fuat Keyman and Ahmet Icduygu, "Globalisation, Civil Society and Citizenship in Turkey: Actors, Boundaries and Discourses," *Citizenship Studies 7*, no. 2 (2003): 225–26.
24. Ioannis N. Grigoriadis and Antonis Kamaras, "Foreign Direct Investment (FDI) in Turkey: Historical Constraints and the AKP Success Story," *Middle Eastern Studies* 44, no. 1 (2008): 53–56.
25. Toprak, "Civil Society in Turkey," 101.
26. Diba Nigar Goksel and Rana Birden Gunes, "The Role of NGOs in the European Integration Process: The Turkish Experience," *South European Society & Politics* 10, no. 1 (2005): 67.
27. Ziya Onis and Umut Turem, "Business, Globalization and Democracy: A Comparative Analysis of Turkish Business Associations," *Turkish Studies 2*, no. 2 (2001): 98–103.
28. Bulent Tanor, *1997 TUSIAD Report: Perspectives on Democratization in Turkey* (Istanbul: TUSIAD, 1997).
29. Serap Atan, "Europeanisation of Turkish Peak Business Organisations and Turkey-EU Relations," in *Turkey and European Integration: Accession Prospects and Issues,* ed. Mehmet Ugur and Nergis Canefe (London: Routledge, 2004), 104–7.
30. Binnaz Toprak, "Civil Society in Turkey," in *Towards Civil Society in the Middle East,* ed. Jillian Schwedler (London: Lynne Rienner, 1995), 79–80.
31. Kemal Kirisci and Gareth M. Winrow, *The Kurdish Question and Turkey: An Example of a Trans-State Ethnic Conflict* (London: Frank Cass, 2003), 113.
32. This was a group of mothers whose children went missing as a result of state security operations. The Saturday Mothers demonstrated every Saturday from 1995 to 1999 in the Galatasaray Square of Istanbul, demanding an account of their children's fate, and became a symbol of Turkey's human rights problems. See Jonathan Sugden, "Human Rights and Turkey's EU Candidacy," in *Turkey and European Integration: Accession Prospects and Issues,* ed. Mehmet Ugur and Nergis Canefe (London: Routledge, 2004), 246.
33. The Turkish Human Rights Association (*Insan Haklari Dernegi—* IHD), one of the most active supporters of human rights for Turkey's Kurdish population, repeatedly faced state persecution, which was frequently documented in the annual reports of the EU Commission.
34. Erdogan, *Turk Sivil Toplum Kuruluslarinin Gelismeleri Uzerine Bazi Notlar.*
35. Jenny B. White, *Islamist Mobilization in Turkey: A Study in Vernacular Politics* (Seattle: University of Washington Press, 2003), 69–76.
36. For more information on Mazlum-Der, see Gottfried Plagemann, "Human Rights Organisations: Defending the Particular or the Universal?" in *Civil Society in the Grip of Nationalism,* ed. Stefanos

Yerasimos, Gunter Seufert and Karin Vorhoff (Istanbul: Orient-Institut & Institut Francais d'Études Anatoliennes, 2000), 451–59.

37. For a thorough portrait of MUSIAD, see Karin Vorhoff, "Businessmen and Their Organizations: Between Instrumental Solidarity, Cultural Diversity and the State," in *Civil Society in the Grip of Nationalism*, ed. Stefanos Yerasimos, Gunter Seufert and Karin Vorhoff (Istanbul: Orient-Institut & Institut Francais d'Études Anatoliennes, 2000), 158–72.

38. Nilufer Gole, "Authoritarian Secularism and Islamic Participation: The Case of Turkey" in Jillian Schwedler, ed., *Towards Civil Society in the Middle East* (London: Lynne Rienner, 1995), 81–82.

39. White, *Islamist Mobilization in Turkey*, 211.

40. On "*the legitimacy crisis of the strong-state tradition*" in Turkey since the 1980s, see Keyman and Icduygu, "Globalisation, Civil Society and Citizenship in Turkey," 223.

41. Sugden, "Human Rights and Turkey's EU Candidacy," 247.

42. Millions of Turkish citizens simultaneously turned off the lights of their houses at 9:00 PM for one minute throughout February 1997. See Tanil Bora and Selda Caglar, "Modernlesme ve Batililasmanin Bir Tasiyicisi Olarak Sivil Toplum Kuruluslari" in *Modernlesme ve Baticilik*, ed. Uygur Kocabasoglu (Istanbul: Iletisim, 2002), 340.

43. Human Rights Watch, *World Report 1998-Turkey*, http://www.hrw .org/worldreport/Helsinki-23.htm.

44. Turkiye Insan Haklari Vakfi, *Press Release on the Manisa Trial*, http:// www.tihv.org.tr/press/press09042003manisa.html.

45. Demir Murat Seyrek, "The Road to EU Membership: The Role of Turkish Civil Society," *Turkish Policy Quarterly* 3, no. 3 (2004): 118.

46. Kubicek, "The Earthquake, Europe, and Prospects for Political Change in Turkey," 38.

47. Hakan Tunc, "The Lost Gamble: The 2000 and 2001 Turkish Financial Crises in Comparative Perspective," *Turkish Studies* 4, no. 2 (2003): 46.

48. Ibid., 47–48.

49. Ziya Onis, "Domestic Politics versus Global Dynamics: Towards a Political Economy of the 2000 and 2001 Financial Crises," *Turkish Studies* 4, no. 2 (2003): 14–15.

50. Ibid., 15.

51. For details on the EU-funded promotion of democratization in the Mediterranean countries through the MEDA program, see Nadim Karkutli and Dirk Butzler, *Final Report: Evaluation of the MEDA Democracy Programme 1996–1998* (Brussels: European Commission, 1999).

52. European Union, *Financial Assistance before Candidacy* (Delegation of the European Commission to Turkey: Ankara, 2004), http:// www.deltur.cec.eu.int/default.asp?lang=1&ndx=12&mnID=3&ord =5&subOrd=1.

53. Accession Partnership documents are signed between the European Union and applicant states. Within the spirit of the Copenhagen Criteria, they identify reform priorities and objectives as well as a roadmap, whose implementation will enable the start of accession negotiations.

54. Official Journal of the European Communities, *2000 Accession Partnership Agreement with the Republic of Turkey [2001/235/EC]* (Brussels: European Communities, 2001), L85/16.

55. The information on the six programs has been obtained from European Union, *EU Funded Programmes in Turkey 2003–2004* (Ankara: European Commission Representation to Turkey, 2004), 39–45.

56. Korel Goymen, "The Third Sector in Turkey: Towards a New Social Contract with the State" (paper presented at the EGPA 2004 Annual Conference, Ljubljana, September 1, 2004), 5.

57. Ozbudun and Yazici, *Democratization Reforms in Turkey (1993–2004)*, 20.

58. Commission of the European Communities, *1998 Regular Report on Turkey's Progress Towards Accession* (Brussels: European Union, 1998), 16.

59. Commission of the European Communities, *1999 Regular Report on Turkey's Progress Towards Accession* (Brussels: European Union, 1999), 13.

60. Commission of the European Communities, *2000 Regular Report on Turkey's Progress Towards Accession* (Brussels: European Union, 2000), 17.

61. The 2002 Copenhagen European Council considered for the first time whether Turkey should be given a date for the start for accession negotiations and decided to move the final decision to December 2004.

62. Turk Buyuk Millet Meclisi (TBMM), *Turkiye Cumhuriyeti Anayasasinin Bazi Maddelerinin Degistirilmesi Hakkinda Kanun* (4709/2001).

63. Commission of the European Communities, *2001 Regular Report on Turkey's Progress Towards Accession [SEC(2001) 1756]* (Brussels: European Union, 2001), 26–28.

64. Turk Buyuk Millet Meclisi (TBMM), *Bazi Kanunlarda Degisiklik Yapilmasina Iliskin Kanun* (4748/2002).

65. See Turk Buyuk Millet Meclisi (TBMM), *Cesitli Kanunlarda Degisiklik Yapilmasina Iliskin Kanun* (4963/2003a).

66. Commission of the European Communities, *2002 Regular Report on Turkey's Progress Towards Accession [SEC(2002) 1412]* (Brussels: European Union, 2002), 35.

67. See Turk Buyuk Millet Meclisi (TBMM), *Cesitli Kanunlarda Degisiklik Yapilmasina Iliskin Kanun* (4778/2003b).

68. Commission of the European Communities, *2003 Regular Report on Turkey's Progress Towards Accession* (Brussels: European Union, 2003), 32.

69. Turk Buyuk Millet Meclisi (TBMM), *Dernekler Kanunu* (5231/ 2004a).
70. Senem Aydin and E. Fuat Keyman, *European Integration and the Transformation of Turkish Democracy [No. 2]* (Brussels: Centre for European Policy Studies (CEPS), 2004), 29–30.
71. Turk Buyuk Millet Meclisi (TBMM), *Dernekler Kanunu* (5253/ 2004b).
72. This referred to Articles 10 (on financial assistance from and to political parties) and 13 (on the minimum number of association members).
73. Derya Sazak, "Egitim-Sen Davasi," *Milliyet*, May 27, 2005.
74. According to Article 89 of the Turkish Constitution, the President of the Republic has the right to return bills to the Parliament on the grounds of unconstitutionality.
75. Tanor, *1997 TUSIAD Report: Perspectives on Democratization in Turkey*, 3.
76. Ibid.
77. See Bora and Caglar, "Modernlesme ve Batililasmanin Bir Tasiyicisi Olarak Sivil Toplum Kuruluslari," 344–45.
78. Ersin Kalaycioglu, "Civil Society in Turkey Continuity or Change?" in *Turkish Transformations: New Centuries, New Challenges*, ed. Brian W. Beely (Walkington, UK: Eothen Press, 2004), 74–75.
79. The empowerment of Turkish civil society also became evident in its impact on Turkey's refusal to join the United States in its 2003 war against Iraq. See Ian O. Lesser, *Turkey in the EU: A New U.S. Relationship* (Western Policy Center: Washington DC, 2004), 2, http://www.westernpolicy.org/Secondary.asp?PageName=Publication&Page=Commentary/Commentary75.asp.
80. Goksel and Birden Gunes, "The Role of NGOs in the European Integration Process," 63.

Chapter 4

1. Giovanni Sartori, *The Theory of Democracy Revisited* (Chatham NJ: Chatham House, 1987), 213–14.
2. Ibid., 132.
3. Robert Alan Dahl, *Dilemmas of Pluralist Democracy: Autonomy vs. Control* (New Haven CT: Yale University Press, 1982), 106–7.
4. Robert N. Berki, "State and Society: An Antithesis of Modern Political Thought," in *State and Society in Contemporary Europe*, ed. Jack Hayward and Robert N. Berki (Oxford: Martin Robertson, 1979), 2–3.
5. Ibid., 3–4.
6. Metin Heper, "The Strong State as a Problem for the Consolidation of Democracy—Turkey and Germany Compared," *Comparative Political Studies* 25, no. 2 (1992): 170.

7. Metin Heper, "Political Culture as a Dimension of Compatibility," in *Turkey and the West: Changing Political and Cultural Identities*, ed. Metin Heper, Ayse Oncu and Heinz Kramer (London: I. B. Tauris, 1993), 15.
8. Heper, *The State Tradition in Turkey*, 15–17.
9. Ozbudun, "Continuing Ottoman Legacy and the State Tradition in the Middle East," 133.
10. Murat Belge, "Intisab: Yaygin ve Dayanikli Iliski," *Radikal*, October 16, 2004.
11. Frank Tachau, "The Political Culture of Kemalist Turkey," in *Ataturk and the Modernization of Turkey*, ed. Jacob M. Landau (Boulder, CO: Westview Press, 1984), 60.
12. Metin Heper, "The State and Interest Groups with Special Reference to Turkey," in *Strong State and Economic Interest Groups: The Post-1980 Turkish Experience*, ed. Metin Heper (Berlin: Walter de Gruyter, 1991), 13.
13. Ozbudun, "Continuing Ottoman Legacy and the State Tradition in the Middle East," 135.
14. The rise of the Greek Phanariot elite in the early eighteenth century was an exception that confirmed the rule.
15. Heper, *The State Tradition in Turkey*, 24.
16. This was the essence of the patriarchal duty of *hisba*. See Heper, "The Ottoman Legacy and Turkish Politics," 65.
17. According to the "circle of justice" argument, a ruler can have no power without soldiers, no soldiers without money, no money without the welfare of his subjects, no popular welfare without justice, and no justice without a ruler. See Ayhan Akman, "Modernist Nationalism: Statism and National Identity in Turkey," *Nationalities Papers* 32, no. 1 (2004): 33–34.
18. Heper, *The State Tradition in Turkey*, 25.
19. The *timar* was "a grant of land, in return for which the *sipahi*, a feudal cavalryman, was bound to render military service in person and with as many men-at-arms as were required by the size and income of his fief." See Lewis, *The Emergence of Modern Turkey*, 90.
20. Heper, "The Ottoman Legacy and Turkish Politics," 65.
21. Opinions favoring decentralization and power devolution as a means to sustain the unity of a multiethnic, multi-religious empire were expressed by Midhat Pasa among the Young Ottomans and Prince Sabahaddin among the Young Turks. Nonetheless, they never appealed to the majority of elites and the public.
22. Akman, "Modernist Nationalism," 34.
23. Ozbudun, "Continuing Ottoman Legacy and the State Tradition in the Middle East," 137.

24. Kemal H. Karpat, *Turkey's Politics: The Transition to a Multi-Party System* (Princeton NJ: Princeton University Press, 1959), 443.
25. Heper, *The State Tradition in Turkey*, 61.
26. Kalaycioglu, "Civil Society in Turkey," 67–69.
27. For the encounters of early republican elites with corporatism, see Kansu, "Turkiye'de Korporatist Dusunce ve Korporatizm Uygulamalari," 260–66.
28. Yuksel Akkaya, "Korporatizmden Sendikal Ideolojiye, Milliyetcilik ve Isci Sinifi," in *Milliyetcilik*, ed. Tanil Bora (Istanbul: Iletisim, 2002), 831–33.
29. For the case of the intellectual movement linked with the magazine *Kadro*, see Mustafa Turkes, "Kadro Dergisi," in *Kemalizm*, ed. Ahmet Insel (Istanbul: Iletisim, 2001).
30. Levent Koker, "Kemalizm/Ataturkculuk: Modernlesme, Devlet ve Demokrasi," in *Kemalizm*, ed. Ahmet Insel (Istanbul: Iletisim, 2001), 108–11.
31. Ali Kazancigil, "The Ottoman-Turkish State and Kemalism," in *Ataturk, the Founder of a Modern State*, ed. Ali Kazancigil and Ergun Ozbudun (London: C. Hurst, 1981), 48.
32. For the purposes of this study, the term "state elite" encompasses civil and military bureaucracies and excludes politicians, for whom are the term "political elite" is used.
33. For an early and valuable study of Turkish political elite, see Frederick W. Frey, *The Turkish Political Elite* (Cambridge, MA: MIT University Press, 1965).
34. Ilter Turan, "The Evolution of Political Culture in Turkey," in *Modern Turkey: Continuity and Change*, ed. Ahmet Evin (Opladen: Leske Verlag + Budrich GmbH, 1984), 105.
35. Metin Heper, "The Consolidation of Democracy versus Democratization in Turkey," *Turkish Studies* 3, no. 1 (2002): 140.
36. Metin Heper, "Conclusion," in *State, Democracy and the Military: Turkey in the 1980s*, ed. Metin Heper and Ahmet Evin (Berlin: Walter de Gruyter, 1988), 250.
37. Serif Mardin, "Opposition and Control in Turkey," *Government and Opposition* 1, no. 3 (1966): 379–80.
38. Mardin, "Center-Periphery Relations," 185.
39. Turan, "The Evolution of Political Culture in Turkey," 98.
40. Heper, "State and Society in Turkish Political Experience," 5.
41. Udo Steinbach, "The Impact of Ataturk on Turkey's Political Culture since World War II," in *Ataturk and the Modernization of Turkey*, ed. Jacob M. Landau (Boulder, CO: Westview, 1984), 81.
42. Ernest Gellner, "The Turkish Option in Comparative Perspective," in *Rethinking Modernity and National Identity in Turkey*, ed. Sibel Bozdogan and Resat Kasaba (Seattle: University of Washington Press, 1997), 241.

---

43. Mardin, "Center-Periphery Relations," 186.
44. Ergun Ozbudun, "State Elites and Democratic Political Culture in Turkey," in *Political Culture and Democracy in Developing Countries*, ed. Larry Diamond (Boulder, CO: Lynne Rienner Publishers, 1993), 257–58.
45. Ozbudun and Yazici, *Democratization Reforms in Turkey (1993–2004)*, 33.
46. Hale, *Turkish Politics and the Military*, 174–75.
47. Heper, *The State Tradition in Turkey*, 102–3.
48. Ozbudun and Yazici, *Democratization Reforms in Turkey (1993–2004)*, 33–34.
49. Hale, *Turkish Politics and the Military*, 208.
50. Articles 141 and 142 of the Turkish Penal Code severely restricted freedom of expression and association. Participation in "any society aiming to establish the hegemony or domination of a social class over the other social classes" or "overthrow any of the fundamental economic or social orders established within the country" or to "carry on propaganda" to the same effect was severely penalized. See Hale, *Turkish Politics and the Military*, 197.
51. Ibid., 318. Some parties came to develop special links with the state, claiming to be protectors of its interest. For the statism of the CHP, see Hasan Bulent Kahraman, "Iki Devletcilik, Iki Populizm," *Radikal*, December 1, 2004.
52. Muftuler-Bac, "The Impact of the European Union on Turkish Politics," 168–69.
53. Heper, "The Consolidation of Democracy versus Democratization in Turkey," 141.
54. On the bifurcated nature of the state, see Metin Heper and E. Fuat Keyman, "Double-Faced State: Political Patronage and the Consolidation of Democracy in Turkey," *Middle Eastern Studies* 34, no. 4 (1998).
55. On the Ottoman roots of clientelism, see Belge, "Modernizasyon'da Intisab."
56. For the limited political role of the Turkish citizen, see Etyen Mahcupyan, "Devlet Sirrindan Devlet Sucuna," *Zaman*, December 12, 2004.
57. Heper and Keyman, "Double-Faced State: Political Patronage and the Consolidation of Democracy in Turkey," 264–65.
58. For a comparison of the populist image of Demirel and Ozal, see Tanil Bora and Necmi Erdogan, "Muhafazakar Populizm," in *Muhafazakarlik*, ed. Ahmet Cigdem (Istanbul: Iletisim, 2003), 644.
59. Ozbudun, "State Elites and Democratic Political Culture in Turkey," 262.
60. Ihsan D. Dagi, "Human Rights and Democratization: Turkish Politics in the European Context," *Journal of Southeast European and Black Sea Studies* 1, no. 3 (2001): 52.

204   NOTES

61. Ozbudun, "Continuing Ottoman Legacy and the State Tradition in the Middle East," in *Imperial Legacy: The Ottoman Imprint on the Balkans and the Middle East*, ed. L. Carl Brown (New York: Columbia University Press, 1996), 137.
62. Etyen Mahcupyan, "Ulusal Cikar 'Sir' Olur mu," *Zaman*, December 10, 2004.
63. Ozbudun and Yazici, *Democratization Reforms in Turkey (1993–2004)*, 34–37.
64. Hale, *Turkish Politics and the Military*, 270.
65. Suleyman Sozen and Ian Shaw, "Turkey and the European Union: Modernizing a Traditional State?" *Social Policy & Administration* 37, no. 2 (2003): 111–12.
66. Ozbudun, "State Elites and Democratic Political Culture in Turkey," 264.
67. Metin Heper, "Trials and Tribulations of Democracy in the Third Turkish Republic," in *Politics in the Third Turkish Republic*, ed. Metin Heper and Ahmet Evin (Boulder, CO: Westview Press, 1994), 236–37.
68. Metin Heper, "The State and Debureaucratization: The Case of Turkey," *International Social Science Journal* 42, no. 4 (1990): 609–12.
69. Ozbudun, *Contemporary Turkish Politics: Challenges to Democratic Consolidation*, 118–19.
70. Ergun Ozbudun, "Turkey: How Far from Consolidation?," *Journal of Democracy* 7, no. 3 (1996): 130–31.
71. Umit Cizre, "Egemen Ideoloji ve Turk Silahli Kuvvetleri: Kavramsal ve Iliskisel Bir Analiz," in *Kemalizm*, ed. Ahmet Insel (Istanbul: Iletisim, 2001), 158.
72. Umit Cizre, "Demythologizing the National Security Concept: The Case of Turkey," *Middle East Journal* 57, no. 2 (2003): 217.
73. Caglar Keyder, "Whither the Project of Modernity? Turkey in the 1990s," in *Rethinking Modernity and National Identity in Turkey*, ed. Sibel Bozdogan and Resat Kasaba (Seattle: University of Washington Press, 1997), 46–49.
74. Cizre, "Demythologizing the National Security Concept," 218–19.
75. M. Hakan Yavuz, "Cleansing Islam from the Public Sphere," *Journal of International Affairs* 54, no. 1 (2000): 37–38.
76. As Admiral Guven Erkaya, who participated in the crucial MGK meeting, reportedly later pointed out: "This time it was not the 'armed' but the 'unarmed forces' (*silahsiz kuvvetler*) that should be activated." See Ahmet Tasgetiren, "YOK'u Ciddiye Almak," *Yeni Safak*, August 21, 2003.
77. Metin Heper, "Turkey: Yesterday, Today and Tomorrow," *Journal of Southeast European and Black Sea Studies* 1, no. 3 (2001): 13–14.
78. On the other hand, it could also be argued that the 1982 Constitution had established such a powerful veto power in politics for the military

that a "crude military intervention had become redundant." See Umit Cizre Sakallioglu, "The Anatomy of the Turkish Military's Political Autonomy," *Comparative Politics* 29, no. 2 (1997): 53–54.

79. Umit Cizre and Menderes Cinar, "Turkey 2002: Kemalism, Islamism, and Politics in the Light of the February 28 Process," *South Atlantic Quarterly* 102, no. 2/3 (2003): 322.

80. Cizre, "Demythologizing the National Security Concept: The Case of Turkey," 219.

81. Cizre and Cinar, "Turkey 2002," 321.

82. Ali Karaosmanoglu, "The Evolution of the National Security Culture and the Military in Turkey," *Journal of International Affairs* 54, no. 1 (2000): 213.

83. Cizre and Cinar, "Turkey 2002: Kemalism, Islamism, and Politics in the Light of the February 28 Process," 321.

84. Ibid., 321–22.

85. Following the works of Bourdieu and Elias, the social *habitus* can be defined as "a system of historically and socially constructed generative principles, granting a symbolic frame in which individuality unfolds." See Dietrich Jung, "The Sevres Syndrome: Turkish Foreign Policy and its Historical Legacies," *American Diplomacy* 8, no. 2 (2003): 3.

86. Ibid., 2. See, for example, Huner Tuncer, "Emperyalizmin Yeni Yuzu," *Cumhuriyet*, December 1, 2004.

87. Dagi, "Human Rights and Democratization," 52.

88. Cizre, "Egemen Ideoloji ve Turk Silahli Kuvvetleri," 160.

89. Heper, "Turkey: Yesterday, Today and Tomorrow," 12.

90. For the mixed Kemalist legacy on military intervention to politics, see William Hale, "Transitions to Civilian Governments in Turkey: The Military Perspective" in *State, Democracy and the Military: Turkey in the 1980s*, ed. Metin Heper and Ahmet Evin (Berlin & New York: Walter de Gruyter, 1988), 160–61.

91. Hale, *Turkish Politics and the Military*, 163.

92. Cizre, "Egemen Ideoloji ve Turk Silahli Kuvvetleri," 177–78.

93. On the conservative transformation of Kemalism, see Murat Belge, "Muhafazakarlik Uzerine," in *Muhafazakarlik*, ed. Ahmet Cigdem (Istanbul: Iletisim, 2003), 100.

94. Heper, "Turkey: Yesterday, Today and Tomorrow," 14.

95. Commission of the European Communities, *2004 Regular Report on Turkey's Progress Towards Accession [SEC(2004) 1201]* (Brussels: European Union, 2004), 23.

96. Hale, *Turkish Politics and the Military*, 256–59.

97. Commission of the European Communities, *1999 Regular Report on Turkey's Progress Towards Accession*, 9–10.

98. Commission of the European Communities, *2000 Regular Report on Turkey's Progress Towards Accession*, 12–14.

99. Commission of the European Communities, *2001 Regular Report on Turkey's Progress Towards Accession*, 16–18.

100. Article 169 (support for illegal armed organizations), for example, was applied to students petitioning for optional Kurdish language courses at their university.

101. Commission of the European Communities, *2002 Regular Report on Turkey's Progress Towards Accession*, 21–25.

102. For more details, see Cizre Sakallioglu, "The Anatomy of the Turkish Military's Political Autonomy," 159–61.

103. Commission of the European Communities, *2003 Regular Report on Turkey's Progress Towards Accession*, 18–22.

104. Commission of the European Communities, *2004 Regular Report on Turkey's Progress Towards Accession*, 23.

105. Commission of the European Communities, *1999 Regular Report on Turkey's Progress Towards Accession*, 9.

106. Commission of the European Communities, *2000 Regular Report on Turkey's Progress Towards Accession*, 12.

107. Commission of the European Communities, *2004 Regular Report on Turkey's Progress Towards Accession*, 22–23.

108. Commission of the European Communities, *2001 Regular Report on Turkey's Progress Towards Accession*, 19.

109. Commission of the European Communities, *2003 Regular Report on Turkey's Progress Towards Accession*, 18–19.

110. Commission of the European Communities, *2004 Regular Report on Turkey's Progress Towards Accession*, 21–22.

111. Commission of the European Communities, *2002 Regular Report on Turkey's Progress Towards Accession*, 21–25.

112. Commission of the European Communities, *2003 Regular Report on Turkey's Progress Towards Accession*, 19–22.

113. Ibid., 21.

114. Commission of the European Communities, *2004 Regular Report on Turkey's Progress Towards Accession*, 23–24.

115. This figure rises up to four if the "soft" coup of 28 February 1997 is also counted.

116. Atilla Yayla, "Bumin, Demokrasi ve Laiklik," *Zaman*, April 27, 2005.

117. Dagi, *Batililasma Korkusu*, 1–3.

118. Murat Gurgen, "Orgeneral Kilinc: Avrupa Bize Uymaz," *Radikal*, March 8, 2002. For a similar approach, see Manisali, "Rusya ile Iliskiler Alternatif mi, Yoksa Bir Denge Arayisi mi?"

119. Metin Heper, "The Military-Civilian Relations in Post-1997 Turkey" (paper presented at the IPSA Armed Forces and Society Research Committee Conference "Globalization of Civil-Military Relations: Democratization, Reform, and Security," Bucharest, June 29–30, 2002), 3.

120. Metin Heper, "The European Union, the Turkish Military and Democracy," *South European Society & Politics* 10, no. 1 (2005): 37–42.

121. The cases of the CHP, DYP, and MHP should be noted in that respect.
122. Ankara Burosu, "'Ulusal Guvenlik Tartisilmali'," *Radikal*, August 5, 2001.
123. Mesut Yilmaz, *'Ulusal Guvenlik Tartismasi'* (Ankara: 2001), http://www.belgenet.com/2001/yilmaz_040801.html.
124. Cizre, "Demythologizing the National Security Concept."
125. Dagi, *Batililasma Korkusu*, 19–20.
126. Mehmet Ali Birand, "Askeri Rahat Birakalim," *Posta*, November 12, 2002.
127. Ibid.
128. Ahmet Insel, "The AKP and Normalizing Democracy in Turkey," *South Atlantic Quarterly* 102, no. 2/3 (2003): 300.
129. On the diachronic question of human rights and Westernization in Turkey, see Tanil Bora, Y. Bulent Peker, and Mithat Sancar, "Hakim Ideolojiler, Bati, Batililasma ve Insan Haklari," in *Modernlesme ve Baticilik*, ed. Uygur Kocabasoglu (Istanbul: Iletisim, 2002).
130. Ankara Burosu, "Emir Ozkok'ten," *Hurriyet*, December 7, 2004.
131. Ahmet Insel, "Cumhuriyet'in Yol Ayrimi," *Radikal Cumhuriyet*, October 29, 2004.
132. Ankara Burosu, "Dusunce Aciklamak Hala Suc," *Radikal*, May 11, 2005.
133. This issue has continued to create friction in EU-Turkey relations and is being used as evidence of Turkey's failure to apply EU norms. The Turkish military refused to endorse a report of an experts' group on Turkey's democratization financed by the Dutch EU Presidency on the grounds that it recommended the subordination of the military to the Ministry of Defense and the transfer of decision-making authority on national security issues to the parliament. See Ozgur Eksi, "Pasalar Rapordan Imzalarini Cekti," *Hurriyet*, June 27, 2005.
134. Hilmi Ozkok, *Harp Akademileri Komutanligindaki Yillik Degerlendirme Konusmasi* (Ankara: 2005), http://www.tsk.mil.tr/bashalk/konusma_mesaj/2005/yillikdegerlendirme_200405.htm.
135. Editorial, "Glosse Politik: Machtwort," *Frankfurter Allgemeine Zeitung*, April 22, 2005.
136. Mehmet Ali Birand, "Asker Kendini Zora Sokuyor," *Posta*, April 26, 2005.
137. Ibid.
138. Mehmet Ali Birand, "Turkiye Artik Tercihini Yapmali," *Posta*, April 27, 2005.
139. See Eduard Soler i Lecha, "Debating on Turkey's Accession: National and Ideological Cleavages in the European Parliament," in *The Role of Parliaments in European Foreign Policy*, ed. Esther Barbé and Anna Herranz (Barcelona: European Parliament Information Office, 2005).

CHAPTER 5

1. This happened in the famous response of Jesus to a man who asked him whether Jews should pay taxes to the Roman Caesar. Jesus then showed him a Roman coin on which Caesar's face and name were inscribed and replied, "Render to Caesar what is Caesar's, and to God what is God's" (Luke 20:20–26). His response clearly recognized that the realms of religion and politics do not overlap.

2. Binnaz Toprak, "Religion and State in Turkey" (paper presented at the Dayan Center Conference "Contemporary Turkey: Challenges of Change," Tel-Aviv, June 20, 1999), 2.

3. Mardin, "Ideology and Religion in the Turkish Revolution," 206.

4. Zurcher, *Turkey: A Modern History*, 83.

5. Gellner, "The Turkish Option in Comparative Perspective," 239.

6. Nuray Mert, "Cumhuriyet Turkiyesi'nde Laiklik ve Karsi Laikligin Dusunsel Boyutu," in *Kemalizm*, ed. Ahmet Insel (Istanbul: Iletisim, 2001), 202–7.

7. Mardin, "Ideology and Religion in the Turkish Revolution," 208.

8. For a thorough account of this process, see Binnaz Toprak, *Islam and Political Development in Turkey* (Leiden: Brill, 1981), 40–58.

9. Suna Kili, "Kemalism in Contemporary Turkey," *International Political Studies* 1, no. 3 (1980): 383–92.

10. Toprak, *Islam and Political Development in Turkey*, 46.

11. Sencer Ayata, "Patronage, Party, and State: The Politicization of Islam in Turkey," *Middle East Journal* 50, no. 1 (1996): 44–45.

12. Andrew Davison, "Turkey, a "Secular" State? The Challenge of Description," *South Atlantic Quarterly* 102, no. 2/3 (2003): 337–39.

13. Aydin and Keyman, *European Integration and the Transformation of Turkish Democracy*, 6.

14. Islam as a social *idiom* maintained its significance throughout the republican years, as Kemalism failed to provide a formidable alternative. See Serif Mardin, "Islam in Mass Society: Harmony versus Polarization" in *Politics in the Third Turkish Republic*, ed. Metin Heper and Ahmet Evin (Boulder CO: Westview Press, 1994), 164.

15. Ronnie Margulies and Ergin Yildizoglu, "The Political Uses of Islam in Turkey," *Middle East Report* 153 (1988): 13.

16. Binnaz Toprak, "The State, Politics and Religion in Turkey," in *State, Democracy and the Military: Turkey in the 1980s*, ed. Metin Heper and Ahmet Evin (Berlin & New York: Walter de Gruyter, 1988), 123–24.

17. These public secondary schools provided—in addition to the regular school curriculum—Arabic and Islamic religion courses so their graduates could qualify to become prayer leaders (*imam*) and preachers (*hatip*).

18. Berkes, *The Development of Secularism in Turkey*, 490.

19. Toprak, *Islam and Political Development in Turkey*, 79–80.

20. For the tension between state secularism and democracy in republican Turkey, see Nilufer Gole, "Authoritarian Secularism and Islamic Participation: The Case of Turkey," in *Civil Society in the Middle East*, ed. Augustus Richard Norton (Leiden: E. J. Brill, 1995), 19–20.

21. Despite being an antisystemic political movement, the National View borrowed many conceptual tools from orthodox Kemalism. See Menderes Cinar, "Kemalist Cumhuriyetcilik ve Islamci Kemalizm," in *Islamcilik*, ed. Yasin Aktay (Istanbul: Iletisim, 2004), 174–76.

22. On the pragmatic approach of the AP, see Umit Cizre Sakallioglu, "Parameters and Strategies of Islam-State Interaction in Republican Turkey," *International Journal of Middle East Studies* 28, no. 2 (1996): 239–40.

23. This was the first time in republican Turkish history that *tarikat*s were involved in party politics. See ibid., 241.

24. Occidentalism is the mirror image of Orientalism, a discourse that essentializes the West as inherently imperialistic, rapacious, unjust, and ultimately uncivilized despite its material affluence and power superiority.

25. Burhanettin Duran, "Cumhuriyet Donemi Islamciligi," in *Islamcilik*, ed. Yasin Aktay (Istanbul: Iletisim, 2004), 144–51.

26. See Necmettin Erbakan, *Adil Ekonomik Duzen* (Ankara: Semih Ofset, 1991), cited in Burhanettin Duran, "Islamist Redefinitions of European and Islamic Identities in Turkey," in *Turkey and European Integration: Accession Prospects and Issues*, ed. Mehmet Ugur and Nergis Canefe (London & New York: Routledge, 2004), 127.

27. Rusen Cakir, "Milli Gorus Hareketi" in *Islamcilik*, ed. Yasin Aktay (Istanbul: Iletisim, 2004), 562.

28. Haldun Gulalp, "Modernization Policies and Islamist Politics in Turkey," in *Rethinking Modernity and National Identity in Turkey*, ed. Sibel Bozdogan and Resat Kasaba (Seattle & London: University of Washington Press, 1997), 59.

29. Turkiye Anayasa Mahkemesi, *Milli Nizam Partisi'nin (MNP) Kapatilma Davasi Gerekceli Karari* (Ankara: 1971), http://www.belgenet.com/dava/mnp_05.html.

30. Ali Yasar Saribay, "Millî Nizam Partisi'nin Kurulusu ve Programinin Icerigi," in *Islamcilik*, ed. Yasin Aktay (Istanbul: Iletisim, 2004), 584–87.

31. Cakir, "Milli Gorus Hareketi," 566.

32. For the role of the Turkish-Islamic Synthesis in the formation of post-1980 conservatism in Turkey, see Yuksel Taskin, "Muhafazakar Bir Proje Olarak Turk-Islam Sentezi," in *Muhafazakarlik*, ed. Ahmet Cigdem (Istanbul: Iletisim, 2003), 398–401.

33. Paul J. Magnarella, "Desecularization, State Corporatism and Development in Turkey," *Journal of Third World Studies* 6, no. 2 (1989): 37–44.

34. Nilufer Gole, "Secularism and Islamism in Turkey: The Making of Elites and Counter-Elites," *Middle East Journal* 51, no. 1 (1997): 53–55.

35. Baskin Oran, "Kemalism, Islamism and Globalization: A Study on the Focus of Supreme Loyalty in Globalizing Turkey," *Journal of Southeast European and Black Sea Studies* 1, no. 3 (2001): 30.

36. Haldun Gulalp, "Globalization and Political Islam: The Social Bases of Turkey's Welfare Party," *International Journal of Middle East Studies* 33, no. 3 (2001): 441–42.

37. Nilufer Gole, "The Quest for the Islamic Self within the Context of Modernity," in *Rethinking Modernity and National Identity in Turkey*, ed. Sibel Bozdogan and Resat Kasaba (Seattle & London: University of Washington Press, 1997), 91–92.

38. Omer Laciner, "Islamcilik, Sosyalizm ve Sol," in *Islamcilik*, ed. Yasin Aktay (Istanbul: Iletisim, 2004), 475.

39. Toprak, "Religion and State in Turkey," 5.

40. Omer Caha, "Ana Temalariyla 1980 Sonrasi Islami Uyanis," in *Islamcilik*, ed. Yasin Aktay (Istanbul: Iletisim, 2004), 479.

41. Huntington, "The Clash of Civilizations?" 42–43.

42. This was hardly a surprise, given that experiments with liberal democracy in the Muslim world often threatened to bring to power governments with stark anti-U.S. policies, such as in the case of the Algerian failed elections experiment in 1992.

43. It should be mentioned, though, that the rise in the RP's vote share was also due to its temporary election alliance with the Nationalist Labor Party (*Milliyetci Calisma Partisi*-MCP), led by Alparslan Turkes.

44. Recep Tayyip Erdogan was the RP candidate who won the elections for the Municipality of Istanbul.

45. See Bahattin Aksit, Ayse Serdar and Bahar Tabakoglu, "Islami Egilimli Sivil Toplum Kuruluslari," in *Islamcilik*, ed. Yasin Aktay (Istanbul: Iletisim, 2004).

46. For more details on Islamist political mobilization, see White, *Islamist Mobilization in Turkey*.

47. This pragmatism even created—ephemeral, in retrospect—hopes that the RP rule could reconcile Islam and democracy in Turkey. See Metin Heper, "Islam and Democracy in Turkey: Toward a Reconciliation?," *Middle East Journal* 51, no. 1 (1997): 44–45.

48. M. Hakan Yavuz, "Political Islam and the Welfare (Refah) Party in Turkey," *Comparative Politics* 30, no. 1 (1997): 73–74.

49. Ziya Onis, "Political Islam at the Crossroads: From Hegemony to Co-Existence," *Contemporary Politics* 7, no. 4 (2001): 285.

50. The signature of a multi-billion dollar trade agreement between Turkey and Iran for the construction of a pipeline for the delivery of Iranian natural gas to Turkey, despite explicit U.S. opposition, was a clear sign of this new policy. See Hale, *Turkish Foreign Policy 1774–2000*, 314–15.

51. While Erbakan condemned the UN sanctions against Libya and declared that Libya was the country suffering most from terror—apparently of Western origin, the Libyan leader Muammar Qaddafi called in Erbakan's presence for the establishment of an independent Kurdish state in Turkey. See Alan Makovsky, "How to Deal with Erbakan," *Middle East Quarterly* 4, no. 1 (1997).

52. The lack of any serious genuine civil society reaction against the military intervention and the alliance of other civil society forces with the military against the coalition government, were clear manifestations of the shortcomings of the democratic political system. See Bekir Berat Ozipek, "28 Subat ve Islamcilar," in *Islamcilik*, ed. Yasin Aktay (Istanbul: Iletisim, 2004), 646–48.

53. Cizre and Cinar, "Turkey 2002," 312.

54. Yavuz, "Cleansing Islam from the Public Sphere," 37–38.

55. Onis, "Political Islam at the Crossroads," 287.

56. Birol Yesilada, "The Virtue Party," *Turkish Studies* 3, no. 1 (2002): 78–79.

57. Turkiye Anayasa Mahkemesi, *Fazilet Partisi'nin (FP) Kapatilma Davasi Gerekceli Karari* (Ankara: 2001), http://www.belgenet.com/arsiv/fazilet.html.

58. Fuller, "Turkey's Strategic Model," 52.

59. Haldun Gulalp, "Whatever Happened to Secularization? The Multiple Islams in Turkey," *South Atlantic Quarterly* 102, no. 2/3 (2003): 389–90.

60. Ismail Kara, "Diyanet Isleri Baskanligi," in *Islamcilik*, ed. Yasin Aktay (Istanbul: Iletisim, 2004), 180–83.

61. This instrumental use of Islam, however, met with the opposition of Islamists. See Murat Yilmaz, "Darbeler ve Islamcilik," in *Islamcilik*, ed. Yasin Aktay (Istanbul: Iletisim, 2004), 637–39.

62. Gole, "Secularism and Islamism in Turkey: The Making of Elites and Counter-Elites," 48–49.

63. Etyen Mahcupyan, "Aleviler, Azinlik, Diyanet," *Zaman*, November 1, 2004.

64. Binnaz Toprak, "Turkiye'de Laiklik, Siyasal Islam ve Demokrasi," in *Uluslararasi Ataturk ve Cagdas Toplum Sempozyumu*, ed. Demokrasi ve Genclik Vakfi (Istanbul: Is Bankasi Kultur Yayinlari, 2002), 289.

65. Commission of the European Communities, *1998 Regular Report on Turkey's Progress Towards Accession*, 10.

66. Ibid., 19.

67. Commission of the European Communities, *2000 Regular Report on Turkey's Progress Towards Accession*, 11.

68. Ibid., 17–18.

69. Commission of the European Communities, *2001 Regular Report on Turkey's Progress Towards Accession*, 27.

70. Commission of the European Communities, *2002 Regular Report on Turkey's Progress Towards Accession*, 37.

71. Commission of the European Communities, *2003 Regular Report on Turkey's Progress Towards Accession*, 36.

72. Commission of the European Communities, *2004 Regular Report on Turkey's Progress Towards Accession*, 23.

73. Ibid., 44–45.

74. Commission of the European Communities, *2002 Regular Report on Turkey's Progress Towards Accession*, 32.

75. Commission of the European Communities, *2003 Regular Report on Turkey's Progress Towards Accession*, 21.

76. Ibid., 36.

77. Commission of the European Communities, *2004 Regular Report on Turkey's Progress Towards Accession*, 44.

78. Ioannis N. Grigoriadis, "AKP and the Paradox of Islamic Europhilia," *Turkish Policy Quarterly* 3, no. 1 (2004): 66.

79. European Court of Human Rights (ECHR), *Registrar's Press Release: Judgment in the Case of Refah Partisi (Welfare Party), Erbakan, Kazan and Tekdal vs. Turkey* (Strasbourg: ECHR, 2001), http://www.echr.coe .int/Eng/Press/2001/July/RefahPartisi2001jude.htm. The full text of the decision is available at European Court of Human Rights (ECHR), *Refah Partisi [Welfare Party] and Others vs. Turkey [No. 41340/98, No. 41342/98, No. 41343/98 and No. 41344/98]* (Strasbourg: Third Section, 2001).

80. European Court of Human Rights (ECHR), *Refah Partisi [Welfare Party] and Others vs. Turkey [No. 41340/98, No. 41342/98, No. 41343/98 and No. 41344/98]* (Strasbourg: Grand Chamber, 2003).

81. Grigoriadis, "AKP and the Paradox of Islamic Europhilia," 68.

82. For parallel developments in the field of *tarikat*s and the Fethullah Gulen movement, see M. Hakan Yavuz, "Towards an Islamic Liberalism? The Nurcu Movement and Fethullah Gulen," *Middle East Journal* 53, no. 4 (1999): 600–605.

83. Effie Fokas, "The Islamist Movement and Turkey-EU Relations," in *Turkey and European Integration: Accession Prospects and Issues*, ed. Mehmet Ugur and Nergis Canefe (London & New York: Routledge, 2004), 154–55.

84. Gareth Jenkins, "Muslim Democrats in Turkey?" *Survival* 45, no. 1 (2003): 53–55.

85. Soner Cagaptay, "The November 2002 Elections and Turkey's New Political Era," *Middle East Review of International Affairs (MERIA)* 6, no. 4 (2002): 44.

86. Yalcin Akdogan, "Adalet ve Kalkinma Partisi," in *Islamcilik*, ed. Yasin Aktay (Istanbul: Iletisim, 2004), 625–31.

87. Metin Heper and Sule Toktas, "Islam, Modernity, and Democracy in Contemporary Turkey: The Case of Recep Tayyip Erdogan," *Muslim World* 93, no. 2 (2003): 173.
88. Ihsan D. Dagi, "Transformation of Islamic Political Identity in Turkey: Rethinking the West and Westernization," *Turkish Studies* 6, no. 1 (2005): 31.
89. Grigoriadis, "AKP and the Paradox of Islamic Europhilia," 67.
90. On the conservative nature of the AKP, see Yasin Aktay, "Islamciliktaki Muhafazakarlik Bakiye," in *Muhafazakarlik*, ed. Ahmet Cigdem (Istanbul: Iletisim, 2003), 348–50.
91. See Onis, "Turkish Modernisation and Challenges for the New Europe," 13–17.
92. Cizre and Cinar, "Turkey 2002," 327.
93. On this, also see Ahmet T. Kuru, "Reinterpretation of Secularism in Turkey: The Case of the Justice and Development Party," in *Transformation of Turkish Politics*, ed. M. Hakan Yavuz (Salt Lake City: University of Utah Press, 2006).
94. Yalcin Akdogan, *AK Parti ve Muhafazakar Demokrasi* (Ankara: AK Parti Yayinlari, 2004), 6, http://www.akparti.org.tr/muhafazakar.doc.
95. Insel, "The AKP and Normalizing Democracy in Turkey," 304.
96. See Sahin Alpay, "AB, Turkiye ve Islam," *Zaman*, October 9, 2004.
97. Heper and Toktas, "Islam, Modernity, and Democracy in Contemporary Turkey," 176.
98. Ali Bulac is a primary example of this shift. His argument on the "three generations of Islamist politics" is illuminating. See Ali Bulac, "Islam'in Uc Siyaset Tarzi veya Islamcilarin Uc Nesli," in *Islamcilik*, ed. Yasin Aktay (Istanbul: Iletisim, 2004), 48–50. See also Ihsan D. Dagi, "Rethinking Human Rights, Democracy, and the West: Post-Islamist Intellectuals in Turkey," *Critique: Critical Middle Eastern Studies* 13, no. 2 (2004): 143–49.
99. This was the phenomenon of "Westoxification," a favorite topic of Iranian political Islam.
100. Some authors even came to the point of discovering human rights courts during the Islamic "Era of Felicity." See Ahmet Sahin, "Islam'da Insan Haklari Mahkemesinden Bir Ornek!" *Zaman*, December 14, 2004.
101. Dagi, "Rethinking Human Rights, Democracy, and the West," 141.
102. Ali Bulac, "CHP, Anadolu Solu ve Basortusu," *Zaman*, July 3, 2002.
103. Dagi, "Rethinking Human Rights, Democracy, and the West," 142.
104. Simten Cosar and Aylin Ozman, "Centre-Right Politics in Turkey after the November 2002 Election: Neo-Liberalism with a Muslim Face," *Contemporary Politics* 10, no. 1 (2004): 66.
105. Heper and Toktas, "Islam, Modernity, and Democracy in Contemporary Turkey," 160; Murat Belge, "Takiye Tartismasi," *Radikal*, November 8, 2002.

106. See European Court of Human Rights (ECHR), *Leyla Sahin vs. Turkey [No. 44774/98]* (Strasbourg: Fourth Section, 2004), 26. This decision came under heavy attack by European human rights organizations, which diagnosed a dangerous illiberal shift in the ruling of the Court, following the emergence of a headscarf question in EU member states like France.

107. In any case, the decision only ruled that headscarf restrictions in higher education did not violate the freedom of religion according to the European Convention. It did not pose any obstacles to the lifting of the restrictions. See Taha Akyol, "Anayasa, Laiklik, Siyaset," *Milliyet*, April 27, 2005.

108. Oran, "Kemalism, Islamism and Globalization: A Study on the Focus of Supreme Loyalty in Globalizing Turkey," 27–29.

109. Rusen Cakir and Irfan Bozan, *Sivil, Seffaf ve Demokratik Bir Diyanet Isleri Baskanligi Mumkun mu?* (Istanbul: TESEV Yayinlari, 2005), 73–74. Nonetheless, the rise in the number of mosques should be attributed not only to increasing religiosity but also to rising welfare. Mosques were also built in Sunni villages that could not afford one before.

110. Kara, "Diyanet Isleri Baskanligi," 194–96.

111. Cakir and Bozan, *Sivil, Seffaf ve Demokratik Bir Diyanet Isleri Baskanligi Mumkun mu?* 110–17.

112. See Timur Soykan, "Alevi Tepkisi Artiyor," *Radikal*, October 9, 2004.

113. Cakir and Bozan, *Sivil, Seffaf ve Demokratik Bir Diyanet Isleri Baskanligi Mumkun mu?* 336–39.

114. Ozkok, *Harp Akademileri Komutanligindaki Yillik Degerlendirme Konusmasi.*

115. Mustafa Bumin, *Bilimsel Toplantiyi Acis Konusmasi* (Ankara: 2005), http://www.anayasa.gov.tr/ydonum/kur43.htm.

116. Ismet Berkan, "Turban: Yine, Yeni, Yeniden . . . ," *Radikal*, April 27, 2005.

117. Ankara Burosu, "Havada Bulut, Turbani Unut!" *Radikal*, April 26, 2005.

118. Yayla, "Bumin, Demokrasi ve Laiklik."

119. Ismet Berkan, "Gereksiz Lakirdilar," *Radikal*, May 3, 2005.

120. Osman Can, "Turkiye Tarzi Laiklik," *Radikal Iki*, May 12, 2004.

121. Ali Carkoglu and Binnaz Toprak, *Turkiye'de Din, Toplum ve Siyaset* (Istanbul: TESEV Yayinlari, 2000), 17.

122. Ibid., 70–75.

123. Ibid., 58.

124. Dagi, "Rethinking Human Rights, Democracy, and the West," 149–50.

125. Ibid., 139.

126. Duran, "Islamist Redefinitions of European and Islamic Identities in Turkey," 131.
127. Dagi, "Transformation of Islamic Political Identity in Turkey," 31–33.
128. Onis, "Political Islam at the Crossroads: From Hegemony to Co-Existence," 293–95.

CHAPTER 6

1. Timothy Baycroft, *Nationalism in Europe 1789–1945* (Cambridge: Cambridge University Press, 1998), 6.
2. Umut Ozkirimli, *Theories of Nationalism: A Critical Introduction* (New York: Palgrave, 2000), 38–39.
3. Lewis, *The Emergence of Modern Turkey*, 335.
4. The Ottoman Sultan had been invested with the title of Caliph (supreme political and religious leader of all Muslims) since the early sixteenth century, although this was mainly symbolic and not universally accepted.
5. Non-Sunni Ottoman Muslims (Alevi, Shiite, and Druze) often faced severe discrimination.
6. David Kushner, *The Rise of Turkish Nationalism 1876–1908* (London: Frank Cass, 1977), 7–9.
7. Yusuf Akcura, *Uc Tarz-i Siyaset* (Ankara: Turk Tarih Kurumu Basimevi, 1976), 19–36, originally published as Yusuf Akcura, "Uc Tarz-i Siyaset," *Turk*, March 15, 1904.
8. Nergis Canefe, "Turkish Nationalism and Ethno-Symbolic Analysis: The Rules of Exception," *Nations and Nationalism* 8, no. 2 (2002): 145–50.
9. Following the Moudros Armistice of October 30, 1918, military forces of Entente states occupied large parts of Ottoman territory, dealing a heavy blow against Ottoman sovereignty.
10. Caglar Keyder, *State and Class in Turkey: A Study in Capitalist Development* (London: Verso, 1987), 79, cited in Ayhan Aktar, "Homogenising the Nation, Turkifying the Economy: The Turkish Experience of Population Exchange Reconsidered," in *Crossing the Aegean: An Appraisal of the 1923 Population Exchange between Greece and Turkey*, ed. Renée Hirschon (New York & Oxford: Berghahn Books, 2003), 81.
11. Akman suggested the use of the term "modernist nationalism" as a more accurate description of Kemalist nationalism. See Akman, "Modernist Nationalism," 24–30.
12. Ayse Kadioglu, "The Paradox of Turkish Nationalism and the Construction of Official Identity," *Middle Eastern Studies* 32, no. 2 (1996): 184.
13. In Ataturk's words: "We will raise our national culture up to the level of contemporary civilization." See Mustafa Kemal Ataturk, *Ataturk'un*

Soylevleri ve Demecleri (Ankara: Ataturk Kultur, Dil ve Tarih Yuksek Kurumu, Ataturk Arastirma Merkezi, 1989), 318.

14. Ioannis N. Grigoriadis and Ali M. Ansari, "Turkish and Iranian Nationalisms," in *A Companion to the History of the Middle East*, ed. Youssef Choueiri (Oxford: Blackwell Publishing, 2005), 314.
15. Mustafa Kemal Ataturk, *Nutuk* (Ankara: Kultur Bakanligi Yayinlari, 1980), 6–7.
16. Kushner, *The Rise of Turkish Nationalism 1876–1908*, 50–55.
17. Anthony D. Smith, *The Ethnic Origins of Nations* (Oxford & Malden MA: Blackwell, 1988), 134–36.
18. Canefe, "Turkish Nationalism and Ethno-Symbolic Analysis," 145–46.
19. For more information, see Peter Alford Andrews, ed., *Ethnic Groups in the Republic of Turkey* (Wiesbaden: Dr. Ludwig Reichert Verlag, 1989).
20. Kili, "Kemalism in Contemporary Turkey," 388–89.
21. Etyen Mahcupyan, "Azinlik Ureten Zihniyet . . .," *Zaman*, December 12, 2004.
22. This call was also addressed to non-Muslim minorities. Tekin Alp, a Jewish-born fervent Turkish nationalist intellectual campaigned for the voluntary assimilation of non-Muslim minorities. Yet the appeal of his efforts was rather limited. See Rifat Bali, "Tekin Alp," in *Milliyetcilik*, ed. Tanil Bora (Istanbul: Iletisim, 2002), 896–99.
23. Kushner, *The Rise of Turkish Nationalism 1876–1908*, 7–9.
24. Tanil Bora, "'Ekalliyet Yilanlari': Turk Milliyetciligi ve Azinliklar," in *Milliyetcilik*, ed. Tanil Bora (Istanbul: Iletisim Yayinlari, 2002), 911–13.
25. Turk Buyuk Millet Meclisi (TBMM), *Iskan Kanunu* (2510/1934).
26. Turk Buyuk Millet Meclisi (TBMM), *Varlik Vergisi Hakkinda Kanun* (4305/1942).
27. Cemil Kocak, "Kemalist Milliyetciligin Bulanik Sulari," in *Milliyetcilik*, ed. Tanil Bora (Istanbul: Iletisim, 2002), 37–41.
28. Educated Muslim elites of the Ottoman Empire preferred the term "Ottoman" (*Osmanli*) and attributed the term "Turk" to the Turco-man nomads, or later, "the ignorant and uncouth Turkish-speaking peasants of the Anatolian villages." See Kushner, *The Rise of Turkish Nationalism 1876–1908*, 20–26.
29. Hugh Poulton, *Top Hat, Grey Wolf and Crescent: Turkish Nationalism and the Turkish Republic* (London: Hurst and Company, 1997), 109–14. For the "revival" of Turkish vernacular in republican Turkey and its political connotations, see Serif Mardin, "Playing Games with Names," in *Fragments of Culture: The Everyday of Modern Turkey*, ed. Deniz Kandiyoti and Ayse Saktanber (London, New York: I. B. Tauris, 2002), 119–25.
30. Ayhan Aktar, *Varlik Vergisi ve 'Turklestirme' Politikalari* (Istanbul: Iletisim, 2000), 130–34.

31. Turan, "The Evolution of Political Culture in Turkey," 101–5.
32. Baskin Oran, *Turkiye'de Azinliklar: Kavramlar, Lozan, Ic Mevzuat, Ictihat, Uygulama* (Istanbul: TESEV Yayinlari, 2004), 84.
33. Jacob M. Landau, *Pan-Turkism: From Irredentism to Cooperation*, 2nd ed. (Bloomington, IN: Indiana University Press, 1995), 221–24.
34. Tanil Bora, "Nationalist Discourses in Turkey," *South Atlantic Quarterly* 102, no. 2/3 (2003): 436.
35. Ziya Gokalp, *Turkculugun Esaslari* (Istanbul: Kum Saati Yayinlari, 2001), 37–53, originally published as Ziya Gokalp, *Turkculugun Esaslari* (Ankara: Matbuat ve Istihbarat Matbaasi, 1920).
36. Poulton, *Top Hat, Grey Wolf and Crescent: Turkish Nationalism and the Turkish Republic*, 76–82.
37. Kadioglu, "The Paradox of Turkish Nationalism and the Construction of Official Identity," 188–89.
38. A significant percentage of the Anatolian population was refugees from former Ottoman territories, which they were forced to flee on the basis of their Islamic religion, which identified them with Ottoman Turks.
39. Bora, "Nationalist Discourses in Turkey," 449.
40. Poulton, *Top Hat, Grey Wolf and Crescent: Turkish Nationalism and the Turkish Republic*, 178–81.
41. Magnarella, "Desecularization, State Corporatism and Development in Turkey," 39–40.
42. Duygu Koksal, "Fine-Tuning Nationalism: Critical Perspectives from Republican Literature in Turkey," *Turkish Studies* 2, no. 2 (2001): 64–65.
43. Murat Belge, "Turkiye'de Zenofobi ve Milliyetcilik," in *Milliyetcilik*, ed. Tanil Bora (Istanbul: Iletisim, 2002), 189–90.
44. Detailed information on the "Turkish-Islamic Synthesis" can be found in the book of one of its ideologues: Ibrahim Kafesoglu, *Turk-Islam Sentezi* (Istanbul: Aydinlar Ocagi, 1985), 159–213.
45. Poulton, *Top Hat, Grey Wolf and Crescent: Turkish Nationalism and the Turkish Republic*, 181–87.
46. Kadioglu, "The Paradox of Turkish Nationalism and the Construction of Official Identity," 189–92.
47. Sam Kaplan, "Din-u Devlet All over Again? The Politics of Military Secularism and Religious Militarism in Turkey Following the 1980 Coup," *International Journal of Middle East Studies* 34, no. 1 (2002): 120.
48. Council of Europe, *European Charter for Regional or Minority Languages* (Strasbourg: Council of Europe, 1992), http://conventions.coe.int/Treaty/en/Treaties/Html/148.htm.
49. Council of Europe, *Framework Convention for the Protection of National Minorities* (Strasbourg: Council of Europe, 1995), http://conventions.coe.int/Treaty/en/Treaties/Html/157.htm.
50. See Checkel, "The Europeanization of Citizenship?" 185.

51. In contrast, the concept of "humanitarian intervention" and its application in the Kosovo and Iraq wars weakened the moral basis of minority rights protection.

52. Western insensitivity to the minority rights situation in Turkey, while "humanitarian interventions" were planned in other parts of the world, was often seen as evidence of Western double standards.

53. Mustafa Saatci, "Nation–States and Ethnic Boundaries: Modern Turkish Identity and Turkish–Kurdish Conflict," *Nations and Nationalism* 8, no. 4 (2002): 559.

54. Many of the leading political and military figures of republican Turkey were claimed to be of—at least partial—Kurdish descent. Ismet Inonu, Cemal Gursel, Suleyman Demirel, and Turgut Ozal were some of the Turkish leaders with alleged or real Kurdish roots.

55. Will Kymlicka, "Misunderstanding Nationalism," in *Theorizing Nationalism*, ed. Ronald Beiner (Albany, NY: SUNY Press, 1999), 134.

56. Mesut Yegen, "Turk Milliyetcilligi ve Kurt Sorunu," in *Milliyetcilik*, ed. Tanil Bora (Istanbul: Iletisim, 2002), 889–91.

57. In the early 1990s, the People's Labor Party (*Halkin Emek Partisi—* HEP) became the representative of moderate Kurds who opposed the use of violence but demanded respect for human rights of Turkey's Kurds.

58. See Hamit Bozarslan, "Kurd Milliyetcilligi ve Kurd Hareketi (1898– 2000)," in *Milliyetcilik*, ed. Tanil Bora (Istanbul: Iletisim Yayinlari, 2002), 866–67. After the closure of the People's Democracy Party (*Halkin Demokrasi* Partisi—HADEP), the political representation of the Kurdish minority was assumed by the Democratic People's Party (*Demokratik Halk* Partisi—DEHAP).

59. Baskin Oran, "Kurt Milliyetcilligin Diyalektigi," in *Milliyetcilik*, ed. Tanil Bora (Istanbul: Iletisim Yayinlari, 2002), 878–79.

60. A Kurdish nationalist historiographic narrative appeared for the first time as a response to established Turkish nationalist historical accounts. See Konrad Hirschler, "Defining the Nation: Kurdish Historiography in Turkey in the 1990s," *Middle Eastern Studies* 37, no. 3 (2001).

61. Orhan Miroglu, "AB Sureci, Dil Haklari ve Kurtler," *Radikal Iki*, October 17, 2004.

62. Mesut Yegen, "Turkluk ve Kurtler: Bugun," *Birikim*, no. 188 (2004): 32–34.

63. Murat Kucuk, "Mezhepten Millete: Aleviler ve Turk Milliyetciligi," in *Milliyetcilik*, ed. Tanil Bora (Istanbul: Iletisim, 2002), 907–9.

64. For more details, see Turkiye Insan Haklari Vakfi (TIHV), *1995 Turkiye Insan Haklari Raporu* (Ankara: Turkiye Insan Haklari Vakfi Yayinlari, 1997), 194–213.

65. David Zeidan, "The Alevi of Anatolia," *Middle East Review of International Affairs (MERIA)* 3, no. 4 (1999): 81.

66. Ibrahim Bahadir, "Alevilige Milliyetci Yaklasimlar ve Aleviler Uzerindeki Etkileri," *Birikim*, no. 188 (2004): 49–55.
67. Kucuk, "Mezhepten Millete: Aleviler ve Turk Milliyetciligi," 901–2.
68. Istanbul Burosu, "Aleviler, Rapordaki Azinlik Ifadesine Itiraz Edecek," *Zaman*, November 20, 2004.
69. Erdogan Aydin, "Alevileri Ne Yapmali?," *Radikal Iki*, October 24, 2004.
70. Michael M. Gunter, *The Kurds and the Future of Turkey* (New York: St. Martin's Press, 1997), 67.
71. Ciller has been one of the most inconsistent and mercurial Turkish politicians, but this does not eliminate the political significance of her statements.
72. William Hale, "Identities and Politics in Turkey," (London: SOAS, 2003), 23.
73. Muhittin Ataman, "Ozal Leadership and Restructuring of Turkish Ethnic Policy in the 1980s," *Middle Eastern Studies* 38, no. 4 (2002): 127–28.
74. Carnegie Endowment for International Peace, "Treaty of Peace with Turkey Signed at Lausanne, July 24, 1923" *The Treaties of Peace 1919–1923* (New York: Carnegie Endowment for International Peace, 1924).
75. William Hale, "Human Rights, the European Union and the Turkish Accession Process," *Turkish Studies* 5, no. 1 (2003): 116–18.
76. Dilek Kurban, "Turkiye'nin Azinlik Sorununun Anayasal Cozumu: Esitlik ile Yuzles(me)mek," *Birikim*, no. 188 (2004): 41–42.
77. Ioannis N. Grigoriadis, "Turk or Turkiyeli? The Reform of Turkey's Minority Legislation and the Rediscovery of Ottomanism," *Middle Eastern Studies* 43, no. 3 (2007): 425–27.
78. Commission of the European Communities, *2002 Regular Report on Turkey's Progress Towards Accession*, 41.
79. Commission of the European Communities, *2004 Regular Report on Turkey's Progress Towards Accession*, 24.
80. Ibid., 38.
81. Commission of the European Communities, *2001 Regular Report on Turkey's Progress Towards Accession*, 29.
82. See Commission of the European Communities, *2003 Regular Report on Turkey's Progress Towards Accession*, 23. Turkey reserved the right to interpret and apply the provisions of Article 27 of the Covenant, which referred to minority rights, "in accordance with the related provisions and rules of the Constitution of the Republic of Turkey and the Treaty of Lausanne of 24 July 1923 and its Appendices."
83. Commission of the European Communities, *2004 Regular Report on Turkey's Progress Towards Accession*, 38.
84. Oran, *Turkiye'de Azinliklar: Kavramlar, Lozan, Ic Mevzuat, Ictihat, Uygulama*, 102.

85. Ankara Burosu, "Erken Kalkan Kurtce Dinler," *Radikal*, June 5, 2004.

86. It is interesting to note that the Laz language was excluded from the list, while both dialects of Turkey's Kurdish population were included. The broadcasting of songs in Laz in state media remained banned. See Ismail Saymaz, "Laz Fikrasi Gibi Olay," *Radikal*, March 28, 2005.

87. Ersan Atar, "Diyarbakir Aciliminin Ilk Somut Adim Atildi: Kurtce TV'nin Yolu Aciliyor," *Sabah*, August 17, 2005.

88. See Oran, *Turkiye'de Azinliklar: Kavramlar, Lozan, Ic Mevzuat, Ictihat, Uygulama*, 113 and Ismail Saymaz, "Bosnaklar Sitemkar," *Radikal*, June 8, 2004.

89. Oran, *Turkiye'de Azinliklar: Kavramlar, Lozan, Ic Mevzuat, Ictihat, Uygulama*, 104.

90. Commission of the European Communities, *2004 Regular Report on Turkey's Progress Towards Accession*, 49.

91. Ibid., 43.

92. Grigoriadis, "Turk or Turkiyeli?" 427–32.

93. Adnan Keskin, "Cesur Azinlik Raporu," *Radikal*, October 17, 2004.

94. Azinlik Haklari ve Kulturel Haklar Calisma Grubu, "Rapor," *Birikim*, no. 188 (2004): 26.

95. Ibid., 26–29.

96. Ibid., 29.

97. Ibid., 29–30.

98. Ahmet Cakmak, "Turk'un Atesle Imtihani," *Radikal Iki*, November 7, 2004.

99. Sadi Somuncuoglu, "Geciken Azinlik Tartismasi," *Radikal*, October 21, 2004.

100. Fikret Bila, "Cumhuriyet ve Kimlik," *Milliyet*, October 30, 2004.

101. Ankara Burosu, "'Turk Ulusu Bir Ustkimliktir'," *Radikal*, October 29, 2004.

102. Murat Yetkin, "Cumhurbaskani ve Genelkurmay Baskani'nin Mesajlari," *Radikal*, October 29, 2004.

103. Sedat Ergin, "Amerikalilik, Turkiyelilik ve Turkluk," *Hurriyet*, October 31, 2004.

104. Istanbul Burosu, "Tolon'dan Azinlik Cikisi," *Milliyet*, November 24, 2004.

105. Baskin Oran, "'Azinlik Haklari ve Kulturel Haklar Raporu'nun Butun Oykusu," *Birikim*, no. 188 (2004): 22.

106. Murat Belge, "Azinlik Degiliz Estagfurullah," *Radikal*, May 4, 2003.

107. Oran, "'Azinlik Haklari ve Kulturel Haklar Raporu'nun Butun Oykusu," 23.

108. Ibid., 24–25. This argument was rebutted by columnists who argued that Ataturk used both terms, so he should not be quoted in the debate. See Taha Akyol, "Ataturk Turk Devleti Demedi!!!" *Milliyet*, November 2, 2004.

109. Ibrahim O. Kaboglu, "Hukumet Saldirganligi Tahrik Etti," *Interview with Nese Duzel, Radikal,* November 8, 2004.
110. Ankara Burosu, "Sivil Toplum: Rapor Yirtma Ilkel ve Irkci," *Hurriyet,* November 2, 2004.
111. Turker Alkan, "Kim Hakiki Turk'tur?" *Radikal,* October 19, 2004.
112. Sahin Alpay, "AB Uniter Devleti Sorguluyor mu?" *Zaman,* November 4, 2004.
113. Murat Belge, "Azinliklar Raporu," *Radikal,* October 26, 2004.
114. Safa Reisoglu, "AB Yolunda Azinlik Kavgasi," *Radikal,* November 11, 2004.
115. Murat Belge, "'Azinlik' Fobyasi," *Radikal,* November 6, 2004.
116. Anzor Keref, "'Asli Unsurlar' ve 'Digerleri,'" *Radikal Iki,* October 31, 2004.
117. Cengiz Candar, "Eskiden 'Turkiyelilik' mi Vardi," *Tercuman,* October 24, 2004.
118. Ahmet Insel, "Ayricalikli Ortaklik ve Icimizdeki Oteki," *Radikal Iki,* December 12, 2004.
119. See Karl Vick, "Turkey Charges Acclaimed Author," *Washington Post,* September 1, 2005; Derya Sazak, "Orhan Pamuk'u Yargilamak," *Milliyet,* September 3, 2005.
120. The Swiss newspaper *Das Magazin,* on February 6, 2005, quoted Pamuk as saying in an interview, "Thirty thousand Kurds and a million Armenians were killed in these lands, and nobody but me dares to talk about it."
121. Istanbul Burosu, "'O Kafa' Serbest Birakildi," *Radikal,* September 8, 2005.
122. Having said that, one needs not to forget that only two months before Pamuk's indictment, the Istanbul Prosecutor's Office had decided that his statements were, indeed, protected by free speech. This provides additional evidence for the deep division within the Turkish judiciary. See Soli Ozel, "Free-Speech Case Can't Hide Progress," *International Herald Tribune,* September 8, 2005.
123. In March 2005, the Ministry of Environment and Forestry decided to unilaterally rename *Vulpes Vulpes Kurdistanica,* a red fox indigenous to southeastern Turkey, as *Vulpes Vulpes. Ovis Armeniana,* a wild sheep indigenous to eastern Turkey, was renamed as *Ovis Orien Anatolicus. Capreolus Capreolus Armenius,* a deer indigenous to eastern Turkey, was renamed as *Capreolus Capreolus Capreolus.* See Umit Cetin, "Bakanliktan 'Bolucu Hayvan' Operasyonu," *Hurriyet,* March 5, 2005.
124. Oran, *Turkiye'de Azinliklar: Kavramlar, Lozan, Ic Mevzuat, Ictihat, Uygulama,* 100–101.
125. Yetkin, "Cumhurbaskani ve Genelkurmay Baskani'nin Mesajlari."
126. Istanbul Burosu, "Tolon'dan Azinlik Cikisi."
127. The case of the students who were criminally charged after applying for Kurdish language courses is illuminating. See Oran, *Turkiye'de Azinliklar: Kavramlar, Lozan, Ic Mevzuat, Ictihat, Uygulama,* 104.

128. For such an event, the assassination of a man with his 12-year-old son at Kiziltepe, Mardin in November 2004, see Hasan Cemal, "13 Kursunu, Ugur'u Sakin Unutmayin," *Milliyet*, December 10, 2004.
129. Oran, *Turkiye'de Azinliklar: Kavramlar, Lozan, Ic Mevzuat, Ictihat, Uygulama*, 100.
130. The ban of Kurdish language by Turkish authorities was a basic theme of PKK's propaganda campaigns.
131. Ibrahim O. Kaboglu, "Cumhuriyetimiz Tek Soya Indirgenemez," *Interview with Derya Sazak, Milliyet*, November 1, 2004.
132. Baskin Oran, "Turkiye'de Herkes Esittir," *Radikal Cumhuriyet*, October 29, 2004.
133. "Peace Be Upon to You," *Economist*, no. 8440, August 20, 2005.
134. See Adnan Keskin, "Erdogan: Kurt Sorunu Demokrasiyle Cozulur," *Radikal*, August 11, 2005.
135. Ankara Burosu, "Diyarbakir Umutlu," *Radikal*, August 12, 2005.
136. Istanbul Burosu, "TUSIAD, Erdogan'a Destek Verdi," *Radikal*, August 17, 2005.
137. See Dogan Haber Ajansi (DHA), "Baykal'in Gorusu: Teroristle Flort," *Radikal*, August 15, 2005. Interestingly, Kurdish nationalists showed the same discontent with Erdogan's statements. See Haluk Sahin, "Diyarbakir'in Kafasi Karisik," *Radikal*, August 17, 2005.
138. Deniz Zeyrek, "Bildiri Sezer Damgali," *Radikal*, August 24, 2005.

CHAPTER 7

1. For the relevance of path dependence theory in the study of political culture, see Pierson, "Increasing Returns, Path Dependence, and the Study of Politics," 260.
2. On contingency in path dependent political processes, see Ibid., 263.
3. For the role of "sunk costs" and the "rising price of exit" in EU politics, see Pierson, "The Path to European Integration," 144–48.
4. The EU reform process was even called the second top-down revolution in Turkish politics after Ataturk's reform program. See Oran, *Turkiye'de Azinliklar*, 94.
5. The only caveat to this point refers to the care of the AKP government not to antagonize the bureaucracy to an extent that a military coup might be considered.
6. Pierson, "The Path to European Integration," 132–35.
7. This problem, which grew even bigger with the accession of many new smaller member states in 2004 through the Eastern Enlargement, was attempted to be resolved through the EU Constitutional Treaty and the Lisbon Treaty.
8. Pierson, "The Path to European Integration," 135–36.

9. Karen Smith, *The Making of EU Foreign Policy: The Case of Eastern Europe* (New York: Palgrave, 1999), 169.
10. Soler i Lecha, "Debating on Turkey's Accession," 55.
11. Gamze Avci, "Putting the Turkish EU Candidacy into Context," *European Foreign Affairs Review* 7, no. 1 (2002): 99.
12. See Stefan Krauss, "The European Parliament in EU External Relations: The Customs Union with Turkey," *European Foreign Affairs Review* 5, no. 2 (2000). This stance had created a lot of friction in Turkey.
13. See Putnam, "Diplomacy and Domestic Politics," 433–35. For a thoughtful application of Putnam's model to a comparative analysis of Europeanization in Poland and Turkey, see Ziya Onis, "Diverse but Converging Paths to European Union Membership: Poland and Turkey in Comparative Perspective," *East European Politics and Societies* 18, no. 3 (2004): 493–506.
14. Heper, "The Ottoman Legacy and Turkish Politics," 82.
15. Onis, "Diverse but Converging Paths to European Union Membership," 495–97.
16. Putnam, "Diplomacy and Domestic Politics," 457.
17. For the incidence of such alliances, see ibid., 444.
18. Ibid., 442.
19. On the definition of win-sets, see ibid., 435–37.
20. Ibid., 442.
21. Ibid., 448–50.
22. For similar cases in the Third World context, see ibid., 440.
23. "Why Europe Must Say Yes to Turkey," *Economist*, no. 8393, September 18, 2004.
24. For more examples where a weak chief negotiator gains considerable leverage, see Putnam, "Diplomacy and Domestic Politics," 458–59.
25. Meltem Muftuler-Bac, "Turkey's Political Reforms and the Impact of the European Union," *South European Society & Politics* 10, no. 1 (2005): 18–19.
26. For the special case of the EU impact on Turkey's human rights situation in Turkey after 1999, see Sugden, "Human Rights and Turkey's EU Candidacy."
27. Aydin and Keyman, *European Integration and the Transformation of Turkish Democracy*, 12–13.
28. The other two were the Human Rights Directorate (*Insan Haklari Baskanligi*) and the High Council of Human Rights (*Insan Haklari Ust Kurulu*).
29. Cengiz Candar, "Azinlik Raporu: Dogru Rapor, Gerekli Rapor," *Tercuman*, October 20, 2004.
30. On the role of the European Union as an external anchor of reform, see Nathalie Tocci, "Europeanization in Turkey: Trigger or Anchor for Reform?" *South European Society & Politics* 10, no. 1 (2005): 79–82.

31. Putnam, *Making Democracy Work*, 182.

32. On the persistence of a subject political culture as displayed in the postponement of a conference on the Armenian question in May 2005, see Murat Belge, "'Sasirma' Konusu," *Radikal*, May 28, 2005.

33. The statements of the CHP leader Deniz Baykal in the aftermath of December 17, 2004 are illuminating. See Murat Yetkin, "Istedigimiz AB Bu Degil," *Radikal*, December 19, 2004. For a powerful critique, see Murat Belge, "AKP ve Muhalefet," *Radikal*, December 24, 2004.

34. The "soft coup" of February 28, 1997 had certainly its own impact on these developments; however, it was the prospect of EU membership that channeled and provided the ideological ground for them.

35. Fokas, "The Islamist Movement and Turkey-EU Relations," 164.

36. Putnam, *Making Democracy Work*, 184.

37. Murat Belge, "Daha Cok Zaman Gerek," *Radikal*, December 21, 2004.

38. Birand, "Turkiye Artik Tercihini Yapmali."

39. Istanbul Burosu, "Bu Konferans Gecikmeyecek," *Radikal*, May 27, 2005.

40. The Euro-Mediterranean Partnership also became known as the "Barcelona Process."

41. European Commission, *Euro-Med Partnership Regional Strategy Paper 2002–2006 & Regional Indicative Programme 2002–2004* (Brussels: European Commission, 2001), 5.

42. Rory Miller and Ashraf Mishrif, "The Barcelona Process and Euro-Arab Economic Relations, 1995–2005," *Middle East Review of International Affairs (MERIA)* 9, no. 2 (2005): 97–100.

43. See European Council, *Common Strategy of the European Council on the Mediterranean Region [2000/458/CFSP]* (Brussels: European Council, 2000), 1–3.

44. European Communities, *The Barcelona Process, Five Years on (1995–2000)* (Luxembourg: Office for Official Publications of the European Communities, 2000), 8–10.

45. Putnam, *Making Democracy Work*, 184.

46. On the historic significance of the decision, see Mustafa Erdogan, "Avrupa Kimligi ve Turkiye," *Tercuman*, December 16, 2004.

47. For arguments in support of the view that finally prevailed at the European Council, see Edgar Morin et al., "Pourquoi il Faut Accueillir la Turquie," *Le Monde*, December 12, 2004 and "A Bit Too Late to Go Cold on Turkey," *Financial Times*, November 26, 2004.

48. Etyen Mahcupyan, "Asil Turkler Sasirtacak," *Zaman*, December 19, 2004.

49. On this issue, see Ahmet Altan, "Die Turkei ist Neurotisch," *Frankfurter Allgemeine Zeitung*, April 10, 2005.

50. Aktar, "Olmayan Avrupa Dusuncesi Uzerine," 273–74.

51. Meltem Muftuler Bac, "Turkey's Accession to the European Union: Institutional and Security Challenges," *Perceptions: Journal of International Affairs* 9, no. 3 (2004): 33–36.

52. This was the suggestion of the then French Minister of Interior and current President Nicolas Sarkozy. See Edwy Plenel, "'Au Vif': Le Cas Sarkozy," *Le Monde*, July 1, 2005.
53. This idea gained popularity within the center-right of France and Germany. See Valéry Giscard d'Estaing, "A Better European Bridge to Turkey," *Financial Times*, November 25, 2004 and Angela Merkel, "Turkei: Partnerschaft statt EU-Mitgliedschaft," *Die Welt*, October 16,2004.
54. Kalypso Nicolaidis, "Europe's Tainted Mirror: Reflections on Turkey's Candidacy Status after Helsinki," in *Greek-Turkish Relations in the Era of Globalization*, ed. Dimitris Keridis and Dimitrios Triantaphyllou (Dulles VA: Brassey's, 2001), 275–76.
55. Mehmet Ali Birand, "Iki Secenegimiz Var: Kavga ve Anlayis," *Posta*, July 1, 2005.
56. Mehmet Ali Birand, "AB Ertelemez, Bize Erteletir," *Posta*, June 30, 2005.
57. Eser Karakas, "En Calkantili 10 Yila Giriyoruz! . . . ," Interview with Nese Duzel, *Radikal*, December 20, 2004.
58. Ignacio Ramonet, "Turquie," *Le Monde Diplomatique*, November 2004.
59. Owen Bowcott, "Turkey in EU 'Would Bridge Cultures,'" *Guardian*, November 21, 2002.
60. Sahin Alpay, "Turkiye ve Uygarliklar Catismasi," *Zaman*, December 18, 2004.
61. Tom Happold, "Straw: Turkey is EU 'Acid Test'," *Guardian*, March 23, 2004.
62. Adam Przeworski, *Democracy and the Market: Political and Economic Reforms in Eastern Europe and Latin America* (Cambridge: Cambridge University Press, 1991), 26, cited in Ozbudun, "Turkey: How Far from Consolidation?" 124.
63. Ozbudun, "Turkey: How Far from Consolidation?" 124.
64. E. Fuat Keyman, "Cumhuriyet Projesi ve Avrupa Birligi," *Radikal Cumhuriyet*, October 29, 2004.
65. Ali Carkoglu, "Who Wants Full Membership? Characteristics of Turkish Public Support for EU Membership," *Turkish Studies* 5, no. 1 (2003): 173–75.
66. Hale, *Turkish Politics and the Military*, 198.
67. Heper, "The Consolidation of Democracy versus Democratization in Turkey," 141–42.
68. On the crucial role of AKP for the future of reform, see Cuneyt Ulsever, "AKP AB'ye Direnebilecek mi?," *Hurriyet*, June 2, 2005.
69. Michael Emerson and Nathalie Tocci, *Turkey as a Bridgehead and Spearhead: Integrating EU and Turkish Foreign Policy [Working Paper No. 1]* (Brussels: Centre for European Policy Studies, 2003), 7.
70. Istanbul Burosu, "Erdogan, 'Santaj' Sorusuna Kizdi: Ne Alakasi Var?," *Zaman*, September 4, 2005.

INDEX

Abdulhamid II, 2, 69, 97, 192
adab, 68, 70
adaptational pressures, 5, 6, 7, 13
AKUT, 54
Almond, Gabriel and Sidney Verba,
    14, 15, 16, 17, 18
Armed Forces. *See* military
Armenia, 78
Ataturk, Mustafa Kemal, 2, 21, 22,
    23, 25, 26, 27, 28, 34, 39, 45,
    71, 79, 88, 98, 101, 106, 126,
    127, 130, 131, 136, 139, 145,
    146, 147, 186, 187, 188, 211,
    216, 218

Basbug, Ilker, 92
Bayar, Celal, 28
bureaucracy, 22, 23, 29, 30, 43,
    52, 60, 61, 63, 66, 68, 72, 73,
    74, 76, 77, 82, 86, 87, 88, 91,
    113, 117, 118, 120, 133, 148,
    150, 151, 156, 157, 161, 162,
    163, 166, 168, 169, 170, 172,
    218
business capital, 47, 61, 62, 63, 64,
    100, 151, 169
Buyukanit, Yasar, 92

Ciller, Tansu, 136, 165, 215
civil society, 3, 20, 33, 41, 42, 43,
    44, 45, 46, 47, 48, 49, 50, 51,
    52, 53, 54, 55, 56, 57, 58, 59,
    60, 61, 62, 63, 64, 70, 73, 77,
    88, 90, 91, 102, 103, 109,
    145, 152, 153, 155, 156, 157,

    158, 161, 162, 164, 166, 167,
    168, 169, 170, 171, 172, 174,
    182, 191, 196, 207
constitutions
    1924 constitution, 29, 30, 45,
        99, 145
    1961 constitution, 29, 30, 45,
        72, 79, 100, 117, 134
    1982 constitution, 30, 39, 45,
        56, 74, 80, 106, 131, 133,
        138, 145, 201
Copenhagen Criteria, 3, 6, 31, 32,
    39, 57, 58, 64, 86, 87, 92, 120,
    121, 139, 153, 155, 156, 161,
    164, 171, 180, 195
coups, 22, 28, 45, 72, 77, 163, 171,
    218
    1913 coup, 79
    1960 coup, 29, 30, 45, 72, 79,
        99, 106, 117
    1971 coup, 30, 39, 80, 101, 117,
        165
    1980 coup, 30, 39, 45, 53, 56,
        73, 74, 117, 131, 165
    1997 "soft" coup, 76, 86, 104,
        109, 114, 117, 167, 202,
        220
Customs Union, 39, 57, 104
Cyprus, 4, 78, 88, 92, 129, 190

Demirel, Suleyman, 49, 73, 136,
    199, 214
democratic consolidation, 42, 63,
    67, 75, 77, 79, 86, 87, 93, 162,
    172, 173, 178, 179

DGM, 72, 73, 81, 82, 84, 85, 88,
    94, 157
Directorate of Religious Affairs, 99,
    106, 108, 109, 116, 121, 138,
    168

Ecevit, Bulent, 54, 88
ECHR, 81, 84, 109, 110, 116, 119,
    208, 210
Egypt, 68, 104
elite, 6, 103, 212
    bureaucratic, 34, 73, 79, 116
    business, 47
    Islamist, 114, 170
    Kemalist, 27, 28, 79, 100, 112,
        169
    military, 45, 92, 125
    political, 51, 71, 164, 198
    state, 23, 34, 60, 70, 71, 72, 75,
        76, 77, 80, 86, 90, 117,
        120, 136, 171
Era of Felicity, 97, 100, 209
Erbakan, Necmettin, 50, 77, 100,
    101, 102, 103, 104, 105, 107,
    109, 110, 130, 131, 205, 207
Erdogan, Recep Tayyip, 105, 107,
    111, 117, 142, 151, 152, 156,
    174, 179, 180, 206, 218
Euro-Mediterranean Partnership,
    55, 173, 174, 220
European Commission, 57, 58, 64,
    81, 82, 83, 84, 85, 94, 107,
    108, 116, 136, 157, 158, 159,
    160, 169, 170
European Council, 20, 35, 57, 58,
    139, 155, 159, 160, 161, 162,
    164, 171, 175, 195
European integration, 7, 9, 13, 37,
    176
Europeanization, 5, 6, 11, 62, 63,
    86, 87, 182
European Parliament, 57, 94, 160,
    161, 203
European Union, 1, 3, 4, 7, 9, 13,
    20, 31, 32, 33, 34, 35, 36, 37,
    38, 39, 40, 42, 46, 55, 57, 58,
    81, 82, 86, 87, 104, 107, 109,
    111, 113, 120, 121, 137, 150,
    155, 157, 158, 160, 161, 162,
    163, 164, 165, 166, 167, 168,
    170, 171, 173, 175, 176, 177,
    178, 179, 180, 181

General Secretariat for the European
    Union, 82, 86, 150, 157
Gokalp, Ziya, 44, 126, 129
goodness of fit, 5, 7
Greece, 39, 78, 92, 190, 211
Gul, Abdullah, 105

headscarf, 106, 111, 114, 115, 116,
    118, 119, 121, 167, 210

IHD, 57, 58, 152, 193
IMF, 54
Inonu, Ismet, 25, 28, 188, 214
instrumentalism, 28, 61, 66, 164,
    169
intelligentsia, 111, 118, 119, 120,
    147, 150, 151, 170
Iraq, 35, 36, 92, 132, 136, 196,
    214
Islamization, 100, 109, 115, 121,
    137

Kutan, Recai, 105

laicism, 96, 170
laïcité, 112, 113. See also laicism
liberalization, 4, 33, 49, 60, 61,
    62, 89, 91, 93, 121, 136, 148,
    149, 150, 151, 155, 158, 161,
    162, 163, 164, 165, 166, 170,
    172, 173
    economic, 31, 46, 47, 74, 136,
    political, 3, 4, 5, 20, 28, 31, 32,
        33, 34, 40, 42, 69, 87, 89,
        93, 120, 121, 136, 151,
        153, 155, 156, 157, 161,

162, 165, 169, 172, 175, 180

liberals, 23, 24, 25, 27, 33, 152, 162, 164, 165, 187

Menderes, Adnan, 28

MGK, 29, 72, 73, 76, 78, 79, 80, 81, 82, 83, 84, 87, 88, 94, 104, 117, 149, 152, 157, 200

military, 24, 28, 29, 30, 31, 33, 34, 36, 43, 45, 48, 67, 68, 72, 74, 75, 76, 79, 80, 88, 89, 90, 92, 93, 108, 117, 132, 133, 134, 149, 150, 152, 153, 156, 164, 165, 167, 200

millet, 24, 44, 124, 186

minorities, 3, 21, 22, 23, 24, 27, 31, 33, 34, 44, 45, 57, 125, 130, 132, 135, 138, 141, 147, 148, 150, 152, 153, 157, 165, 168, 170, 172, 188, 215

Alevis, 21, 33, 106, 107, 108, 109, 116, 117, 127, 131, 134, 135, 136, 138, 186, 211

Armenians, 24, 92, 126, 128, 129, 138, 160, 172, 217, 220

Assyrians, 126, 138

Bosnians, 21, 142

Chaldeans, 138

Circassians, 21, 141

Greeks, 4, 24, 68, 126, 128, 129, 138, 190, 197

Jews, 109, 128, 129, 138, 186, 204, 212

Kurds, 21, 22, 24, 26, 28, 31, 33, 36, 48, 49, 50, 52, 76, 77, 92, 102, 131, 132, 133, 134, 136, 138, 141, 142, 147, 150, 152, 153, 160, 186, 188, 193, 202, 207, 214, 216, 217, 218

Lazes, 21, 216

Moudros, Armistice of, 70, 187, 211

multiculturalism, 1, 37, 119

MUSIAD, 51, 194

national identity, 3, 9, 20, 21, 22, 23, 24, 27, 32, 33, 106, 123, 124, 125, 126, 127, 128, 129, 130, 131, 133, 136, 137, 143, 144, 147, 148, 149, 150, 151, 153, 155, 157, 158, 165, 168, 170

nationalism, 22, 24, 37, 123, 125, 126, 127, 129, 130, 131, 132, 133, 134, 139, 187, 211

national security, 3, 30, 56, 72, 73, 74, 76, 77, 78, 80, 82, 84, 89, 108, 133, 139, 140, 151, 163, 169, 171, 203

ethnic, 16, 106, 123, 124, 128, 129, 143

territorial, 123, 126, 127, 128

Ocalan, Abdullah, 49, 76, 134, 153

OHAL, 76, 133

Okyar, Fethi, 25, 26, 27

Oran, Baskin, 147, 148, 150

Orbay, Rauf, 25

Ottomanism, 125, 165, 187

OYAK, 72

Ozal, Turgut, 31, 39, 50, 74, 75, 76, 136, 199, 214

Ozkok, Hilmi, 88, 91, 92, 93, 118, 146, 149

PKK, 33, 36, 49, 76, 92, 132, 133, 134, 136, 150, 153, 218

pluralism, 3, 25, 69, 120, 145

political culture, 3, 4, 5, 7, 11, 14, 15, 16, 17, 18, 19, 20, 21, 22, 23, 27, 28, 31, 32, 33, 42, 67, 155, 156, 158, 159, 161, 162, 163, 166, 167, 168, 169, 170, 171, 172, 173, 175, 179, 180, 188, 218, 220 political Islam, 50, 51, 76, 92, 100, 101, 102, 103, 104, 105, 106, 109, 110, 111, 112, 113, 117, 130, 131, 172, 209

political parties, 29, 30, 45, 51, 56, 57, 62, 72, 73, 100, 104, 110, 111, 120, 176, 177, 192, 196

AKP, 51, 59, 61, 63, 88, 90, 105, 111, 112, 113, 114, 115, 116, 117, 118, 119, 121, 156, 157, 161, 163, 164, 166, 170, 179, 180, 221

ANAP, 31, 45, 74, 88, 102, 103, 136

AP, 100, 101, 205

CHP, 22, 26, 27, 28, 29, 45, 59, 61, 70, 73, 101, 121, 152, 167, 188, 199, 203, 220

DP, 28, 29, 30, 71, 72, 79, 99, 100, 130

DSP, 61

DYP, 103, 104, 109, 203

FP, 51, 105, 107, 110, 111, 114, 156, 167, 207

HADEP, 133, 214

MHP, 61, 129, 203

MNP, 100, 101, 130, 205

MSP, 101

RP, 50, 51, 76, 102, 103, 104, 105, 107, 109, 110, 131, 156, 167, 206

SP, 51, 105, 111

privileged partnership, 1, 177

Putnam, Robert, 10, 11, 12, 18, 19, 166, 171, 175, 183, 219

reform, 3, 5, 6, 10, 11, 19, 20, 22, 27, 34, 39, 40, 48, 50, 55, 56, 57, 58, 59, 60, 61, 64, 68, 69, 70, 81, 82, 83, 85, 86, 87, 88, 89, 91, 92, 93, 94, 95, 97, 98, 99, 105, 107, 108, 109, 111, 112, 114, 115, 116, 118, 120, 121, 123, 128, 133, 136, 137, 139, 140, 141, 142, 143, 144, 145, 146, 149, 150, 152, 153, 155, 156, 157, 158, 159, 160, 161, 162, 163, 164, 165, 166, 167, 168, 169, 170, 172, 173, 174, 175, 176, 178, 179, 180, 183, 186, 187, 195, 218, 221

RTUK, 82, 83, 142

secularism, 20, 21, 33, 55, 80, 92, 95, 96, 97, 98, 99, 100, 103, 104, 106, 107, 108, 110, 111, 112, 113, 114, 116, 117, 118, 119, 120, 121, 131, 155, 157, 163, 167, 170, 205

secularization, 24, 45, 96, 97, 98, 99, 120, 127, 129, 130, 178

Sevres syndrome, 78, 79, 133, 145, 201

Sezer, Ahmet Necdet, 54, 61, 146, 152, 167

Sheikh Said, 24, 25, 26, 186, 187

takiyye, 115

Tanzimat, 2, 34, 39, 44, 67, 82, 97, 186

tarikat, 44, 45, 50, 99, 100, 106, 187, 205, 208

terrorism, 75, 77, 103, 110, 134, 140, 152

TESEV, 63

theories of European integration
constructivism, 7, 9
functionalism, 7, 9, 10
historical institutionalism, 5, 7, 9, 10, 12, 13, 42, 64, 158, 183
liberal intergovernmentalism, 7, 8, 9, 12
path dependence, 10, 11, 42, 64, 93, 121, 153, 155, 183, 218
two-level game, 5, 11, 42, 64, 161, 162

TMSF, 54

Tolon Hursit, 146, 149

transcendentalism, 23, 66, 91

Treaty of Lausanne, 126, 128, 129,
    137, 138, 139, 143, 144, 146,
    147, 148, 215
Treaty of Sevres, 24, 25, 34, 78,
    145, 146, 147
Turkish-Islamic Synthesis, 50, 101,
    106, 130, 131, 205, 213
TUSIAD, 48, 62, 151, 152

ummah, 124
United States, 11, 14, 15, 18, 28,
    34, 35, 36, 37, 75, 87, 92,
    176, 181, 189, 196

veto points, 5, 6
VGM, 82

Westernization, 2, 3, 21, 22, 39, 45,
    68, 87, 100, 112, 126, 127,
    129, 169, 181, 187, 203, 209

Yilmaz, Mesut, 89
YOK, 74, 81, 83, 116, 200
Young Turks, 2, 22, 24, 39, 44, 69,
    79, 96, 97, 98, 99, 125, 128,
    129, 130, 197

LaVergne, TN USA
10 February 2010
172605LV00003B/13/P